WC X

WA
100
WIL

THE ETHICS OF
COMMUNITY CARE

WITHDRAWN

Stephen Wilmot

WITHDRAWN

CASSELL

Cassell
Wellington House
125 Strand
London WC2R 0BB

127 West 24th Street
New York
NY 10011, USA

© Stephen Wilmot, 1997

All rights reserved. No part of this publication may be reproduced or transmitted in any form or by any means, electronic or mechanical, including photocopying, recording or any information storage or retrieval system, without prior permission in writing from the publishers.

First published 1997

British Library Cataloguing-in-Publication Data
A catalogue record for this book is available from the British Library.

ISBN 0–304–33889–3 (hardback)
    0–304–33890–7 (paperback)

Typeset by Action Typesetting Limited, Gloucester
Printed and bound in Great Britain by
Redwood Books, Trowbridge, Wiltshire

CONTENTS

A selection of related titles published by Cassell

Care in Chaos: *R. Hadley and R. Clough*

Cities of Pride: *D. Atkinson (ed.)*

Coping with Crisis: *J. Samoff (ed.)*

Making Sense of Research: *G. Hek, P. Moule and M. Judd*

Raising Educational Standards in the Inner Cities: *M. Barber and R. Dann (eds)*

Who Cares? *H.-J. Schulze and W. Wirth (eds)*

Young People Leaving Home: *P. Ainley*

ACKNOWLEDGEMENTS

I want to express my gratitude to Suzanne Hall and Michael Key for their help in the preparation of this book. Their knowledge, practice wisdom and good sense helped to keep me in touch with reality. I also record my thanks to my partner Gilly for her unfailing support, and to my stepson Robin for his practical help and encouragement.

INTRODUCTION

WITHDRAWN

THE FOCUS OF THE BOOK

My aim in this book is to map out some of the ethical issues that arise in and around community care. By the term 'community care' I mean those principles, policies, procedures and practices that have developed since the late 1980s in the field of health and social care for older people, people with enduring mental health problems, people with learning disabilities and people with chronic and/or terminal illness. Specifically, I mean those principles, policies, procedures and practices that have arisen out of the White Paper *Caring for People* (HMSO, 1989) and related documents. Clearly the general concept of community care predates those developments by several decades, and it bears a relation to the developments of the last six years, not least in that some of the aspirations of that long-established principle are expressed in post-1990 policy. The ethical issues raised by recent policy are sufficiently extensive and complex to justify a book devoted to them. I intend that this shall be that book.

THE NATURE OF ETHICS

The notion of mapping ethical issues may seem an odd one. First I need to discuss those dimensions that appear to me to be characteristic of ethics, in order to make sense of the kind of mapping that I propose. A discussion of ethics may draw on areas from a number of academic disciplines. It may enter the territory of the sociologist or social researcher in looking at what people believe to be right or wrong and at how people's views in that area are formed by experience, upbringing and culture. It may draw on the work of theologians, moral philosophers and political theorists in attempting to identify a set of guiding principles in making moral judgements. It may draw on a range of sources in looking at the moral arguments for and against particular courses of action – looking at the concepts used, and the connections between them – in order to understand more clearly the possibilities of consensus or disagreement.

The heart of my discussion will be the last of these. The other areas will play parts of varying importance. I shall, where possible, make use of evidence that may tell us what people believe to be right and wrong, and what may influence them in that. I shall certainly make extensive use of other people's efforts to identify basic guiding principles for distinguishing right and wrong. However, my own agenda is to consider how we might arrive at our own judgements of right and wrong in given situations, in the light of arguments, beliefs and analyses. The main concerns of my analysis will be:

1. Through what processes might we establish what is morally the right course of action for ourselves?
2. Through what processes might we scrutinize the moral justifications put forward by others for their actions and decisions, to establish whether they do in fact justify those actions?
3. How do we identify and validate criteria for making these judgements?

AN EXAMPLE

We are likely to find ourselves descending through several levels of analysis in this process. That probably needs some explaining. I shall do this initially by offering an example.

Let us suppose that I am working to help Mrs Brown regain her skills and confidence in self-care after a stroke and a period in hospital. She says she wants to get back her ability to be self-sufficient and expresses keenness to work with me to achieve this. We agree a plan, but on occasions she shows lack of interest, lack of confidence and a desire to be left alone. There is little progress. The commitment required seems absent, but Mrs Brown does not want to revise or abandon the plan. What should I do?

Let me first of all list some questions that occur to me:

1. How much weight ought I to give to what Mrs Brown wants?
2. How much weight ought I to give to what I believe is good for her?

3. If 1 and 2 above differ, how much skill and effort ought I to put into persuading her that my analysis is the correct one?
4. If she is inconsistent about what she wants, ought I to allow that to affect my decisions in 1–3 above?
5. Ought I to confront her about her inconsistent behaviour?
6. Does the fact that such confronting seems to distress her alter what I should be doing – should I be giving particular weight to whether or not she is happy?
7. Should I be giving extra weight to whether it is my own actions/statements that distress her (as against other circumstances having that effect)?
8. Do I give any weight to undertakings I have given to her, or undertakings she has given to me. Should I keep my promises and should I confront her if she breaks hers?

DISTINGUISHING MORAL AND PRACTICAL QUESTIONS

To work effectively with the above list, we need to be able to distinguish between moral questions and other sorts of questions. I shall illustrate this distinction with regard to questions five and six above by extending the example.

Let us suppose that there is disagreement in the team about the right way to proceed with Mrs Brown. Jeni says, 'You ought to tell Mrs Brown that you are going to stop this programme of work with her unless she makes up her mind to stick to the contract.' Jaswinder says, 'You ought to stay alongside Mrs Brown and encourage her to participate when she loses interest, and don't be put off by her changes of mind.' Is that an ethical disagreement?

It depends on why Jaswinder and Jeni are saying what they are saying. It may be that both think Mrs Brown ought to be persuaded to continue with the programme, but they disagree about the method. Jaswinder thinks consistent support will keep her involved. Jeni thinks that a warning about support being withdrawn will be more effective in keeping her committed. They don't disagree about what is a morally right outcome, simply about what is a practically effective way of achieving that outcome. It is a disagreement over cause and effect; a practical disagreement. They may well agree that it is desirable to keep Mrs Brown in the programme.

However, we can imagine a situation where their reasons for disagreeing are rather different. For instance, we might have a situation where Jeni says, 'You ought to tell Mrs Brown that you will pull out unless she commits herself; and you ought to do that because by doing that you are recognizing and encouraging her to accept what is a basic part of being a competent adult – making decisions and taking responsibility for those decisions. By avoiding that you are treating her as something less than a competent adult.' Jaswinder says, 'You should keep alongside Mrs Brown because she has a right to change her mind, to be awkward and inconsistent, after a lifetime of unremitting responsibility and burdensome decisions; she has a right to be free from all that, to be irresponsible and happy.' We are then dealing with a very different sort of disagreement. Jeni and Jaswinder disagree about what are essentially moral priorities – the importance of competent adulthood as against the importance of happiness and self-expression.

We will see below that this disagreement is fundamental in western ethics, and is likely to show itself in community care practice in numerous guises. It relates closely to question number two in the list of questions posed below about my own practice with Mrs Brown. If I give priority to the 'responsibility' side of life – to promise-keeping on Mrs Brown's part and truth-telling on mine – this might lead me to a fairly confronting approach. If I lean toward the happiness priority I may well take a more supportive and accommodating role with Mrs Brown. Therefore my basic moral orientation may have a considerable effect on the strategy I follow.

So how do we distinguish moral and practical questions? It is clear from this example that moral and practical questions can look exactly the same. It is the reasons behind the answers we give that reveal the difference. We use the words 'ought' and 'should' in two ways: the practical way, in asking what I should do if I am to achieve a particular goal; and the ethical way, in asking what is morally right. Each of the eight questions above could be either a practical question, about which courses of action are most likely to ensure Mrs Brown continues with the programme, or a moral question, about which courses of action are morally right.

ASKING QUESTIONS AT A DEEPER LEVEL

If I want to maximize the likelihood that Mrs Brown completes the agreed programme (provided my concern is a practical one), there are some courses of action that may achieve this, and there are general principles which might help me to predict the effect of particular actions on Mrs Brown's behaviour. Social and physical sciences, such as psychology and physiology, will give me some principles and some information that will help me to maximize the probability of that outcome. These are practical concerns. They cannot tell me whether that is what I ought to do morally.

In order to obtain answers to the moral questions I need to try to find a different set of general principles, and in order to find those I need to pose a more general set of questions. For instance:

1. How do we decide what is good for people?
2. How do we balance such values as well-being and happiness against such values as freedom, truth-telling and promise-keeping in resolving situations where they are in conflict (e.g. where freedom is being used in a self-damaging way, or happiness is achieved through dishonest behaviour)?
3. In what circumstances ought I to question the ability or fitness of someone to know what they want, or what is in their interests or to make a considered decision about that. Having questioned that ability, how ought I to act?
4. What else ought I to expect of myself, and others expect of me, because I am in a professional role (e.g. nurse, social worker, occupational therapist)?
5. What special permissions, tolerances, considerations should Mrs Brown expect from me because she is a user?

ASKING QUESTIONS ABOUT GENERAL PRINCIPLES

Beyond the above questions lie another set, which have very similar wording; but instead of asking 'How do I decide?', 'How do I balance given values in certain situations?,' and so on, I ask the following questions:

1. Can we agree a principle that enables me to decide what is good for people?
2. Can we agree a principle that allows me to find a balance between conflicting values?
3. Can we agree a principle that enables me to decide when to question someone's competence, and how to act in that situation?
4. Can we agree a principle that enables me to identify moral requirements characteristic of the worker and user roles?

If we seek answers to these last four questions, we shall find ourselves dealing with some of the more theoretical and philosophical aspects of ethics. If we explore these aspects, they will not necessarily give us answers to the questions in the earlier lists, but they will help us to map the territory to which the earlier questions refer.

This is an example of the way in which we can pursue an ethical analysis from a set of specific questions about a situation, to sets of increasingly general and abstract questions.

ARE THERE ANY GENERAL PRINCIPLES THAT WE CAN AGREE?

The case against

Clearly the last set of questions above is crucial, and many people would respond to those with a resounding 'no'. They would argue that our answers to the second set of questions, and even the first set, will legitimately vary from person to person in that those answers will depend entirely on personal feelings, attitudes, inclinations and prejudices, and these will reflect experience, upbringing and socialization, all the social and biographical components that make each individual unique. That is one way of dealing with those questions.

The people who offer this argument tend to use one or more of the following principles:

1. Moral beliefs vary widely between individuals and communities.
2. Morality is essentially an expression of individual feelings and inclinations. (The philosopher David Hume stated this principle in the eighteenth century. See Norton, 1993.)
3. Morality is essentially located in communal beliefs. (See Kuthakas, 1994 and Rorty, 1992 for perspectives on this principle.)

Given that these experiences vary enormously across cultures and, indeed, across individual biographies, we can expect that moral beliefs will vary a good deal also. There is empirical evidence available to support this proposition (see, for instance, Miller, 1991). If we think this evidence is satisfactory, we could make a step from accepting this as an empirical fact to accepting it as a definition of morality – i.e. that because moral beliefs vary, morality in its very nature is likewise variable.

The case in favour

However, there are counter-arguments suggesting that it is worth exploring these questions and looking for general principles. Points for this argument are:

1. We can find principles that everyone agrees on irrespective of personal or community experience.
2. We can identify principles that allow our disagreements to be differently framed and managed, if we are willing to go an extra stage in the exploration of these questions.

I have started to do the latter with the example of Mrs Brown. The question that I posed about the balance between happiness on the one hand, and principles such as honesty on the other, reflects a deeper issue about the usefulness of basic general principles (such as happiness) as moral touchstones.

In order to see how this works out in practice we need to look at some of the most important attempts to find general moral principles that might transcend individual and communal beliefs.

ATTEMPTS TO IDENTIFY GENERAL MORAL PRINCIPLES

Since religion began to lose its hold on the western mind, there have been numerous attempts to arrive at beliefs about moral right and wrong using means other than divine revelation and spiritual reflection. Various aspects of human experience and ability have been recruited as substitutes for God's instructions. I shall list some of these, together with an example of a moral theory that emphasizes that faculty:

1. The faculty of reason (Kant).
2. The faculty of empirical observation and experience, applied to
     - Human desires and priorities (utilitarianism)
     - The overall design of the universe (natural law)
     - The planet's ecosystem (modern ecological ethics).

3. The capacity to feel, to experience and express emotion (Hume, emotivism).
4. The capacity to perceive the absurdity of existence (existentialism).
5. The capacity to interact and share with other human beings in groups and communities (pluralism, cultural relativism, communitarianism).

All of these have been identified at various times by various moralists as the road to moral insight. Spiritual reflection and prayer remain the prime source of moral guidance for many people, though in the western world this is increasingly a matter of individual choice rather than of general social practice.

CHOOSING AND FOCUSING IN

I propose to discuss systems of moral philosophy which seem to me to have been, and to be still, influential in the development of health and social care in the UK. I cannot be comprehensive in this, and I don't think it would be helpful if I were. My hope is that the reader will have an opportunity to look at some of these systems in two ways:

1. To identify which might approximate most closely to your own personal moral philosophy.
2. To recognize the sort of influence these philosophies have had in moulding policies and practices over many years. Even when they have not been consciously adhered to, the shape of their influence can be detected.

UTILITARIANISM: JUDGING BY RESULTS

Utilitarianism began at the end of the eighteenth century, and developed especially during the nineteenth century. It is the philosophy of reformers, of the advocates of efficiency and rationality in government and commerce. Jeremy Bentham, its founder, advocated wide-ranging reforms in the society, economy and politics of Britain at the end of the eighteenth century. His successor in the development of utilitarianism, John Stuart Mill, was likewise a reformer, in particular an advocate of democracy and equality (Mill, 1962).

Their philosophy was based on one of the human capacities that I mentioned above as substitutes for divine revelation; the capacity to observe human beings empirically in a systematic way, and to explain and predict on that basis. This was a capacity greatly valued by British philosophers during the eighteenth century, and Bentham took it as his starting-point. He suggested that morality ought to be based on observable fact. He observed that human beings appeared to value and pursue pleasure over and above any other desirable end. This in his view provided the basis for a system of morality in which actions can be judged morally on the basis of the amount of pleasure, as against pain, that they produce in their consequences (Bentham, 1962). This is utilitarianism. Mill subsequently refined this system to focus on the concept of happiness rather than pleasure (Mill, 1962) and more recent utilitarians have in some cases sought to substitute other goods (Sprigge, 1990). But the basic principle has remained. Utilitarianism has several specific characteristics which distinguish it from the other philosophies we shall be considering. These are as follows:

1. It takes as the criterion for right and wrong something which humans can be observed to value: utilitarianism is in that sense based on empirical observation.
2. It takes as its criterion for right and wrong something that in itself can in principle be observed, and even in some respects measured (i.e. happiness).
3. It focuses its moral judgements on actions (rather than other possible foci such as character traits) and specifically on the results of actions, and their impact on the world (rather than other possible foci such as their intention or their actual moral characteristics).

In these ways utilitarianism has a claim to be quintessentially a philosophy for the practical empirically minded individual. It heavily influenced nineteenth-century social policy in the UK (see Roberts, 1979) and is still widely influential. Utilitarianism's appeal to civil servants and planners (not necessarily under that explicit title) lay precisely in this practical orientation toward results. It offered a sense of pragmatism, of relative simplicity and rationality, and freedom from awkward tangles with absolute principles.

UTILITARIANISM AND MRS BROWN

If we return to Mrs Brown's situation we can start to see how a utilitarian approach might show itself. This approach allows me to focus on maximizing Mrs Brown's happiness, and on following only those courses of action which achieve that end, without diminishing the happiness of any other person. If I believe that I will achieve that by being accommodating rather than confronting – allowing her to be inconsistent and ambivalent about her commitment to our agreed programme – then that is what I ought to do. Principles such as responsibility, autonomy and fairness take second place to happiness, and only have weight in so far as their pursuit serves to maximize happiness. So Mrs Brown's somewhat 'irresponsible' or 'immature' behaviour becomes an issue only in so far as it affects her or others' happiness.

If we assume that Jeni and Jaswinder are both utilitarians, we are then in a position where we can agree on our goal. We are all seeking to maximize happiness. However, a utilitarian approach provides numerous grounds for disagreement on the practical level – in particular with regard to the likely effect of any specific action. For instance, my colleagues may believe that confronting Mrs Brown will maximize her happiness in the long run because it will increase the likelihood of her learning a more useful pattern of relating to people, or because it will increase the likelihood of her being effectively helped. Predicting the effects of every available option offers plenty of scope for utilitarians to disagree.

A problem with utilitarianism

A number of problems arise with utilitarianism, some of which we need to explore. First, utilitarianism can lead us into making moral judgements which, while justified by the principle of utility, seem at an intuitive level to be reprehensible. We can imagine certain actions which may well have consequences that maximize happiness, but we feel that they are wrong in some essential way.

A famous example identified by Feldman (1978) is the policy of framing and punishing an innocent person as a deterrent to criminals. If we cannot catch real culprits, but we know that deterrence works given a sufficiently severe punishment, and we know that crime causes great unhappiness, why not simply set up one individual as an ersatz culprit and punish them with unprecedented severity? If this works, and sufficiently deters crime, we could argue that we have reduced the unhappiness of a great many people at the price of greatly increasing the unhappiness of only one person. If many thousands or millions of people are living in fear of crime and this fear is greatly reduced, that surely must outweigh the anguish of one individual, however deep.

There seems to be something intrinsically wrong with sacrificing one individual, even when many benefit as a result. But the utilitarian would apparently feel obliged to commend this act.

Act utilitarianism and rule utilitarianism

Utilitarians have recognized this problem, and have looked for ways of using the principle of utility that are more in tune with most people's moral intuitions. One way that has been identified is to apply the judgement of utility not to individual acts, but to rules ordaining that such acts should be performed in given situations. So, if we institute a rule that innocent individuals must be sacrificed every time we have a serious crime problem, we can see that we end up with rather a different balance of outcomes. The probability is that the policy would become known to the public so the element of deception would be lost. Nobody would feel safe from being snatched and sacrificed, and the law would be brought into disrepute. To perform an act as a rule has very different practical consequences from performing it in a one-off situation. On the whole, where actions contain the potential for evil which might on one occasion be outweighed by good consequences, the likelihood of those good consequences predominating when a rule is observed becomes much less. To judge the rule is in that sense a stricter test than to judge the individual action. This has led to a variation of utilitarianism, known as rule utilitarianism, which applies the test of utility not to individual actions but to rules.

An example

A utilitarian may think it justified on one or two occasions to omit to tell users that the services for which they are being assessed are in fact unavailable owing to lack of resources. They might argue that if people knew that these services were not available they would see no point in giving information, that such information is necessary to identify shortfalls and that identification of shortfalls will help arguments for more resources for the benefit of many users who suffer these shortfalls. So, at the cost of being dishonest with a few users, many users potentially benefit. However, if it became a rule that users should be assessed without being told that services are not available, the effects would be different. The deception would be more likely to be known about generally, and so simply fail to work. Community care agencies and their employees would become discredited, and all assessment would become impossible as trust broke down. Such a situation would clearly not maximize happiness – quite the contrary. Therefore, the rule fails the utility test so cannot be justified morally.

Another problem with utilitarianism

The apparent pragmatism of utilitarianism is based on a funda-mental moral assumption – that happiness is synonymous with moral good. This is rather different from saying that happiness *is* morally good. No doubt many people would agree that the maxi-mizing of happiness is (other things being equal) morally desirable. But that is not the same thing as equating happiness with moral good. It is simply saying that maximizing happiness is, alongside many other qualities and actions, morally desirable. The utilitarian view is much more fundamental than that. Strictly speaking it is impossible for a utilitarian to say that happiness is a good thing, because that, for him or her, would simply be to say that good is a good thing – a tautology.

The fundamental utilitarian proposition is that we can equate moral good with something that exists 'out there' in the world. This decision, to define moral judgements in terms of practical judge-ments, certainly has an appeal in the pragmatic, practical culture of British policy, and perhaps of British society to some degree. But it begs a huge question – what is so special about happiness? We can see that human beings value many things, happiness being only one in a long list. The concept of happiness is culture-specific, and to some extent historically specific. Two hundred years ago it was seen as an unproblematic good (*vide* the American Declaration of Independence), now it is seen as highly problematic. As our empir-ical knowledge of human cognition, affect and behaviour develops, we cannot continue to see happiness as a pure given good.

The attractions of utilitarianism

I have identified a number of problems with utilitarianism. But it retains a degree of credibility and currency as a moral philosophy, and the utilitarian mindset arguably remains influential in the dominant culture of the UK. It is worth considering why that is. I think the following characteristics work in its favour:

1. Utilitarianism focuses on the results of actions. In a culture which values goal-oriented action this fits in with many people's beliefs about what matters. In an activity such as community care which is publicly funded and closely monitored, the achieving of desirable results is basic to the activity. It makes sense for moral judgements to share that focus.
2. Happiness does make sense to many people as an overarching good. In practice many of our day-to-day moral judgements can probably be reduced to that criterion. Users, as members of the community, presumably value happiness as much as anyone else.
3. We tend to feel that happiness is real and that, in theory at least, we can apply some sort of measurement to it, however much the psychologists question that proposition. In the practice of community care it is usually apparent when provision improves a user's well-being and, in effect, maximizes their happiness.
4. If we have problems with happiness as a subjective experience, we can always create alternative versions of utilitarianism based on other criteria, perhaps relating to physical well-being, health or quality of life, all of which are directly relevant to community care. None are unproblematic in terms of measurement, but that is not to say that they are non-existent or unidentifiable (see Sprigge, 1990, for discussion of this).
5. Utilitarianism is concerned with the distribution of well-being among people and, where relevant, across large populations. Any activity, such as community care, which involves the manipulation of resources for the benefit of large numbers of people, lends itself to analysis through the utilitarian perspective.

In the end we need to decide whether or not utilitarianism is a workable basis for moral judgements, and for an ethics of practice in community care. We may make that choice, at least in part, through a reasoned assessment of its strengths and weaknesses, or we may make it on the basis of our pre-existing moral intuitions. I shall say more about our choices in this respect in Chapter 5.

KANT: REASON AS THE KEY TO ETHICS

In health and social care ethics the influence of utilitarianism is balanced by the ethical theory of Immanuel Kant. Kant was a German philosopher who lived in the latter part of the eighteenth century. His impact on western philosophy as a whole was enormous, and his ideas retain a good deal of currency in modern western philosophy. His theory of ethics forms only a part of his overall output, though it is through this that his name is probably most widely known. I shall outline his position, then consider the attractions and difficulties of his system.

Kant was a rationalist. He took the view that reason is the key to understanding, in ethical matters as in other matters. Emotion will not guide us to appropriate moral perceptions, nor is there a moral key to be found in empirical observation of the world as a utilitarian might argue. Reason alone will lead us appropriately.

Why reason?

In Kant's view the very existence of morality as a realm of definition depends on the existence of reasoning beings. Reason alone confers meaning and purpose on actions. Only reasoning beings can make choices and perform actions that have meaning and purpose. Therefore only reasoning beings can make choices between right and wrong action, and be held responsible for those choices, and so be said to have acted rightly or wrongly (Paton, 1956).

Other beings may perform actions which cause harm, damage, death or mayhem, but if they are not reasoning beings they cannot be said to have acted wrongly or to be in any sense due for punishment. So we may kill or confine animals that have harmed us but this is not punishment.

Reason in action: the categorical imperative

The special status of reason in this respect allows us to identify fundamental moral principles through the use of that very faculty. Kant called those bedrock principles the 'Categorical Imperative'.

Because they are by their nature definers, or in a sense even creators of morality, reasoning beings have a special moral value as ends in themselves. Kant offered a logical proof as to why reasoning beings ('persons') are ends in themselves, summarized by Feldman (1978) as follows:

1. If people are not ends in themselves, then nothing is an end in itself.
2. If nothing is an end in itself then there is never any reason to act in one way rather than any other.
3. There is sometimes a reason to act in one way rather than another.
4. Therefore people are ends in themselves.

This summary gives a flavour of the combination of reason as framework and reason as method which characterizes Kant. It also gives us one component of his categorical imperative: 'Act so that you treat humanity, whether in your own person or in that of any other, always as an end and never as a means only' (Sullivan, 1994, p.29). This clearly entails an outlawing of actions which involve violence towards persons. The more serious the harm to another person, the more likely it is that the actor is taking no account of that person as an end.

The test of universalizability

Another part of the categorical imperative focuses on the concept of universalizability. Kant derived this from formal logic. Pursuing the principle that logic, the ultimate expression of reason, can give us fundamental moral principles, he applied the principle to moral rules. This part of the categorical imperative can be stated as follows: 'I ought never to act in such a way that I could not also will that my maxim should be a universal law' (Sullivan, 1994, p.29).

Kant's test of universalizability involves a test of self-contradiction. Actions which are wrong are those which, if willed as a universal rule, would become self-contradictory. Kant's most famous example of such an action is that of false promising. He argued that we can establish the moral wrongness of this action (making a promise that we do not intend to keep) because we can establish that if such an action became a rule, it would promptly become impossible. We can only make false promises if the concept of promising retains its meaning. The concept of promising depends on the intention of keeping the promise. If it became a rule that we do not intend to keep the promise in given circumstances, the concept of promising becomes meaningless and it will become impossible to promise at all. If it is impossible to promise, it is impossible to falsely promise. So the willing of that rule is self-contradictory because it makes the willed action impossible.

We can apply the same test to the actions that go to make up false promising – lying and promise-breaking – with the same result. Lying fails the test because if we all lied all the time the activity would become meaningless and nonsensical. Language itself would become unusable and lose its meaning if we made a rule of saying the opposite of what we meant. Lying would lose its meaning. Likewise with breaking promises which creates, in a more specific way, the same contradiction as lying. Kant argues that suicide creates a similar problem. A reasoned decision to end one's own existence as a reasoning being is a self-contradictory act even if performed only once, and would certainly be so as a rule. It also offends against the first part of the categorical imperative, as it treats the self as a means to the achievement of the self's end (self-destruction) – a formulation which again emphasizes its self-contradictory nature.

Kant's concepts of good will and duty

Given the abstract and rational basis of these principles, one might wonder how we can expect real human beings to experience any personal commitment to them. Kant dealt with this issue through the concept of duty. Duty in his system defines the relation of the rational being to the moral principle that this being is motivated to obey. The valid motivating factor is will. Desire, emotion and passion are not the true basis for right action. Only the ability to understand the moral principle, and the will to observe it, constitutes such a valid basis. The concept of duty is the link between the will and the principle. We perceive a duty to observe that principle which we thereby will ourselves to obey. This focus on duty has led to Kant's system being included under the 'deontological' family of moral theories, 'deon' being ancient Greek for 'duty'.

Problems with Kant

A number of problems arise in attempting to make use of Kant's system.

Persons, humans and sentient beings

Kant identifies that persons have specific duties to other persons. He does not thereby exclude all other sentient life from the protection of morality, but he does focus primarily on the behaviour of person to person as being the most morally mapped of the areas of human behaviour. His definition of person is one that excludes a significant part of the human race. The list of those who do not have the cognitive capacity or skills to count as a 'reasoning being' is a long one. Babies and young children, people with severe learning disabilities, people suffering from Alzheimer's disease, constitute only some of this list. Kant's system seems to exclude them from the right to be treated as an end.

Rationality and moral feelings

Kant's denial of moral significance to emotion seems also to be somewhat counter-intuitive in that the desire to do right seems to be experienced by most of us as an emotion of some sort – whether a felt commitment to the rightness of a certain action or a desire to be acceptable to others.

Conflicting duties

Kant has no system of prioritizing those duties which are based on his universalizability principle (mostly duties *not* to do something). So if I find myself in a situation where keeping a promise involves me in telling a lie, Kant's principles do not help me to decide which I should do.

The attractions of Kant

Kant's principles, like those of the utilitarians, retain a good deal of currency in modern health and social care ethics. I suspect that the following are the features of his system that sustain that currency.

First, Kant provides a rationale for respecting the individual. As such, it is a useful counterweight to arguments which lead us toward sacrificing the interests of the few or the one in favour of the interests of the many. Community care, ironically, frequently involves working with individuals about whom the community does not care – in fact, whom the community actively dislikes and seeks to reject. Kant's principles provide a basis of argument for supporting the marginalized.

Second, as a closely related point, Kant's ethics provides us with a rationale for the ascription of equal rights and equal worth to all persons, irrespective of lifestyle and contribution to the community. This again can provide a basis for commitment to the equal worth of users, and others, in the community care context where social and political forces may try to propel workers in a different direction.

Third, Kant expresses rationally a view that is felt intuitively by many people – that some actions are right and some are wrong in themselves, irrespective of their consequences. Utilitarianism does not accomodate that perception, but the Kantian approach does. For community care workers who are under pressure from agency or community to let the end justify the means, an argument against such a position may prove supportive and sustaining.

I intend now to consider some alternative views that have taken shape in response to the dominance of utilitarian and Kantian ethics. I shall consider two perspectives, one a specific philosophy and the other a collection of ideas with important common characteristics.

EXISTENTIALISM

I shall give this philosophy briefer treatment than the others discussed, as its focus is narrower and its relevance more limited. Existentialism has existed in various stages of development since the nineteenth century (see Macquarrie, 1972). A salient characteristic of existentialism is that it develops Kant's emphasis on the individual autonomy and moral responsibility of the person to a point considerably beyond that envisaged by Kant. For the existentialist, the individual is responsible not only for his or her actions, but for his or her very existence. This rather startling concept is based upon the proposition that the person ('being') does not exist in the way that other parts of the universe exist. Persons do not have identifiable characteristics which define them, as do chairs, tables and nuclear reactors. They are in constant flux, constantly changing and in a real sense undefinable. Only through self-definition can they achieve 'reality', and that is achievable through the conscious making of choices and the accepting of responsibility for those choices. The freedom to make these choices is not only real, it is inescapable. If the individual does not choose to choose, he or she has still so chosen and cannot escape that responsibility. That individual choosing and acceptance of responsibility for choice constitutes the highest good in existentialist ethics. The kind of choices that are made, the nature of the actions that follow from those choices, are of much less importance than the fact of choice itself.

For the existentialist, the individualism that is a feature to varying degrees of utilitarianism and Kant's system, is pursued considerably

further. Existentialist writers have varying views on the kind of responsibility that individuals might have towards one another. Of its main
exponents Sartre (1991) takes perhaps the most individualistic stance.
Heidegger (1967) identifies the concept of 'solicitude', denoting a kind
of authenticity, a 'real presentness' in relationships. Buber (1971)
develops this idea into a powerful philosophy of authenticity and commitment in interpersonal relationships. However, social and
communal demands are seen by existentialists as barriers to personal
autonomy and interpersonal authenticity. The social elements of the
dominant philosophies, especially of utilitarianism, are largely absent
from existentialism.

Relevance to community care

It may well seem that existentialism has little relevance to community care, an activity which of all things must surely require an ethic
of social and interpersonal interaction. Its relevance is partial only,
but the existentialist emphasis on freedom and choice does have a
bearing on situations characteristic of community care.

First, in a situation where someone may be having more freedom
imposed on them than they wish to exercise, existentialism may be
relevant, though it may not give a welcome message to that person.
The move from institutional care to community care – a move which
is expressly intended to increase freedom and responsibility – raises
this issue. How should we view this? Existentialism might cast a
helpful light on this.

Second, where an individual is using their freedom in a way that
appears self-destructive – where they are neglecting themselves and
refusing help – existentialism may have something to say about individual freedom and apparently self-damaging behaviour (up to and
including suicide) as an expression of that freedom.

COMMUNITY ETHICS

The final set of ideas I shall introduce is not in any sense a single philosophy as are the other philosophies I have discussed so far. It is a
collection of ideas with varying origins, but with important common
features. These common features are built around some of the propositions that I put earlier in the chapter concerning the location of
morality, with a particular focus on social, cultural and community
ethics. I shall try to identify the main strands in this body of thinking.

Communitarianism

A strand of thinking known as communitarianism, argued by writers such as MacIntyre (1985), Taylor (1992) and Waltzer (1983), has sought to move ethics away from theories which emphasize individual rights and universal rules, toward theories which give moral importance to culture, community and specific relationships (for instance, family relationships and neighbourly relationships). Morality in this view is to be found in the beliefs and practices of communities. Moralities which bind people to their communities, neighbours and families within relationships characterized by loyalty, caring and obligation are cited as having greater validity than moralities that atomize people through ascribing to them unboundaried autonomy and personal responsibility. Ancient Greek ideas about civic virtue have been rediscovered in this context (see MacIntyre, 1985, for discussion of this).

Embodied and located ethics

An emphasis on the specificity of moral agents as inhabiting a particular body, time, place and set of relationships has been brought forward against Kant's rather disembodied and abstract idea of the person. This focus on the concreteness and locatedness of the person brings in also the significance of such factors as gender, race and sexual orientation. Women might approach moral issues in a way that is legitimately different from the way men approach them (see Benhabib, 1992 and Noddings, 1984 for discussion of this perspective).

These arguments are concerned with challenging the method we use to arrive at moral judgements and do not, by their nature, offer a complete set of moral propositions to compete with those of the utilitarians, the Kantians and the existentialists. There are several quite specific moral concepts which are emphasized by writers in this tradition, often in response to a belief that Kantians and utilitarians have neglected those concepts. One is the idea that moral obligations are moulded by specific relationships existing in specific situations (see Noddings, 1984). The concepts of community and of care are both emphasized in this tradition. Clearly these have considerable relevance to community care, as we shall see. I shall develop them further in later chapters.

Relativism

The other important idea to be drawn from this strand of thinking is that of ethical relativism – the view that there is no single morality which we are all struggling to discover, but rather a multiplicity of moralities specific to culture, religion, community, family, even individuals. In the relativist analysis it is nonsense to judge another person's action by one's own moral code, if ours is different from theirs. Their actions can be judged only by their code. This approach has a great deal to commend it in a multicultural society and the ethics of multiculturalism look, on the face of it, to be essentially relativist. The most difficult ethical dilemmas that present themselves in this context concern the morality of imposing the majority values on minority communities whose values may be very different. It could be strongly argued that for a number of reasons relativism is the most appropriate moral stance for a society that is becoming increasingly diverse in terms of culture and religion, and in a world where, through the development of trade, travel and communication, different moralities come into increasing contact with one another. If we are to survive, there needs to be mutual tolerance and an avoidance of the situation where the more powerful impose their moralities on the less powerful.

Two kinds of relativism

There are difficulties with the relativist position. First, it is not one but (at least) two positions. True relativism attempts to define and locate morality at the level of community, religion or culture and argues that it is meaningless to seek overarching moral principles on the basis of which we might feel it right to criticize someone else's moral code where it offends such principles. This argument proposes that it is absurd to try to do this.

The other version, which is not strictly relativist, posits a moral virtue of tolerance – what Taylor (1992) refers to as a 'presumption of equal worth' between cultures. This implies that it is morally wrong to condemn or criticize the actions of others if they are acting in accordance with their own moral code which is different from ours. I have characterized this as not strictly relativism because it requires one universal moral principle – tolerance – in order to argue that there should be no others. It also implies that we impose this principle on other cultures as well as our own. That single principle clearly cannot be justified through relativism. The 'relativist' of this sort would therefore need to have recourse to some other system, perhaps utilitarian, to justify the principle of tolerance. So it is not really relativist. I suspect that the belief in intercultural tolerance is based generally on the moral principle thereof rather than on a definitional proposition about morality.

Problems with tolerance

We need to consider the problems around this important concept. First, we have the problem of justifying the paramountcy of universal tolerance. If we use, for instance, utilitarian principles to justify it, we may then find that other principles in various situations have greater utility. So there is a real problem in sustaining that principle.

Second, tolerance presents difficulties in situations where universal tolerance and other principles that help to sustain a practical relativism seem to be unacceptable within certain cultural or religious belief systems which preach intolerance and the imposition of beliefs. Logically those of us who regard tolerance as a moral value in its own right should have no problem in condemning such behaviour in people of other cultures, since we have already accepted that the principle of tolerance is truly universal. However, the problem is that culture and religious systems of belief are in some respects indivisible. A belief in one's own superiority may be fundamental to some cultures and religions, and a duty to strenuously oppose manifestations of wickedness and unbelief may be fundamental to the beliefs of some religious groups. Requiring them to be tolerant liberals is requiring them to stop being what they are. In effect it is being intolerant.

Problems with relativism

The true relativist, who sees relativism as following from the nature of morality rather than from its dictates, is free of the problems experienced by the believer in tolerance. The intolerant are not being immoral; on the contrary, they are being entirely moral, if that is what their system requires. If the tolerance of our system makes us vulnerable to intolerant fanatics of other systems, that is too bad. It is not a process that can be regulated by moral principles since there is no 'supermorality'.

However, the true relativist cannot escape another problem. The location of morality, he or she argues, belongs in the concrete beliefs of people. But which beliefs of what people. Where do we draw the boundaries around a real system of morality? If we use religion, we are corralling a large part of the human race into a small number of systems; if we use culture, we have much greater diversity and much greater problems of boundary and definition. However we do it, we create restrictions. If we define right as 'that which is approved by my moral reference group' (whatever that might be) that makes it impossible for me to decide that my reference group is immoral. In other words it excludes the possibility of individual morality unless we treat every individual as their own reference group and have a completely atomized relativism, in which case some of the basic characteristics of morality, particularly its shareability, come into question. In practice we may have real problems in knowing where to locate individuals in terms of their culture, religion and moral reference group. Without that location, relativism becomes unworkable. And we may also have a problem in responding to the individual who wishes to assert his or her moral independence against his or her community. How far can it make moral sense to leave to the individual the choice of that reference group?

Relevance to community care

Despite all these problems, relativism must have particular appeal to the professional in the care field, who has endless opportunities to offend and interfere. Where others' beliefs must constantly be encountered and negotiated, the priority of avoiding offence and giving the benefit of the doubt is high. For all its contradictions, therefore, the practical attraction of relativism remains. On the policy level also relativism has appeal as a source of legitimacy in a diverse society (Donnison, 1994). I shall attempt to explore its implications in practice in Chapters 5 to 9.

WITHDRAWN

REFERENCES

Benhabib, S. (1992) *Situating the Self.* Cambridge: Polity Press.

Bentham, J. (1962) 'Introduction to the principles of morals and legislation', in M. Warnock (ed.) *Utilitarianism.* London: Collins.

Buber, M. (1971) *I and Thou.* Edinburgh: T & T Clark.

Donnison, D. (1994) 'By what authority? Ethics and policy analysis'. *Social Policy and Administration* 28(1), 20–32.

Feldman, F. (1978) *Introductory Ethics.* Englewood Cliffs: Prentice-Hall.

Heidegger, M. (1967) *Being and Time.* Oxford: Blackwell.

HMSO (1989) *Caring for People.* (White Paper) London: HMSO.

Kuthakas, C. (1994) 'Explaining moral variety', in E. Paul, F. D. Miller and J. Paul (eds) *Cultural Pluralism and Moral Knowledge.* New York: Cambridge University Press.

MacIntyre, A. (1985) *After Virtue: A Study in Moral Theory.* London: Duckworth.

Macquarrie, J. (1972) *Existentialism*. Harmondsworth: Penguin.

Mill, J. S. (1962) *Utilitarianism* (ed. M. Warnock). London: Collins.

Miller, J. G. (1991) 'A cultural perspective on the morality of benificence and interpersonal responsibility', in S. Ting-Toomey and F. Korzenny (eds) *Cross-Cultural Interpersonal Communication*. Newbury Park: Sage.

Noddings, N. (1984) *Caring: A Feminine Approach to Ethics and Moral Education*. Berkeley: University of California Press.

Norton, D. F. (1993) 'Hume, human nature and the foundations of morality', in D. F. Norton (ed.) *The Cambridge Companion to Hume*. New York: Cambridge University Press.

Paton, H. J. (1956) *Groundwork of the Metaphysics of Morals*. New York: Harper.

Roberts, D. (1979) 'The utilitarian conscience', in P. Marsh (ed.) *The Conscience of the Victorian State*. London: Harvester.

Rorty, A. O. (1992) 'The advantages of moral diversity', in E. F. Paul, F. D. Miller and J. Paul (eds) *The Good Life and the Human Good*. New York: Cambridge University Press.

Sartre, J.-P. (1991) *Being and Nothingness: An Essay on Phenomenal Ontology*. London: Routledge.

Sprigge, T. L. S. (1990) *The Rational Foundation of Ethics*. London: Routledge.

Sullivan, R. (1994) *An Introduction to Kant's Ethics*. New York: Cambridge University Press.

Taylor, C. (1992) *Multiculturalism and the Politics of Recognition*. Princeton: Princeton University Press.

Waltzer, M. (1983) *Spheres of Justice: A Defence of Pluralism and Equality*. Oxford: Blackwell.

CHAPTER 1
Key Concepts: Care and Community

KEY CONCEPTS

In the first four chapters I shall introduce a number of key concepts which are relevant to community care. These are not dependent on a particular theory for their significance but carry a substantial ethical freight in their own right. I shall outline the significance of these concepts as I perceive them and also suggest how they interact in the context of community care ethics. My discussion of that interaction will also be an explanation of the structure of the rest of those chapters.

The concepts that will provide the structure of Chapters 1 to 4 are as follows: care and community, justice, autonomy and responsibility. My choices are partly dictated by the subject-matter, partly by the issues that arise. I have, for instance, left out concepts relating to matters of life and death – personhood and death criteria for instance. None of these is necessarily irrelevant. Community care can certainly be a matter of life and death. But the provider of care, while making decisions that may prove retrospectively lethal or life-saving, is unlikely to have to make decisions about (for instance) life-sustaining treatment for an irretrievably comatose user.

The concepts that I have selected work in pairs, providing alternative perspectives on particular issues and therefore, I hope, providing a further degree of illumination. I shall try to illustrate this. The relevance of care and community appears to be self-evident but we may initially be concerned with some basic questions about why community care is being provided in the first place. What is its justification? The principle of care may provide a justification, and the principle of justice might provide us with an alternative justification. Why should we care for others? Is it because they are 'our own folk', members of our community, towards whom we have a duty of care? Does that mean we have no duty towards 'outsiders' (however defined)? Or is it because they are human beings who have a right, in justice, to reasonable provision, irrespective of their specific relationship with us? Here we have to wear two rather different sets of spectacles to look at the same set of questions.

Since community care is a good which is to some degree divisible we are faced not only with questions of who gets it, but also of how much they get. Justice is the most comprehensive and accommodating concept available to address moral questions of who gets what. Issues of right and need can be explored within its remit. As we are also faced with a question of who should provide what, the concept of responsibility seems the most helpful to match against justice and care on the 'who provides' question. Again, this equips us with two viewpoints.

Finally, in the process of providing and receiving community care, what behaviour can we reasonably expect from the professional providers, the recipients and others? What are the professional's responsibilities to the recipients and to the rest of the community? What sort of response to one another's behaviour is appropriate? Can the professionals or the community expect any degree of conformity from its members who receive this care or should the autonomy of the individual take precedence over any notion of responsiblity to the rest of the community or to the State? Again, we have concepts balancing against each other in tension; autonomy against community, and autonomy against responsibility.

I intend that this process of using concepts to illuminate each other will characterize the structure of the first four chapters and that the concepts from the four theories of ethics I have identified will be brought into that discussion.

In the rest of this chapter I shall explore community and care as concepts, in order to begin to gain some ethical purchase on the idea of community care. Clearly the idea of community care is likely to mean a good deal more than the sum of its constituent words. None the less those two words both have enormous power to evoke complex and compelling ideas, and I would suggest that that has shaped our thinking about community care.

CARE

Care can be understood in many different ways:

1. It can refer to a relationship between persons, where one cares for or cares about the other.
2. It can refer to an attitude. We might say that a person cares about another person, or some other creature, or a thing or an idea.

3. It can refer to actions which constitute care – taking care of someone – or actions which express care – acting in a caring way toward another.
4. It can stand for responsibility – I have care of someone.
5. It can stand for custody or tutelage – he is in my care.
6. It can denote solicitude, empathy and identification.
7. It can denote anxiety, even unhappiness.

It is a remarkably flexible and variable word. In the professional context Pellegrino (1985) identified four versions of care:

1. Care as compassion.
2. Care as doing for others what they cannot do for themselves.
3. Caring for the patient's problem – directing skill and resources to the problem and seeking to address and share the burden of the patient's anxiety.
4. Care as taking care – providing our service with care and attention.

Caring and being careful

If we focus on behaviour and relationships reflecting care, we can identify an enormous range of phenomena that can be referred to in this way. At one extreme I may behave in a careful circumspect way, taking care and watching my back, as a kind of defensive self-care that we would describe as 'careful'. At the other extreme, I might follow Buber (1971) and commit myself with total authenticity to a relationship with another human being where convention is irrelevant and there is a complete and unmediated prehension of the other person, where caring for the other is complete. In between those extremes there are varying degrees of selfishness and selflessness – devotion to persons, to ideas, to principles – all of these could be described as characterized by 'care'. Fox (1995) captures something of the contradictions of care when he identifies its opposites as, respectively, the 'vigil' – authoritarian and controlling – and the 'gift' – a generous celebration of otherness.

The ethics of care

In essence care denotes a relation, an exchange of energy, of giving and receiving. The giving of energy may involve a burden, a discomfort, a labour. The receipt of that energy may involve a maintenance, a nurturance, an enfolding (even entrapment) and preserving. The predisposition to provide is often taken as morally laudable, whether we value the motive, the desire, the attitude or the action, and what is received is often taken as a moral good, as happiness is for the utilitarian, or freedom for the existentialist. We may take a predisposition to care as in some sense definitive of the moral profile of a person or a group. Noddings (1984) identifies the predisposition to care as being constitutive of a feminine morality which contrasts with the more masculine moralities of Kantian rule-following or utilitarian calculation. She emphasizes the person-to-person end of the caring dimension which involves a close recognition of the other, showing something of Buber's existentialist commitment. But there is also a recognition of caring as part of a network of social and personal relationships, which both include and exclude – something very different from Buber's approach, and historically perhaps more characteristic of the experience of women than of men in western society. Care in this sense can be considered as providing a base for an ethics alternative to the rules and rights-based moralities of Kant and the utilitarians, though this is a matter of debate (Allmark, 1995).

COMMUNITY

Community as institution

We can place the community alongside the family, the State and other configurations of people, as a social institution. As such it may be geographically concentrated (neighbourhood) or dispersed, as ethnic or religious communities might be. The community as a social institution has characteristics which distinguish it from other institutions.

The community as social institution comes in many different forms, some of which are mapped out by Mayo (1994). It can manifest itself as anything between the world community and ten people living in a commune. The moral freight of the word in this context is ambiguous. Sometimes it seems to be morally neutral, simply a collective noun like the formerly named 'European Community'. But even in those contexts, it often proves to have a strong emotional undertow. Sometimes it is heavily laden with values, often of a contradictory sort. For instance, the traditional village community as a shared image carries a curious ambiguity between the values of hierarchy and intimacy. Likewise there is a contradiction between exclusion and inclusion. A community, like any group, must exclude somebody or something. A close community where people know each other is by its nature exclusive. But community is also seen as welcoming, accepting and valuing. Some of this ambiguity is perpetuated by post-modern cultural developments which emphasize images of tradition. However, it has deeper roots than that. The first sociologist of the community, Tonnies (1957), helped to create the image of the community as a close, natural, informal, non-negotiated institution embodying a deep, almost mystical togetherness ('Gemeinschaft') which he contrasted with the impersonal, negotiated nature of modern organizations ('Gesellschaft').

Community as value

Much of the language used in discussing the community is value laden. It may therefore help if we separate out the value of community from the institution of the community. Community as a value implies valuing what is communal and that which involves communing. A sense of community might mean a sense of living as part of a particular collection of people who care about each other and know each other. Or it might mean a sense of sharing, of mutual concern and connectedness with one anothers' lives which might be experienced in any collection of people. Yeo and Yeo (1988) identify this use of the term as going back at least to the sixteenth century.

What sense might we make morally of community as a value? It could be placed alongside individuality and collectivity as competing values in western society and politics. Where the former two values show the footprint of the universalist moralities – Kant and the utilitarians – who seek to identify principles which will apply to all persons irrespective of location or relationship, community has a more particularist focus. It implies that we have a particular moral relation to particular others – fellow members of whatever communal unit has moral significance – and that this moral relationship is different from the relationship I might have with someone outside that communal unit. In that sense community as a moral concept seems to belong more comfortably in the tradition represented by communitarianism and relativism. Whereas the universalist theories are all-inclusive in terms of categories of persons, the community tradition is exclusive. Some people are left out. That seems to be an important feature which may be significant in looking at the ethical implications of community care.

Community and care

My final task in this area is to attempt to explore the moral 'fit' between the ideas of community and care. Some kinds of care fit more comfortably with community as both value and institution than do other kinds. Bureaucratic carefulness and principles do not sit comfortably with the personal and particularist dimension of community. They tend to minimize the element of felt bonds and obligations that seem characteristic of community. At the other extreme the intense care of Buber's existential encounter is so exclusive that it seems to preclude the notion of a network of relationships and obligations with varying degrees of closeness. The kind of caring that fits best with the idea of community is perhaps one which contains an element of personally felt commitment, but is also containable within a system of balances and limitations.

But what does this do to my options as a caring member of the community? I may feel an obligation or desire to take a caring interest in my neighbours in the village or suburb where I live, if I subscribe to the value of community. How do I fulfil that obligation? On the basis of the point I made in the previous paragraph, am I required to give care which is personal, particular and concrete, like visiting, helping with shopping and taking a caring personal interest? There are after all various forms of behaviour that might be indicative of a caring commitment. It may be equally caring for me to lobby the Government to provide better practical care for my neighbours. If I am acting for the benefit of my neighbours in my lobbying activities, rather than for a universal category (e.g. of elderly people), I am arguably expressing community care in a concrete way, even though my actions belong in a more impersonal frame of political activity.

A major thrust of community care has been to move away from institutional care. Institutions do create communities of a sort, but they are seen as artificial in that they are created through formal mechanisms to achieve agreed ends. They conform to Tonnies's notion of 'Gesellschaft' – the formal organization – rather than 'Gemeinschaft' – the organic community. This idea seems to have been a powerful engine of government policy since 1989. An assumption behind recent government policy is that users are better off where people 'naturally' co-operate and communicate in a variety of ways and 'most care is provided by family, friends and neighbours' (HMSO, 1989, p.9). There is a clear expectation here that it is better for people to be cared for in this type of community because it is in some sense real, natural and authentic in the way that institutions are not, and it helps those individuals to maintain moral links, which are truly characteristic of community, with other people. These are particularistic, informal and felt – the kind of relationships described by Bulmer (1987).

Community values

Another moral framework is provided by the specific values held by different communities. There is still a good deal of variation in norms of behaviour relating to the support given to the needy, and the location of those obligations, between different sorts of communities. This can be seen in communities characterized by class and location. For instance, there are histories of mutual aid and care for the vulnerable among certain kinds of traditional working-class community. This has tended to be associated with a high level of shared experience and shared risk (for instance in mining or fishing communities), and a fair degree of homogeneity and physical proximity. There are also communities of a more dispersed kind – consisting of particular ethnic or religious groups, for instance, who have distinctive traditions of mutual aid and obligation. However, it is not always easy to distinguish between norms of community care and norms of family care that are strongly adhered to in particular communities, and there is a great danger in making assumptions about the propensity of particular minority communities to 'look after their own'. The value of community care may be difficult enough to specify; the practice is even more elusive.

Community care as a policy

The Government that introduced the policy of community care in its present form is explicitly anti-collectivist in its ideology, and the community does not appear to have prospered during its period of office, either as institution or as value. This is not surprising. Walker (1989) argues that the Government's agenda for community care has been characterized by, among other things, increased emphasis on self-help and family support, extension of the market and commodification of social relations. The first of these does not necessarily relate to community and can function as an alternative to community care. The latter two are antithetical to community. Labour mobility and industrial restructuring have ensured that many long-established communities (for instance mining villages and small towns) have suffered considerable social dislocation and, often, dramatic changes. By contrast individual opportunities (for some people) have been maximized. The idea that there are obligations that exist outside those to one's family (an obligation recognized and endorsed by the Government) and those to the State, seems not to have much space in this world-view. Indeed, Hammond (1995) argues that the value of community has little to do with the Government's community care policies which are informed rather by values of individual choice.

But there seems to be some degree of inconsistency. On the one hand the Government has promoted individualism at the expense of traditional community ties. On the other hand it appears to have worked on the assumption that community ties will provide a substantial part of the care needed under the new policy. As part of this process, voluntary activity has been encouraged. This comes nearer to a recognizable version of community than individual self-help or commercial care, in that it draws on the individual's sense of moral obligation to specific groups of people, and therefore differs considerably from commercial or state activity which is usually motivated by prudential rather than moral forces, and is morally regulated (if at all) by universalist notions such as that of contract.

However, for many users community care has not been character-ized by the moral commitment of community, at least not in the sense of streets, districts, villages or towns. Rather they have experi-enced the moral commitment of family members, whose sense of obligation, though eminently particularistic, informal and felt, exists irrespective of community involvement. In those cases it is families – and, as pointed out by Qureshi (1990), especially female relatives – who are taking on that obligation, not 'the community' in any real sense. It is not clear whether the Government intended anything other than this.

The only care-giving system that shows any characteristics of community as institution or value is the voluntary sector. Otherwise care-giving is through state, family or commercial activity. So the rela-tionship between the policy of community care and community (either as institution or value) seems tenuous. However, there are points at which there is a connection. The value of community is likely to enhance the acceptance and support of vulnerable people living outside of institutional care. And by the same token, the nature of the relation-ship between those people, and the people who may constitute their community, is one of considerable moral significance. This is an area we shall explore further in Chapters 2 and 8.

The moral significance of the community

Accepting that community care policies so far have treated the community as a passive element in the situation, it is none the less worth considering how far the community has the potential to become morally significant in the process of care provision. At present, the structure and operation of community care has been focused on individual users, involving, where possible, individual relatives and individual neighbours. There has been work in various places to develop models of care which genuinely involve the community as an organized collectivity, rather than treating the community merely as a context for individual care. But the mainstream of service provision is still individually focused.

The community as participant in care

The community could be approached more positively as a participant in care from two directions, as recipient of care and as provider of care. A system of individual care requires someone to have the responsibility of providing that care, and for that responsibility to be clearly focused on the recipient of care. For the community to be morally significant in this process I think the community would need to be the focus of responsibility (that is, it would need to make sense for me to say 'I have a responsibility to this community') as recipient, and the community would need to have responsibility (perhaps 'a duty of care') as provider.

Community as provider of care

Let us first consider community as provider of care. What does it mean for me to say that community X has a duty of care to Mrs Smith? I could use it to indicate that every member of community X individually has a duty of care to Mrs Smith. Or I could mean something different – that community X as a collective entity has a duty of care to Mrs Smith. For the moment I shall focus on this second meaning and consider its coherence. The first thing to say is that we often ascribe duties to collective entities. My employer, if it happens to be a community care trust, could quite sensibly be said to have a duty of care to Mrs Smith. The analogy seems promising at first sight.

However, the analogy does not hold up. In each case where the community care trust is the carrier of responsibility, it can assume this role because it can enter into a commitment. The community cannot do that. To explain this further I intend to follow Peter French's (1984) theory of collective responsibility in this analysis. He argues that only a particular kind of collective grouping of people can truly have collective responsibility. This body is what he terms a 'conglomerate collectivity': an organized entity with a clear identity and boundary, a formal decision-making structure and an organized system of storing and accessing information which provides an organizational memory. All these characteristics allow such a grouping to be held responsible. The trust would meet these requirements but the community in this case would not.

Situations may arise where informal groupings of people without organizational structure none the less share responsibility for an event or action because they were all involved in the event or action as individuals, but that kind of grouping (which French terms an 'aggregate collectivity') cannot hold collective responsibilty. The responsibility lies with each individual, and it is shared in the sense that it is divided between those individuals. However, it is not collective responsibility in the sense that it lies with the collectivity as a whole.

It is likely that community X will have neither the characteristics of the aggregate collectivity or of the conglomerate collectivity. In practical terms it will almost never be the case that every member of a neighbourhood community like community X is individually party to a responsibility to provide care, or a failure to do so. Modern communities are simply not small enough or integrated enough to involve every inhabitant in that way. Even if community X consists of only a few streets it will be too diverse and insufficiently integrated to achieve that level of shared responsibility. So it is not an aggregate collectivity.

Likewise community X is unlikely to have the characteristics of conglomerate collectivities. Its boundaries will probably be unclear – if I live on the south side of the ring road, I might see myself as belonging to community X or community Y or both. If we cannot be sure of the boundaries of a particular collectivity, it seems difficult to place a duty on that collectivity because we do not, in a literal sense, know upon whom we are laying that duty. More important, community X as a neighbourhood community will almost certainly have no decision-making mechanisms which can reasonably be said to belong to that community. There may be within it organizations which to some degree or other seek to give a voice to that community, or to parts of it. One of these – perhaps the community association – might see itself as the brain and mouthpiece of the community, as actually constituting the organized decision-making aspect of that community. However, for as long as it is possible to be a member of that community without being a member of the community association, they are different things. Whatever the relationship of the community association to the community, it is not one of identity. So even the best organized and most active community cannot be seen as a conglomerate collectivity. This means that they cannot enter into obligations, or exercise responsibilities.

I would equally argue that a community cannot be blamed for the actions of its members. Let us suppose that the people of a particular neighbourhood are resisting the creation of a proposed group home for people with mental health problems in its midst. Let us suppose that a community organization is set up to oppose this proposal. It is quite arguable that everybody who joins that organization in full knowledge of its purpose, and supports it in pursuing that purpose, is open to blame for prejudiced and oppressive behaviour. It is conceivable that everyone in the neighbourhood might join the organization – everyone who could be said to be a member of a particular community. Does this mean that the community can now be collectively blamed for this particular behaviour? The organization may have a strong claim to represent the community on the basis of saturation membership, but it is still the case that the organization and the community are different things. The members of the organization can be blamed but, even if they are co-terminous with the population of the neighbourhood, we still cannot blame the community. They are different things and as soon as one member of the community resigns, that difference becomes clear.

I am arguing, then, that most communities cannot be said to have characteristics that would allow us to hold them collectively responsible in terms of duty, accountability or blame. However, there are exceptions to this. Some communities are structured in such a way that they could be held responsible as collective entities. Some religious communities, for instance, have structures which involve all members and which allow for collective responsibility. These include decision-making procedures, boundaries and records. But the distinctiveness of this kind of community highlights its difference from the neighbourhood community, or even the ethnic or cultural community, which is more likely to be the focus of community care.

We may question how far representative institutions at community level might make it possible for communities to become morally responsible for community care. If we consider larger communities – that of the city, say, with its local representative institutions – we might argue that every individual elector has a duty to participate in elections and has a portion (very tiny) of the responsibility for the outcome of the election. However, it would be difficult to find many citizens of the average town who feel any responsibility for the actions of their city council and it would be difficult to argue, between elections, that they should feel any. The city council is not the community. It may reflect that community in many respects, and it clearly has a very close relationship with it, but it is not the same thing and its actions are not the actions of the community. The difficulties of justifying collective community responsibility seem insurmountable.

Community as recipient of care

Let us next consider community as recipient of care. What does it mean for me to say that I have a duty to community X? I could use the term as a collective way of saying that I have a duty to every individual living in the neighbourhood of community X – perhaps because my office serves that area – or I could mean that I have a duty to community X as a collective entity, just as I have a duty to my employer as a collective entity. The idea seems quite sensible.

I think we have similar problems in accepting a responsibility to a community as a collective whole as we have in giving that community responsibility. If I as an employee of the community care trust have a responsibility to community X as a collective whole, what can that mean? If there is no organized and recognizable focus to the community to which I can agree and fulfil that responsibility, in what sense do I have it? If there is no way of the community as a whole holding me responsible, in what sense am I so? I may regard it as my duty to work with the community as a structured whole rather than a collection of individuals – perhaps developing and supporting support-structures within the community – but I am answerable to the trust, not to the community, and the trust is answerable to the purchasing authorities and to the Government, not to the community. On the basis of this argument it seems impossible to sustain the idea of responsibility to the community as a collective entity. Again we might make an exception for those communities (such as some religious communities) which do have a focus for acknowledging responsibility and holding accountability.

Community obligation

We shall not get far trying to involve the community as a collective entity in the moral transactions of community care. However, it may still be possible to argue that the community does have significance in the distribution of responsibility, if we could establish that individuals have special responsibilities in relation to others on the basis of community membership. In moving to this focus we are considering the community as a category that people belong to or do not belong to, rather than as a collective entity. The issue is, then, do members of a particular community have particular responsibilities by virtue of that membership and, conversely, does anybody have particular responsibilities to other persons because those other persons are members of a particular community? It is worth considering the possible ways in which it can be approached.

It is clear that Kantian, utilitarian and existentialist ethics, by virtue of their concern with the fundamentals of the human condition, give relatively little weight to the 'special relationships' that such special responsibilities might entail. Writers in all traditions have acknowledged the predisposition of humans to care more about the well-being of those close to and similar to themselves. This has been variously viewed as a sign of moral weakness to be overcome, as an unavoidable characteristic to be made the best of or as a sign of essential moral soundness that then needs to become universal. However, there are other dimensions to this. Although these philosophies do not identify community preference as morally good, they are predicated on the basis that their definition of moral behaviour is something to be realized in the world, by people living their lives. Morality is not in that sense transcendental but belongs in the world. That means it belongs in people's lives and relationships. It also means that actions which are morally commendable are most practically possible with people with whom we are in contact – and the closer and more frequent the contact, the more the opportunities. Right actions are most likely to be performed towards people near me – people in my family, community, workplace and so on. In practice any morality which recommends a quantitative approach – to do right as often as possible rather than to 'save up' toward moral heroism – will enhance community relationships because the community offers one of the main opportunities for achieving that goal. This must give some support to the concept of community responsibility, simply because general responsibilities can most effectively be exercised towards our neighbours.

However, the effects of utilitarianism and Kantianism in this context will be rather different from those of existentialism. In the context of routinized and regulated relationships of the sort we tend to have with our neighbours and families in western society, the utilitarians and Kantians would tend to aim for the avoidance of anti-social or dishonest behaviour, rather than for the achievement of excellence or heroism. In ordinary day-to-day dealings the options that are available within the law will seldom have a life or death significance. I may be a friendly or a grumpy workmate, reliable or capricious. I may be inclined to compromise with my neighbour over boundaries and trees, or I may be awkward and demanding. All this can have a great deal of effect on quality of life but is seldom tragic. The Kantian and utilitarian approach will guide us, if we let them, in making these discriminations. The practicalities of community care may demand something more than this – a degree of proactive altruism, even self-sacrifice, which may not sit easily with either philosophy. Utilitarianism and Kant may, in fact, direct us away from close engagement with our more vulnerable neighbours. For Kant, obligation to a specified individual is based on duties which in some ways are quite distancing – on promise, on respect. It may be more appropriate not to make relationships than to make them while in doubt that those duties can be adhered to. For the utilitarian the focus is more likely to be on the interests of a range of people than on those of one person.

The existentialist may be propelled in rather a different direction, probably not toward any engagement with a duty toward one's neighbours as a generality but, possibly, towards an engagement with another individual. A choice to make a commitment to another person, involving recognition and engagement on a number of different levels, is part of the existentialist tradition and is articulated particularly by Buber (1971), but that commitment cannot be recruited to a wider moral framework for community care. The impact of mutual recognition and commitment is something that simply could not be 'distributed' in any sense that worked on a community level.

A contractarian approach

Another possible way of supporting collective responsibility on a theoretical level might involve the use of an approach which I have not introduced before, but which seems relevant here. This is the contractarian approach. This is a tradition which includes a diverse range of ideas, with one common feature – that of the contract. This involves the idea that commitments and obligations are rooted in a notional contract – an agreement by all members of a polity to live together in a certain way – which forms the basis of a social, political or moral order. No such contract was signed by our ancestors at any specific time, and none exists in a material sense, but the idea of such a contract provides a justification for the mutual expectations which we place on one another (Hampton, 1993). This can be a way of suggesting particular arrangements in a society as best expressing the likely rational judgements of its members were they to actually agree the terms of a contract. Rawls's (1971) theory of justice is based on just such a principle.

A contractarian approach allows for a set of mutual rights and obligations, and could also include particular distributions of obligation and accountability. An example might be for every citizen to have certain obligations, for instance to ensure that no member of our collectivity is allowed to suffer particular disadvantages or oppressions. Any actions to support and help people in danger of such problems could be seen as an action on behalf of the whole collectivity.

If we reframe our coexistence in communities to become based on an implicit contract, such a contract is likely to involve some commitment to mutual aid and support. If we use Rawls's approach to establish what are the most appropriate arrangements for community life – to ask what a rational individual would choose if they had no idea of their own particular circumstances – then it is possible that a rational choice for a high degree of mutual obligation within the community would be chosen. But it may be that the most rational way of organizing that mutual aid is not through individual and small-group acts of care, but through the resourcing of adequate state machinery for care. A rational decision of this kind is likely to be influenced by justice. The communitarian writer Sandel (1982), who argues the priority of the community virtues of benevolence and solidarity over formal concepts such as rights and justice, none the less accepts the need for justice as a 'remedial virtue' where the community is demanding the community virtues in an inequitable way. If we leave it to members of the community to provide care on an individual basis, the burden of obligation will inevitably be distributed very unevenly. If I happen to live next door to vulnerable and needy people on either side, I may reasonably feel that the principle of community mutual aid has not worked equitably. The personal demands made by a general duty to others will never fall equitably in the real world. The State has sought in the past to equalize at least the heavier demands of care. This is becoming less so, and the expectation of individual duty replacing the State's duty is also an expectation that individuals will accept the inequity of luck and chance, and also of more systematic factors such as class and gender. It is hard to imagine a workable contract with such inequitable application. A contract embodying mutual obligations in the community, if it expresses the rationality of its 'signatories', would have to accomodate the justice issue and in doing so may well need to restore the State's role in equalizing the burden of care.

A communitarian approach

We could abandon our attempt to identify a universal set of community obligations based on rational criteria that apply in all situations, and look instead to the patterns of belief and behaviour that actually obtain in different kinds of communities, basing an ethic of mutual aid upon these. This would involve a greater emphasis on feelings of care and obligation, and on shared habits and norms. It is likely to have to accomodate a good deal of cultural variation. Michael Waltzer (1983), arguing from a communitarian standpoint, suggests that communities vary a good deal in their understanding of social goods, and the justice of their arrangements for the sharing of these goods must be judged by the values of that community. Those perceptions are not necessarily going to connect directly with the idea of community as far as the members of those communities are concerned. People may be active in community care without having any commitment to the community. They may provide a good deal of support to other people in the community, and contribute to community care in that sense, but that could be on the basis of some other bond, such as church membership, and feelings and habits of obligation and/or care may be based on that fellow membership rather than on any more general conception of community duty. Other specific ties of membership, connection and loyalty will be at work in different parts of society – some formally organized into charities and organized groups, some remaining informal. The depth and nature of obligation will vary in accordance with personal experience and relationships, but also with culture and the way relationships and obligations are culturally defined.

Family obligations as community cement

A good deal of care in feeling and action will be fuelled by family relationships of various sorts, and there is no guarantee that these will enhance a sense of community solidarity. Family involvement can enhance community involvement, for instance at the school gate. But the trend for decades in western societies has been for families to shrink down to nuclear proportions, and to close their front doors on the rest of the community. Government ideology in the 1980s clearly encouraged this movement. As Finch (1990) points out, there is now pressure, also from government, to reconnect generational obligation in a way that reverses the move to the nuclear family and to encourage the 'middle' generation to acknowledge more obligation to their elderly relatives. Can we, then, see family obligation as being an alternative to community obligation, something that will provide the moral cement for a caring community? It would exclude a lot of people without families but its effectiveness as a community cement depends on its acceptance by the people who do the caring. It is easy to get most people to look after their children but much more difficult to get them to look after their elderly parents, so perhaps the norms and practices of family obligation as they exist are not sufficiently strong or extensive to create a caring community.

If we seek to underpin family obligation with ethical arguments, we are back where we started, looking for a universal rational principle that supports interpersonal obligation in a reliable way. These are not easy to find in the case of the family. Arguments of repayment for parental care seem not to hold up. Children do not ask to be born and starting a family is understood, in western society, as an expression of choice and desire rather than obligation. To create and nurture children for one's own satisfaction who then must pay for their creation and nurturance, seems not to make sense in contractual or Kantian terms. The children are not being treated as ends and are not party to the contract. It may make more sense in utilitarian terms but that will depend on who gains and who loses. In any case not all parents are effective nurturers, so we must decide if we exclude incompetent or uncaring parents from this moral equation. In terms of maximizing well-being filial obligation and care may or may not work better than state obligation and care, or commercial care. Partly this will depend on the degree of satisfaction and dissatisfaction created within the population by such obligations. In a dominant culture that values individual fulfilment and development – a culture that is rights based rather than obligation based – such obligations will probably generate a good deal of dissatisfaction. However, if culture changes and becomes more obligation centred, this equation may change. What will not change with that is the inequity of a general obligation creating very different demands in different situations. This creates a problem of justice which in turn is likely to create disutility, because it causes resentment in those directly affected and insecurity in those who so far have escaped its effects. Any implicit contract, with my parents or with the rest of the community, must accommodate that inequality and either accept or remedy the injustice. Otherwise it does not seem a particularly viable basis for a shared moral obligation.

REFERENCES

Allmark, P. (1995) 'Can there be an ethics of care?', *Journal of Medical Ethics* 21(1), 19–24.

Buber, M. (1971) *I and Thou.* Edinburgh: T & T Clark.

Bulmer, M. (1987) *The Social Basis of Community Care.* London: Allen & Unwin.

Finch, J. (1990) 'The politics of community care in Britain', in C. Ungerson (ed.) *Gender and Caring.* London: Harvester Wheatsheaf.

Fox, N. (1995) 'Post-modern perspectives on care: the vigil and the gift', *Critical Social Policy* 44/45, 107–25.

French, P. (1984) *Collective and Corporate Responsibility.* New York: Columbia University Press.

Hammond, M. (1995) 'Care in the community: an ironic project'. Paper given at conference 'Ethics and Community', University of Central Lancashire, October.

Hampton, J. (1993) 'Contract and consent', in R. Goodin and P. Pettit (eds) *A Companion to Contemporary Political Philosophy.* Oxford: Blackwell.

HMSO (1989) *Caring for People.* (White Paper) London: HMSO.

Mayo, M. (1994) *Communities and Caring.* London: Macmillan.

Noddings, N. (1984) *Caring: A Feminine Approach to Ethics and Moral Education.* Berkeley: University of California Press.

Pellegrino, E. D. (1985) 'The caring ethic: the relationship of physician to patient', in A. H. Bishop and J. R. Scudder (eds) *Caring, Curing, Coping: Nurse, Physician, Patient Relationships.* Birmingham: University of Alabama Press.

Qureshi, H. (1990) 'Boundaries between formal and informal caregiving work', in C. Ungerson (ed.) *Gender and Caring.* London: Harvester Wheatsheaf.

Rawls, J. (1971) *A Theory of Justice.* Cambridge, MA: Harvard University Press.

Sandel, M. (1982) *Liberalism and the Limits of Justice.* New York: Cambridge University Press.

Tonnies, F. (1957) *Community and Society.* (trans. C. P. Loomis) East Lansing: Michigan University Press.

Walker, A. (1989) 'Community care', in M. McCarthy (ed.) *The New Politics of Welfare*. London: Macmillan.

Waltzer, M. (1983) *Spheres of Justice: A Defence of Pluralism and Equality*. Oxford: Blackwell.

Yeo, E. and Yeo, S. (1988) 'On the uses of community', in S. Yeo (ed.) *New Views of Co-operation*. London: Routledge.

WITHDRAWN

CHAPTER 2
Justice and the Allocation of Resources

INTRODUCTION

In this chapter I shall consider how the actual provision of community care can be carried out in a way that makes moral sense. I shall focus primarily on what people get in relation to what they ought to get; also how much they get in relation to how much they ought to get *and* in relation to how much other people get. The conceptual focus for this is justice.

REDISTRIBUTION OF RESOURCES

A major change in the welfare state, such as the 1990 National Health Service and Community Care Act, produces (among other things) changes in the way services are targeted and distributed (Hudson, 1994). Some of this involves a redistribution between age cohorts. There is good reason to suppose that the Government was seeking, through its reforms, to limit the resource demands of an increasing elderly population by residualizing services to them (Jack, 1991). A ceiling was placed on certain sources of resourcing for residential care of the elderly (HMSO, 1989), for instance, which meant that people entering the category of need after 1993 would get a different mix of resources per head from those for whom services were established before that year. There is also good reason to suppose that those resources are less than they were and that, therefore, the slightly younger cohort are receiving less than their elders. Part of the rationale for these changes was the perceived effect of the expansion of the elderly as a proportion of the population, and their predicted impact on state resources. There is also reason to believe that the effects of the redistributed cost and charge structures of residential care for the elderly are having a redistributive impact on their offspring, whose expectations in terms of inheritance may well be substantially affected (Challis and Henwood, 1994).

In this process there are gainers and losers. Some groups get an improved service, and some individuals get services that they find personally congenial. Some groups get a service which is less congenial. Sometimes the service is more congenial, but cheaper, which frees resources to be spent on something else.

EQUALITY AND INEQUALITY

These changes – these losses and gains – do not happen on a level playing field. Western societies are characterized by complex patterns of differing resources, differing access to services, differing degrees of choice, differing qualities of goods available. In other words, we live in societies characterized by inequality along a number of different dimensions.

The concepts of equality and inequality are relevant to our discussion primarily in so far as they relate to the degree to which equality as a moral principle might guide us in deciding how we distribute the goods and services of community care. However, we are inevitably going to be concerned also with people's access to a wider range of goods and services by virtue of their income and wealth, as that access provides the context for their need.

Any claim about equality between people warrants close examination. First, we need to consider whether such a claim relates to similarity or equivalence. If a person makes the claim 'all human beings are equal' are they saying that all human beings are similar, or the same? If so, in what way are they similar, or the same? Or is the person saying that all human beings are equivalent; that they are all of equal worth, irrespective of other differences?

We may also need to establish whether such a statement is descriptive or prescriptive. A descriptive statement of equality would signify that people are, in fact, equal to one another. A prescriptive statement of equality would signify that people *ought to* be equal. Here we are saying something rather different from a statement that people *are* equal.

A statement that human beings are similar or the same can be sustained in relation to certain basic species-specific biological facts, but once we move beyond that level, human diversity and societal complexity makes such statements very hard to sustain.

A statement that human beings all have the same moral worth raises different problems, in that it is hard to see what factual evidence might be used to either support or refute such a statement.

This statement seems to be one of moral belief rather than of fact. Clearly delineating between descriptive and prescriptive (particularly moral) claims of equality has been a major issue for many years. Barry (1984, p.141) offers one view of this: 'In political discourse the word [equality] has little descriptive meaning because in all their most important respects men [*sic*] are most certainly not equal. Therefore its use is mainly prescriptive.'

ARGUMENTS FOR EQUALITY

I shall now pursue further the proposition that people ought to have equal access to goods and services, and I offer two types of moral argument that might support it.

A Kantian argument

The first argument is based on the claim of moral equivalence which I mentioned above. It relates to the moral nature of human beings, and asserts that people deserve to be equal to one another in particular practical ways because they are morally equal, and practical equality expresses that moral equality. This kind of argument has ancient roots, but in its modern non-religious manifestations owes a good deal to Kant's concept of the person as having an irreducible moral significance which is characteristic equally of every person, irrespective of their behaviour, qualities and abilities. Therefore, runs this argument, people are of equal worth. In that sense they are already equal, and from the statement that they are equal in that fundamental respect it follows that they ought to be equal in any practical respects which thereby are entailed.

This leads us into another question – in what practical ways ought people to be equal? One possible answer based on this argument is that people ought to be equal in those characteristics that allow us to fulfil our moral natures as rational beings. The three areas of equality necessary for social justice set out by the Commission on Social Justice (1994) seek to reflect the principle of equality of moral worth. They identify equality of liberties and political rights, equality in the meeting of basic needs, and equality of opportunity. All of these reflect aspects of human moral worth, in particular autonomy and dignity.

However, this argument also countenances some inequality, particularly in the economic sphere. We can argue that inequalities of wealth and income result from the exercise of equal opportunity and, therefore, it is not appropriate to seek to create or impose equality in these areas, by virtue of the fact that that would involve unequal limitation of autonomy. We do not, on the whole, view income as a reflection of moral worth in any case. So we could argue that if people are equal in the ways that do follow from their moral equality – equal before the law, equal in terms of freedom and rights – then that is sufficient, and we ought to accept inequality in terms of material circumstances as a result of equality of autonomy. Given people's diversity, equality of autonomy will produce diverse outcomes. However, this argument would not countenance patterns of inequality related to factors such as ethnicity or gender, or to situations of multiple or cyclical deprivation. All of these would be denials of equality of opportunity as well as moral equality.

It is important to emphasize that the argument I have just been setting out does not depend on any supposition of actual equality between people in other respects. There is no claim that people are equal in terms of character, ability or other practical respects, or even in relation to what we may regard as moral qualities, such as honesty, courage and so on. It would not be possible to sustain such an argument for long, and there is no need.

Utilitarian arguments

The other moral arguments for equality that I shall mention are essentially utilitarian, and are of two sorts. The first argument, set out by Baker (1987), runs to the effect that inequality is a source of unhappiness, resentment and instability in society, therefore, the State and society will be rendered more harmonious, stable and efficient because of the removal of a major source of resentment and conflict.

The second argument is not accepted by all utilitarians, and is adhered to by some non-utilitarians, but it uses utilitarian principles and is relevant to our purposes. Its most influential statement is probably that of Rawls (1971) who uses it as a crucial foundation of his theory of justice. It runs to the effect that extreme inequality tends to be inefficient in terms of maximizing utility. In a very unequal society gains by the well off are unlikely to add to their well-being as much as would similar gains to the worst off. Clearly an extra £500 a year will make much more difference to the life of a very poor person than it will to the life of a very rich person. The poor person's happiness will be more substantially increased. So the utilitarian argument would always be to favour the worst off in redistributions of wealth.

Both utilitarian arguments depend on the practical accuracy of their predictions (unlike the earlier argument which rested entirely on moral principles) and it is equally easy to construct utilitarian arguments against equality, or at least against the imposition of material equality through policy. The classic free-market argument – that overall wealth will be maximized if people are free to create and accumulate wealth in a competitive economy – is essentially utilitarian. However, it is possible to imagine an intermediate situation where enough inequality exists to provide an incentive to the enterprising, but not enough to create instability or the inefficient conversion of wealth into happiness.

INEQUALITY AND COMMUNITY CARE

Where do provisions such as community care come into this? I have already said that changes in the organization of care inevitably involve some redistribution, whether this is intended or desired, or not. Some gain and some lose. In a situation where inequalities exist already, we may wish to consider whether those changes have had an impact on any of those existing inequalities. We can ask if there is an impact on the relative position of the better off as against the worse off and we can ask the direction of that impact. On a slightly more complex level, we might ask whether the change represents anything else of moral significance. For instance, are there any groups who have been ignored or disadvantaged in the past whose position can now be rectified in terms of justice?

Community care as a response to inequality

So far I have talked about changes in community care as if they were accidental by-products of administrative changes, but it is clear that community care can be used as a response to inequality, and we need to consider it in that regard.

Providing community care but accepting inequality

At a simple level care may be a compensation for, or counterbalancing of, misfortune and impairment – for the bad luck involved in being ill, and the difficulties of old age. Or it might go further and follow a straightforward utilitarian rationale, advancing the utilitarian agenda of social work (Clark and Asquith, 1985), increasing happiness and reducing the unhappiness resulting from inequality. The poor suffer more from the worst side of these misfortunes, and it might therefore reduce the impact of inequality if care is available from the State. So care can be an attempt to reduce or remove the worst effects of poverty or other misfortunes of inequality. The impact on health may be reversed if good health care is available. Or we might follow Waltzer's (1983) 'spheres of justice' approach and take the view that inequality in the sphere of income is in some sense just, but we think it unjust if this reproduces itself in other spheres – in worse health for the poor, in worse educational prospects, in more family breakdown and so on – so we provide services that will ensure to some degree that inequality of income does not reproduce itself in every sphere of human life. Or we may follow Daniels's (1985) concept of fair equality of opportunity and take the view that in order to compete in a society which we accept as justly unequal, some basic goods must be matters of equal access – particularly health care.

Providing community care to reduce inequality

We may go a stage beyond the above agenda and decide to use a system of public care as part of a process of moving wealth indirectly from the better off to the worse off, taking the collectivist view that 'redistribution is thus an inevitable and proper function of social policy' (George and Wilding, 1992, p.88). If we have a system of graduated taxation the better off will pay more. If, as we might suppose, need is greater among the worse off and the availability of care relates to need, then there will be a flow of resources from the better off to the worse off which will act as an instrument of indirect redistribution – indirect because no money actually arrives in the pockets of the worse off. More of the needs of the worse off are met without cost to them.

HOW DO WE DECIDE WHO GETS WHAT?

The allocation of resources to different groups in the community needs to be considered in some depth, and that will be the focus of the rest of this chapter. Knowing what inequalities exist does not automatically tell us what proportion of funds that sector of society ought to have allocated to meeting what sorts of needs for what reasons. We need to consider these claims in relation to community care in order to make sense of the moral impact of the changes that have brought the new system into being.

Affected groups

We have considered the dimension of wealth and poverty, and the possible redistributory or compensatory functions of the welfare state in that context, but there are other dimensions which relate to both groups and individuals.

Age

One of the groupings most relevant to community care is that of age. There is every reason to suppose that the community care system as it was conceived in 1989 was a response in part to the cost of caring for the increasing number of frail elderly in the population (Jack, 1991).

In some respects age can be seen as analogous to wealth. Youth can be seen as an advantage – a wealth of prospective years, and often of health also. In some societies the old tend also to be materially poor. In the USA an increasing proportion of the old are well off, and their lack of future years and sometimes of health is in some sense balanced by being rather a well-off group materially. In Britain that is less so.

In the USA the issue of dividing resources between the generations has become a matter of open controversy. For instance, Daniel Callahan (1988) has argued that no public resources should be spent on life-saving or life-preserving treatments for people who are beyond the 'natural life span', which he puts at around 75 years. Anxieties are being expressed in the western world about the cost of pensions to the increasing over-60 population during the next half-century. It is likely that similar issues will arise in relation to other aspects of health and social care, and it seems appropriate at this stage to consider the arguments.

So what is the appropriate relationship between generations in terms of the movement of resources? Space does not allow this to be fully explored now, but I would suggest three major issues for consideration in this area:

1. In terms of justice there seems to be some balance between generations in modern, welfare state societies, in that every generation in its youth and prime to some degree benefits from the efforts of the previous generation, while every generation in its old age to some degree depends on the

efforts of the next generation. Resourcing changes may well change this balance, and we might consider whether such a change enhances or diminishes the justice of the situation.

2. We are not dealing here with constant and identifiable sectors of the population, as we are in the case of race or gender groupings. We are talking to some degree about the distribution of benefits across a lifetime. Most people belong to every generation, and every age group, at some time in their lives. So the distribution of goods between generations could be considered from the point of view of a just distribution of goods across a lifetime. Norman Daniels (1988, p.40) has suggested a 'prudential lifespan account' which offers a way of establishing what sort of goods a reasonable person might require at different times of the life cycle, as a guide to deciding on a reasonable distribution of goods between age groups.

3. It may not make much sense to talk about collective obligations between age groups. Intergenerational obligations are normally understood in the individual context, as existing between individual members of family or comparable groupings. If we try to extend the idea to aggregate age groups in a population, we find ourselves talking about obligations by aggregates toward aggregates, a concept which I suggested in Chapter 1 does not make much sense. People may or may not have duties to their parents or offspring. But any wider duties to the elderly or the young are hard to make sense of unless we conceive them as duties of citizenship – perhaps a duty toward each of our fellow citizens to contribute as best we can (which may only be voting in elections) toward justice between generations.

Gender

Women as a group may be affected by changes in community care provision in a number of ways. Viewing women as a disadvantaged group, we may wish to argue that social and health care ought, to some degree, to rectify or counterbalance those disadvantages, in accordance with the principles of equality I set out above. It is clearly a matter of debate whether the welfare state has achieved anything in that respect in the past half-century. Recent changes in the distribution of benefits seem to alter the balance in a clearer way, however. It has been argued by many commentators that community care is, in many instances, family care, predominantly provided by female relatives (Qureshi, 1990). So it may be that some younger women will find themselves increasingly under pressure to give large parts of their lives to caring, because state care resources are being limited (Baldwin and Twigg, 1991). Part of the problem here is that the 'pressure' I mentioned is not directly applied by the State, though the State may create the conditions that generate it. The pressure is often experienced by women as social expectation. The State could argue that it is simply conserving resources, and family care could mean care by sons as much as care by daughters. The inequality is within our cultures, not in state policy, it might be argued.

Women tend to live longer than men, so anything that disadvantages the old disadvantages women disproportionately. Therefore, we can envisage two generations of women caught in a process which disadvantages both.

Some health needs, and consequently care needs, are distinctive to women. Arguments may arise about the allocation of resources to the areas of health care distinctive to women, as a means of reducing their dependency on care in later life.

Race and ethnicity

As with women, the fundamental reality for many Black and ethnic minority members is one of disadvantage, in this case created by racism and ethnocentricity. This shows itself in a number of ways. The most relevant in this context are probably as follows:

1. Some Black and ethnic minorities are disproportionately located in the poorer parts of the population, and are therefore subject to the same considerations as other groups experiencing poverty, social deprivation and lack of opportunity (Jones, 1993).
2. Where we might see health and social care as ways of counterbalancing or compensating poverty and deprivation, there is reason to suppose that for many Black and ethnic minority members it has the opposite effect, for the following reasons:
   – Provision is insensitive to the health, cultural and other needs of Black and ethnic minority members.
   – Sometimes care is provided in a way that actively amplifies inequality (Ahmad, 1993).

The 1990 reforms are seen by many as exacerbating rather than ameliorating these problems. Williams (1992, p.47) comments on the introduction of contracting that 'in an increasingly competitive sector responsiveness and commitment to race equality and equal opportunities are potential casualties'.

If the community care needs of members of particular ethnic groups are distinctive, and that distinctiveness might in some cases cost more money, is there a reasonable expectation that the population as a whole will contribute something to that extra element? The established principle in our system of health care is that the risk is spread – that people who are at greater risk of developing expensive illnesses or other resource-hungry needs are not expected to pay more, as they would under a private insurance system. Rather, the risk is spread across the community. This applies to groups who choose to do risky things, like smokers and rock-climbers; so it presumably can apply also to groups who have not chosen their group membership in terms of race, ethnicity or culture. However, if the principle of spreading the risk is abandoned by government, as is possible, we may find ourselves in a very different situation.

Other groups of users

I have confined myself so far to social and demographic groups. But there is also another major set of groupings identified by their specific characteristics that are more directly relevant to community care. Those experiencing particular illnesses and those with particular disabilities are clearly part of this. If I have diabetes, I may well have community care needs that are specific to this condition. If I suffer from schizophrenia, my community care needs will probably be shaped by that. If I have a disability, this may have considerable implications for my community care needs at some point. In all such cases these needs may be long term and are likely to have a considerable impact on my life, and I am going to have the option of identifying with a 'group' with whom I share this need. Even if I do not so identify, my interests may well be profoundly affected by the kind of treatment that my group receives within the community care system. It is probable that there will not be enough resources to meet all the needs that each of these groups (and others) will perceive as being real. An increase of resourcing for one group may then mean a diminution for another. So again issues arise of how this is decided.

The arguments may be similar to those of other groups:

1. That people with a particular need are more likely to be poor and, therefore, less able to supply their own needs, and may also suffer worse general health for similar reasons.
2. That people with a particular need may be more likely to be old, or young, or Black, or women.
3. That a particular group may be large in comparison to other groups, and claim some consideration on that basis.
4. That a particular group may have been largely ignored and neglected up until now, and claim consideration on a basis of compensation for past mistreatment.
5. That the needs of a particular group are relatively inexpensive to meet – that they can be rehabilitated and helped to be independent of the State or that the quality of their lives can be greatly improved for a relatively low investment – and therefore present a good investment for the State.
6. That the needs of a particular group are relatively expensive to meet, and that they therefore require a rather greater investment per person to achieve an equivalent level of well-being and/or independence than other groups.

Where diametrically opposed arguments can apparently be used to justify the same thing, we are clearly in an area of considerable difficulty.

Carers

There are other groups with an interest. Perhaps the most important is carers. To some extent, carers' interests may correspond with the interests of users. Those caring for the elderly infirm will probably have the same resourcing interests as the elderly infirm as a group – they may in effect form a common interest group. However, we can follow through a spectrum of situations in which difference of interest between carer and user increases. In many cases what is good for the carer is good for the user, and vice versa. In general state support to carers must be motivated on the State's part by a desire to sustain carers in their caring role. But the carer, him or herself, is presumably able to formulate a set of interests distinct from the users and even, at times, contradictory to those of the user. Carers may argue that they ought to have specific benefits to recompense their efforts or compensate their sacrifices, even though the witholding of those benefits will not lead to the users suffering, and there is therefore no practical benefit for the State in providing them. Certainly the evidence of what the carers may be sacrificing is not lacking (e.g. McLaughlin and Ritchie, 1994). A moral right and a moral obligation may be argued. A moral debt on the part of the State to carers is not difficult to argue on that basis. Matters become more difficult where carers' desires or demands might be seen to conflict with the interests of users. For example, some people caring for users with schizophrenia argue in favour of the use of hospitalization in some circumstances, in conflict with organizations claiming to work for the interests of users, who tend to argue in favour of community care. Neither party would entertain the suggestion that their argument implies the sacrificing of the interests of the other party in this instance, but from the outside it might look like this. It would be difficult to argue that a moral debt by the State to carers could justify acting against the interests of users.

Individual issues

In the end, group issues manifest themselves in day-to-day practice as individual questions. Individual users may believe that they are getting less in terms of services than they ought, or having to wait too long, or pay too much, or are presented with too narrow a choice, in comparison with someone else. They or others may feel that this is because they are a member of an underserved group. But they may simply think they are being underserved as individuals. How can that be considered coherently? I propose to consider individual issues of resource allocation in the context of distributive justice, which now requires focused attention.

JUSTICE

I have raised the foregoing questions without attempting to offer a systematic framework for considering them, but we need such a framework to analyse the sort of questions that arise. To make a judgement as to whether a set of social policies is morally right or wrong requires that we attempt to identify principles by which we can make that judgement. I am going to suggest that the concept of justice provides a structure to make such judgements. It provides a measure of moral appropriateness which can be translated into shared principles operable in formal procedures such as case conferences. Rawls (1971, p.3) says that justice is 'the first virtue of social institutions'. Clearly justice is not the only concept that we need in this process – concepts such as love and care may allow equally morally appropriate judgements, but are less susceptible to a systematic and consistent approach. Justice can subsume a number of other important concepts in this context, and as a formal principle it regulates a significant part of our society through law and the courts. I would suggest that justice is the ethical concept most suited to the consideration of social, political and economic arrangements in a complex society.

Distributive and retributive justice

We need to be clear about what sort of justice we are dealing with. Raphael (1981) makes a distinction between two kinds of justice. Retributive justice is concerned with the allocation of blame, responsibility, liability and compensation. This may on occasions be relevant to our concerns but we shall be concerned more often with distributive justice, that is, with the allocation of material rather than moral burdens – who should receive more, who should receive less to allow others to receive more and who should provide. On the whole we more readily associate justice with its retributive manifestation. This is not surprising. Retributive justice is the business of some of our oldest and most prestigious institutions – the courts and the legal profession. They dispense justice in a way that is visible and explicit, everyday as they have done for many centuries. It is familiar, indeed central to our culture and polity. Distributive justice by contrast is seldom the business of courts in our system, and is primarily the business of government and its offshoots such as local government and related authorities.

Just process and just outcome

There are other ways in which we need to categorize and specify the particular variety of justice we are dealing with. Particularly we need to take account of the distinction made by Edwards (1987) between justice in the process of making decisions and justice in the outcome of decisions. In retributive justice we can see that distinction clearly. It is possible for an innocent person to be convicted in criminal proceedings (an unjust outcome) even when all procedural requirements of natural justice have been adhered to (just process). This can happen even though the rules of procedural justice are partly intended to maximize the likelihood of a just outcome.

The distinction also exists in distributive justice. The most basic characteristic of a just process is arguably the basic principle of formal justice – that of equality of treatment. Since Aristotle it has been widely believed that equality of treatment in relevant respects is at the heart of justice. This leaves open the question of what respects are relevant. In that sense the concept is somewhat empty and leaves much space for argument. We may wish to argue that such features as democracy, consultation, the consideration of the interests of all groups, the careful gathering of evidence and the weighing of alternatives are just ways of arriving at distributions of goods at a policy level. Or we may say that such things as equal opportunity and open competition are the most just mechanisms for deciding the distribution of goods. We cannot guarantee that these processes would produce a distribution which is in accordance with our own conception of justice. On the other hand we may see just outcomes from unjust methods. The toss of a coin may produce a result that, as it happens, reproduces the kind of distribution we would regard as just.

Justice in assessing individuals

Implementing a just policy in practice will ultimately involve providing community care services to individuals in a just way. This brings us back to the individual issues of distribution I mentioned earlier. The first necessary element of justice at that level is justice in assessment. The principle of formal justice would require equality of treatment between those being assessed. In practice ensuring that equality would seem to require at least the following elements:

1. That the same method of assessment is used for every potential user.
2. That the method does not discriminate against any group.

In addition, justice for the potential user must involve empowering them to participate in the assessment on as equal footing as possible. This would involve the potential user knowing:

1. That they are being assessed.
2. What information is required for the assessment.
3. What services they are being assessed for.

This degree of explicitness in the assessment process will also help contribute to what Key (1990) terms 'affirmative assessment', in that the user is empowered to deal with the subject-matter of assessment on an explicit verbal level.

Social consensus about justice

There is clearly not a consensus in our society about the appropriate severity of punishment for particular crimes, but there is a known tariff. And there is at least a roughly shared understanding as to the just relationship between crime and punishment in general. In the case of distributive justice there is by contrast no agreement as to what characteristics constitute the equivalent of 'guilt' or 'liability' in retributive justice. In other words, there is no agreement as to what are the characteristics in individuals or groups which justify their receiving a particular distribution of goods. Instead debates about distributive justice centre around a number of concepts which, while being subsumed under justice for these purposes, are in fact ethical concepts in their own right. We cannot appreciate the complexities and conflicts around distributive justice in community care without exploring these.

Discussions of distributive justice touch on a wide range of concepts in various combinations. Edwards (1987) identifies eleven different combinations in the literature. For our purposes I shall work with those which writers such as Edwards (1987), Miller (1976) and Rawls (1971) variously emphasize: rights, need, desert, equality/equity, utility. I shall consider what reference these may have to the situations discussed earlier in relation to winners and losers in community care.

RIGHTS

I shall give a good deal of attention to rights because they constitute the moral concept which is, I suspect, most widely employed after need. But what does it mean to have a right to something?

Positive rights and ideal rights

Rights are generally understood to be legitimate claims to some good. The legitimacy of the claim is in itself worth consideration. I may say that I have a right to free speech. If I made that claim in the USA my statement could refer to the fact that freedom of speech is guaranteed in the Constitution. I am in that case referring to a right that exists in a material, enforceable and enforced form – it is part of a formal system of rules. If anyone tries to prevent me from speaking freely I may presumably invoke the Constitution and, if necessary, seek legal redress. Miller (1976) calls rights of this kind positive rights. If I say the same thing in a country ruled by a repressive dictatorship the statement must be rather different. If it was a reference to something existing within the system, enforceable and protected by the State, my statement would quite simply be untrue. That state does not allow, let alone protect, freedom of speech. However, my statement could still be true in a different sense. It might be that I am protesting at being arrested by the police of that country for criticizing the Government. I may protest that the Government's restrictions on my self-expression are a breach of my right to free speech. If the Government is sovereign, I cannot be appealing to a higher legal authority that guarantees my freedom of speech. So in what sense could my claim be true? I think it could be true in the sense that I could claim a right that exists independently of any sovereign authority; a moral right, or in Miller's terminology an ideal right. A belief that such rights exist provides the justification for reform and revolution.

The problem is that, while we can verify the existence of legal or constitutional rights through scrutiny of documents and decisions, we cannot verify the existence of ideal rights in any empirical sense. We may be able to argue logically for their existence and we may be able to verify that people believe they exist, but statements claiming such rights are moral statements – statements of right and wrong – rather than factual statements. Our belief in these rights is, therefore, always a matter of argument.

Liberties, claim-rights, welfare rights

In this section I shall use Miller's (1976) version of Hohfeld's (1964) classification of rights, somewhat simplified.

Liberties

Let us say that I have a right to do certain things and not to be prevented from doing those things by anyone else. At a basic level I have the right to walk down the street unimpeded and the right to speak as I wish. In some countries they are positive rights, in others they are not. We might believe them to be ideal rights everywhere. They are rights to perform an action rather than rights to be provided with a good, and they usually only require non-interference from others in general rather than active provision by others in particular. Rights of this kind are referred to as 'Liberties', and Waldron (1993) refers to them as 'first generation rights' because they have the longest pedigree in modern western thought. In terms of a just distribution of community care the relevance of liberties is not as immediately obvious as that of some other sorts of rights. But freedom is something that can be redistributed also, and it is clear that it can be compromised by oppressive practices of welfare agencies.

Claim-rights

A second group of rights is identified by Hohfeld (1964) as claim-rights. These arise out of a particular relationship with specified others. For instance, I may have a right to have a promise kept, a debt paid, privacy and confidentiality respected by other individuals or bodies. If I hand over the agreed price of a good as part of an agreed transaction, I have a claim-right to that good which lays a duty upon the vendor to give me the good. If a doctor examines me as part of an agreed strategy to ascertain and communicate to me my state of health, I have a claim-right to that doctor's opinion as to my state of health and the doctor has a duty to give me his or her opinion. Rights of this sort clearly have relevance to justice in community care because there are situations where a user has a claim on a worker or agency, perhaps on the basis of equality of treatment or the keeping of promises. Such rights may or may not be legally enforceable, but their moral significance is what is most relevant to our purposes.

Welfare rights

In a sense welfare rights are a subcategory of claim-rights, in that they relate to goods which the citizen can legitimately claim from the State in given situations. I have a right to income support in certain circumstances. Those circumstances are laid down by government regulation. I have a right also to free health care. In general, welfare rights only makes sense between citizen and state, and it might be argued that they only make sense in the context of a state welfare system. It does not on the face of it make much sense to say that I have a right to income support, when there is no such thing included in any state provision. Sim (1995, p.34) argues that 'if the correlative duty it imposes on others to provide a certain benefit or service is simply not feasible, then this casts doubt on the validity of the right itself'. So it could be argued that welfare rights only exist where the State provides for them and in that sense they are legal or positive rights only, not ideal rights. If I went to Somalia it would be nonsense for me to claim a welfare right to free health care because the Government there does not, and almost certainly cannot, provide such a thing. No such right could exist.

There is an argument that suggests welfare rights can exist independently of state provision. After all, on what basis can I argue that the State ought to provide benefit X, which it does not at present provide? Could I argue that the State should provide X because people have a moral right to X? This is what the United Nations (UN) Declaration of Human Rights implies in relation to such rights as education and health care. These rights are set out clearly even though many governments do not provide for them. These look very much like welfare rights.

Recognizing rights

How can we establish who has what rights? In the case of positive rights, recipients will often be defined along with the rights themselves. In the case of ideal rights it is less clear. However, we can identify some guidelines. If we follow the UN declaration, then a wide range of rights are due to all members of the human species, by virtue of their membership. The fact of being a human being confers those rights, which include both liberties and welfare rights. Claim-rights must arise from the specific relationship between the beneficiary and others who have the duty of providing what is the subject of the right.

Is there a right to community care?

This question could be answered in one of two ways. First, we could argue that there is a welfare right to a particular set of arrangements and procedures, which are embodied in the law and administrative arrangements, and which are called 'community care'. This makes no assumptions about how much community care any one individual receives. Second we could argue that there is a welfare right to community care up to a particular level, in terms of quality and quantity. This is quite different from saying that we have a right to a system of community care that does not specify how much care we receive.

The second version of this right is clearly going to present more ethical problems than the first version, particularly for whoever has the job of finding the resources to make that provision. The Government may well argue that the nation cannot afford the kind of resourcing that would satisfy everyone's definition of adequacy. Can there then be a right to something that cannot be provided? What does it mean to say that a citizen has a right to state health care when the state is poverty-stricken and cannot conceivably provide what I have a right to? Our government is clearly not in that position, but it could quite properly argue that it will need to reduce the resourcing of other provision – education perhaps, or transport – in order to respond to a notion that those of us in need of community care have a right to it in a given quantity and quality. Do we have that right at the expense of schoolchildren, or road users?

Whatever we may conclude about our rights to scarce resources in the second version of our right to community care, we might argue for the existence of rights applying to the first version above. If we have machinery to deliver community care and there is not enough community care to go round, what rights might we claim in relation to the way that machinery operates? If we take a Kantian view that there are rights attaching to people by virtue of their humanity or personhood, then we could argue a right to equality of treatment for all persons of equal worth (which in this context means all persons); also a right to honest treatment for all persons. This does not depend on the availability of resources, but does clearly depend on the honest and equal use of what resources are available. It also implies a right to honest and equal consideration for those resources on the part of all potential users. This applies in particular to the way assessment is carried out, and is a claim-right rather than a welfare right, implying a duty on both the agency and the individual assessor.

The relevance of rights

Welfare rights

I would argue that the concept of welfare rights works well when we are looking for arguments for improved provision or new provision. To say that a group of people have a right to a service, or a better service, makes some sense where that can be linked to more basic rights of the sort listed (for instance) in the UN declaration. Such basic rights might help us to make decisions about the allocation of resources. If everyone has a right to basic accommodation, for instance, then perhaps we could argue that nobody can claim a right to state funding for higher education while any of their fellow citizens is involuntarily homeless. Such rights-based arguments might help us decide on the allocation of resources between education and community care.

Liberties and claim-rights

I would argue that the concepts of claim-rights and liberties work well when we are looking at the obligations of agencies and workers to individuals. These apply in two ways.

First, they apply to liberties (many of which can be reframed as respect for user autonomy), and to claim-rights in terms of the agencies', and workers' obligation to treat users and others fairly and equally, and with honesty. To a large extent these reflect the sort of duties that Kant argued are owed by persons to other persons. We can view liberties, including a right to control over one's own life, as among the basic rights of citizenship. So these might include the right to participate in decision-making about one's own life and, in this context, one's own care. Biehal (1993) argues that a recognition of such basic rights on the part of the user are a necessary basis for just provision.

Second they apply to recognition of the specific obligations that agencies and workers have to specific individuals on the basis of their eligibility for services. In essence it is a recognition that where someone meets the criteria for provision which the State and the agency have publicly declared to be such, a moral obligation exists to respond to that eligibility, and to provide what is due to the individual. It may in practice be impossible to fulfil that moral obligation because of resource problems, but it is important (on the basis of fairness and honesty) to acknowledge that the right exists even though the matching obligation cannot be fulfilled.

Rights are less useful when we are trying to distinguish between the rights of different individuals in terms of priority and rationing.

NEED

This is likely to be the most generally acceptable of the criteria for a just distribution of community care. The system was created, ostensibly, to respond to need. Many people would argue that need is prior to rights in this context, in that a legal right depends on need, moral right may well be inseparable from need, and that claims to a right based on any other criterion is at best secondary to need, and at worst unjust. Miller (1976) argues that among the criteria for distributive justice, need is most closely related to the principle of equality, while the Commission on Social Justice (1994) identifies the meeting of basic needs as the second essential component of social justice.

Problems with need

However, the apparent firmness of the concept of need (when compared with rights) is illusory. The idea that need is an objective criterion is particularly problematic. When we talk about 'needs' as a noun we increase the impression that they are solid real things. If we keep to its original use, as a verb, it exposes the uncertainty rather more. This allows us to ask a particular question: if you say 'I need X ...' I can respond with 'why?' and that clarifies one characteristic of needs, that they are *for* something. I need X in order to achieve Y. Y might be survival. Or it might be guarding my health, maintaining my self-esteem or avoiding boredom. There are various things that we value sufficiently to talk about in this way, and which, thereby give extra moral force to our requests or demands for certain things. But these valuations are culture-specific, and it would be unwise to assume that they are reproduced in the same way in all cultures.

Our biological nature leads us instinctively to place great priority on survival, though we know that it is not always everyone's personal priority. When we get beyond survival into the other valued characteristics of existence people's priorities vary a great deal, both as individuals and in cultural terms.

Need and justice

In terms of justice, then, we should consider whether provision ought to reflect a common and consistent set of needs even though they may not reflect everyone's (or, exactly, anyone's) priorities, or whether it is more just to respond variously to individual priorities. The argument in favour of the first option would be that justice requires a degree of consistency and comparability (the principle of equal treatment). The argument against this is that consistency is, in fact, not achieved because the notion of need as consistent is false, and that justice cannot be based on a false criterion. However, the problem with an individually tailored definition of need is that we lose the distinction between need and desire. And we are forced back, in real terms, into using desire as criterion.

However, even if we work to a common set of needs, we still have the problem of agreeing a common set of causal links between need and that which will meet need. The need for oral gratification is met in one case by champagne (because Mrs Smith was brought up on it), in the other by lemonade (because Mrs Brown was brought up on that). Do we ensure that the day centre is supplied with both, so that Mrs Smith can have her daily glass of champagne (which she has had for 70 years) and Mrs Brown her daily glass of lemonade? It is perfectly reasonable to argue that individual differences of taste mean that the same needs are met in very different ways. The quality of the experience is the same for the two individuals. The fact that the cost of supplying that experience is different in each case ought not to impinge on the concept of need.

Once we are at this point we lose all hope of consistency of process, even though we might be able to conceive of a situation where outcome is consistent. One requirement for the justice of process is that there is some possibility of objective verification of the facts that are being made use of. Personal values are by their nature not verifiable. If I say that I value something, it is very difficult to know what would be reliable evidence that I am lying or telling the truth. We are dealing with something that is truly, and legitimately, subjective. On a level of practical politics it is unlikely that the tax-paying population as a whole would agree to their resources being allocated on this basis.

It seems, then that need, unlike rights, is a good instrument for distinguishing between what different individuals ought to get in terms of community care. However, it is not good at doing that in a way that satisfies justice, despite the fact that there seems to be something intrinsically just about the idea that people receive according to need.

Theories of need

One way out of this impasse is to go back to my earlier comments about need – that it is subjective, and culture-specific – and to try to find a way out of this by means of something that can be agreed and accepted as objective within our society. This has been tried in various ways. Maslow's (1954) hierarchy of needs is the centrepiece of a theory of need that purports to be based on evidence of human behaviour. If it holds good – that higher needs cannot be met until the lower ones have been met – then it offers a practical framework that seems to solve the moral problem. Only one scale of priorities is possible, and people's varying values and preferences are not 'true'. So we can ignore them and follow a consistent policy that, because it is both consistent and 'real', serves distributive justice. However, this relies on the soundness of the theory.

Another theory of need, that of Doyal and Gough (1991), rests more firmly on moral reasoning, and depends less on empirical evidence. Drawing on Kant's focus on the person, and in particular on autonomy as the focal characteristic of personhood, Doyal and Gough base their concept of need on social participation, suggesting that this can be seen as universal, and entails a need for autonomy and for physical health. So, with health and autonomy we have a rather shallower hierarchy than Maslow's, with far fewer empirical claims and an explicit moral base. If we could agree on the moral universality of those needs it would provide a better basis for needs-based justice than that of Maslow. Spicker (1993) also accepts that need is essentially a moral concept but centres his model of need on the idea of legitimacy of claim, therefore seeming to reduce needs to rights. It appears that need is no firmer a moral concept than it is an empirical one.

UTILITY

This principle – derived as its name might suggest from utilitarianism – identifies justice with the maximization of happiness and, more recently, of other goods such as welfare, well-being and health. Specifically it requires that our decisions will be just if they generate more of those goods and less of their opposites than the available alternatives. Its implications are in some respects rather different from those of need. For instance, we take account of the interests of a wider range of people using utility as our guide than we would if we focused purely on need. If we focus on need we favour the needy. If we focus on utility we take account of everyone affected by community care. We give consideration not only to those who will receive the services but also to those who pay for them – the taxpayers who, presumably, will be happier if their money is spent to the best possible effect – and to those who might not receive them. Need will tend to draw the resources to those with the most serious problems, who may take up more resources to relatively less effect.

Two problems arise with utility as a yardstick of distributive justice. First, there is an issue about which particular good will constitute utility. Will it be happiness, well-being, welfare, health?

They are closely related but not necessarily coterminous. Which we choose will have considerable implications in terms of justice. Second, there are considerable difficulties with making interpersonal comparisons of utility, however we constitute it. Interpersonal comparisons of well-being, for instance, raise numerous problems, particularly with regard to the relationship between subjective and objective states of well-being (see Elster and Roemer, 1993).

Balancing need and utility

In terms of distributive justice, utility has the same problem that it has in morality generally – it allows us to sacrifice one in order to benefit many. In this context we can imagine situations where we may prevent a great deal of unhappiness if we use our resources to maintain users at a reasonable level, and prevent deterioration to a level of extreme need. That may be a more productive use of resources than spending everything on comprehensive care for one badly deteriorated individual. So we can see that need and utility are to some degree mirror images of each other. Their close relationship in community care planning is acknowledged by Lightfoot (1995) who offers a model of planning which seeks to balance the two principles. They can distinguish between individuals (unlike rights) and they focus on closely related aspects of people's situations. They are both principles which seem consonant with distributive justice. However, I think we would suffer more intuitive moral discomfort if we discarded need as a criterion than if we discarded utility. A situation of extreme shortage, in which only the most infirm and needy received any resources, and others were left unsupported until they deteriorated to the required level, would be exasperating in the extreme, but we would blame the shortage, not the prioritizing of the neediest. If on the other hand we allowed the most infirm to deteriorate – perhaps to have to go into institutional care – in order to use our resources to benefit and maintain more people at a better level, we might I think find that unjust.

However, if in the first scenario we found in due course that our resources were increasing and devoted every extra pound to the care of those at the eligible level of need without wondering whether it could be more usefully spent elsewhere, we would again have reason to question the justice of our actions. Once we are out of minimal scarcity, utility starts to look just. Need gives due weight to the moral importance of threat to life and autonomy in a way that utility does not. That must give it some priority. However, utility takes account of the well-being of a wider range of people, so is a principle it seems important to make use of.

EQUALITY

I have discussed this at some length in the first part of the chapter, so I shall limit my comments now. My intention earlier was to look at community care as a means of achieving social equality, but this may be quite a different process from that of using equality as a criterion for the allocation of community care, which is what I am concerned with now. In terms of justice, equality relates closely to need, as Miller (1976) points out, in the sense that need-based justice would require that we apply the criterion of need to every individual in an equal way. Some rights are not equal – rights arising from particular relationships such as contract, for instance – but there are others that are – liberties, and certain claim-rights.

I suggest that the right to equal treatment in such processes as assessment (in a way that is analogous to equality before the law), is another manifestation of the basic Aristotelian principle that justice entails treating everyone alike in the relevant respects. This can be linked to the Kantian idea of equality of worth, which may not require everyone to have the same income and wealth, but does require that they be treated the same in certain essential areas such as law. This principle would require us not to treat people differently unless they are different in a relevant respect (in terms of rights, need, utility) and to avoid differences in treatment which do not correspond to relevant differences in the situation. So we might argue that differences in the standard of service provided by one authority as against another is not likely to correspond to relevant differences in the populations who are receiving these unequal services. In which case if those inequalities are to be justified, we shall need to draw on a moral principle other than justice – democracy, perhaps, or liberty. If discrepancies in services exist between smaller units than this – for instance between residential establishments – then there is again a good argument for claiming injustice, and we must again search for another moral principle to justify this. There may be situations where utility is served through a certain degree of inequality between establishments, where centres of excellence and innovation offer the prospect of better services for all in the future.

DESERT

Are there ever situations where people get a service because they deserve it or have a service withheld because they do not deserve it? It seems difficult to apply the concept of desert to community care. For a start, it is difficult to imagine qualities or actions which may lead someone to deserve this particular good. It seems to make sense in the context of retributive justice to impose a punishment which is deserved by the offender. It seems to make sense to confer deserved honours on a hero or public benefactor. In both cases what is received is something which has as its purpose a moral response – to good or bad behaviour. Punishment or reward exist as part of a moral reciprocation and only make sense in that context. The privation or provision of material goods – a fine, or a pension, perhaps – could be used to fulfil that moral purpose, but community care by its nature – in particular by its relationship to need – could not constitute such a moral response. It is essentially a practical good which raises moral issues (like most practical goods). The notion of community care being a reward or punishment does not sit with its other functions. Desert therefore does not seem to have any relevance to justice in the distribution of community care.

A THEORY OF JUSTICE

So far I have applied concepts of justice independently. However, there are theories of distributive justice which work at least some of these concepts into a consistent system. Probably the most widely known such theory is that of John Rawls (1971). He gives significant weight to the demands of utility, equality and need in his system, and works them into a relation to one another which makes some moral sense.

He argues that in both empirical and rational terms redistribution of goods to the worst off is worth more than redistribution of goods to the better off. In terms of utility, a given additional quantity of goods is likely to augment the material well-being of someone who has very little more than the same quantity will do for someone who already has a great deal. In that sense the greater relative need of the worse off augments the utility of such a redistribution. So the pressure of Rawls's argument is always towards equality. He is not egalitarian, in that he does not object to the rich being rich, and even getting richer, as long as the poor benefit as well. He bases this on the view that inequality is acceptable in so far as it is useful or necessary in terms of incentives. It has no intrinsic moral value, in that the rich do not in any strict sense deserve to be rich, or the poor to be poor.

Rawls is mainly concerned with the distribution of wealth across society as a whole, and on the face of it his theory does not seem particularly relevant to the business of distributing care resources between individuals. However, if we regard community care as an instrument of redistribution we would be justified in Rawls's terms in ensuring that every additional resource and indeed every redistributed resource benefited the poorest, the sickest, the most infirm, the most alone. It also provides an argument for seeing redistribution as a morally justifiable process in the first place. Rawls's theory provides us with a strong moral base for characterizing as unjust any community care system which functions to perpetuate or exacerbate the relative disadvantages of the worst-off.

REFERENCES

Ahmad, W. (1993) *Race and Health in Contemporary Britain.* Buckingham: Open University Press.

Baker, J. (1987) *Arguing for Equality.* London: Verso.

Baldwin, S. and Twigg, J. (1991) 'Women and community care', in M. Maclean and D. Groves (eds) *Women's Issues in Social Policy.* London: Routledge.

Barry, N. P. (1984) *An Introduction to Modern Political Theory.* London: Macmillan.

Biehal, N. (1993) 'Changing practice: participation, rights and community care'. *British Journal of Social Work* 23(5), 443–58.

Callahan, D. (1988) *Setting Limits: Medical Goals in an Ageing Society.* New York: Touchstone.

Challis, L. and Henwood, M. (1994) 'Equity in community care'. *British Medical Journal* 308, 1496–9.

Clark, C. and Asquith, S. (1985) *Social Work and Social Philosophy.* London: Routledge & Kegan Paul.

Commission on Social Justice (1994) *Social Justice: Strategies for National Renewal.* London: Vintage.

Daniels, N. (1985) *Just Health Care.* New York: Cambridge University Press.

Daniels, N. (1988) *Am I my Parents Keeper?* New York: Oxford University Press.

Doyal, L. and Gough, I. (1991) *A Theory of Human Need*. London: Macmillan.

Edwards, J. (1987) *Positive Discrimination, Social Justice and Social Policy*. London: Tavistock.

Elster, J. and Roemer, J. E. (1993) *Interpersonal Comparisons of Well-Being*. Cambridge: Cambridge University Press.

George, V. and Wilding, P. (1992) *Ideology and Social Welfare*. London: Routledge.

HMSO (1989) *Caring for People*. (White Paper) London: HMSO.

Hohfeld, W. N. (1964) *Fundamental Legal Conceptions as Applied in Judicial Reasoning*. New Haven and London: Yale University Press.

Hudson, B. (1994) 'Management and finance', in N. Malin, (ed.) *Implementing Community Care*. Buckingham: Open University Press.

Jack, R. (1991) 'Social services and the ageing population'. *Social Policy and Administration* 25(4), 284–99.

Jones, T. (1993) *Britain's Ethnic Minorities: An Analysis of the Labour Force Survey*. London: Policy Studies Institute.

Key, M. (1990) 'The practice of assessing elders', in O. Stevenson, (ed.) *Age and Vulnerability*. London: Edward Arnold.

Lightfoot, J. (1995) 'Identifying needs and setting priorities: issues of theory, policy and practice'. *Health and Social Care in the Community* 3(2), 105–14.

McLaughlin, E. and Ritchie, J. (1994) 'Legacies of caring: the experiences and circumstances of ex-carers'. *Health and Social Care in the Community* 2(4), 241–54.

Maslow, A. (1954) *Motivation and Personality*. New York: Harper & Row.

Miller, D. (1976) *Social Justice*. Oxford: Clarendon Press.

Qureshi, H. (1990) 'Boundaries between formal and informal care-giving work', in C. Ungerson (ed.) *Gender and Caring*. London: Harvester Wheatsheaf.

Raphael, D. D. (1981) *Moral Philosophy*. Oxford: Oxford University Press.

Rawls, J. (1971) *A Theory of Justice*. Cambridge, MA: Harvard University Press.

Sim, J. (1995) 'Moral rights and the ethics of nursing'. *Nursing Ethics* 2(1), 31–40.

Spicker, P. (1993) 'Needs as claims'. *Social Policy and Administration* 27(1), 7–17.

Waldron, J. (1993) 'Rights', in R. Goodin and P. Pettit (eds) *A*

Companion to Contemporary Political Philosophy. Oxford: Blackwell.

Waltzer, M. (1983) *Spheres of Justice: A Defence of Pluralism and Equality.* Oxford: Blackwell.

Williams, A. (1992) *Caring for People: Caring for Profit.* London: London Voluntary Service Council.

CHAPTER 3
Autonomy

INTRODUCTION

The first part of this chapter consists of an exploration of the concept of autonomy. This is followed by four sections which consider the implications of autonomy in the context of four issues: autonomy and consent; autonomy and influence; unwanted autonomy; autonomy, integrity and privacy.

THE CONCEPT OF AUTONOMY

In modern liberal societies – certainly in those characterized by free-market economies – autonomy is widely valued as a right that takes priority over most other considerations, and a necessary prerequisite (at least in economic terms) to achieving prosperity and maximizing well-being. In Chapter 1 I suggested that the concept of autonomy is important because it counterbalances a number of other principles which we are using in this exploration. It counterbalances justice because it can be used to temper strict distributive justice – for instance when we are seeking to achieve justice through egalitarian policies. It counterbalances the value of community because it emphasizes individual choice against obligation to the group. It counterbalances care because it puts a boundary round the degree to which being cared about should limit the options of the individual.

The priority of autonomy

A traditional view in European political theory is that autonomy matters because it is prior to the State and the community. It is a 'state of nature' characteristic that would have moral force even if no states or communities existed. This perspective has a history reaching back to the political philosophy of Thomas Hobbes in the seventeenth century (Hampton, 1990) and could be characterized as individualistic and Eurocentric, but it gives us a sense of the significance of autonomy.

In terms of community care, autonomy matters because it defines the person – whether user, carer or any other member of the public – as the professional encounters them. Irrespective of whether they have need, right, or any other just claim on help, and irrespective of whether or not the worker has any specific responsibility to that person, the presumption must be that the person is autonomous. Whereas the burden of proof in terms of justice and duty may lie in such a way that the worker must find reasons why that person should receive a service, and that service should come from this agency, the burden of proof with autonomy lies in quite the opposite direction – that their autonomy should not be respected – and any departure from that principle requires very good reasons indeed.

Autonomy in context: the utilitarian view

We need to put autonomy in the context of some of the moral philosophies that we have encountered. For utilitarians autonomy is one of a number of principles which need to be tested against the principle of utility – the maximizing of happiness. Traditional liberal utilitarians worked on the assumption that people needed liberty to maximize their own happiness and that, on the whole, the happiness of the community in general would be enhanced by liberty, and its diminution would generally be a threat to utility.

However, the utilitarian analysis also allows us to place limits on autonomy. It might in some circumstances be justified, in utilitarian terms, to limit the exercise of autonomy where it causes unhappiness to others. John Stuart Mill (1946, p.16) took the view that 'the only freedom which deserves the name is that of pursuing our own good in our own way, so long as we do not attempt to deprive others of theirs, or impede their efforts to attain it'. There are circumstances where the general utility of having secure liberties might well counterbalance the individual annoyance caused by the exercise of those liberties, and a utilitarian may be willing to tolerate some antisocial behaviour in the name of utility. However, there must come a point where general utility is threatened by such antisocial use of autonomy, and it maximizes happiness to limit it. A rule utilitarian may accept a set of rules that protects autonomy, if he or she can calculate that such rules will maximize utility overall, even though there may be individual cases where their observance has the opposite effect. An act utilitarian will make his or her judgement on the utility of the particular action, which may have different consequences on different occasions. The presumption that liberty is the friend of utility is the product of nineteenth-century liberal assumptions about human nature. A modern utilitarian may be less sanguine about this and more likely to see the limitation of autonomy as likely to achieve utility.

The Kantian view

Autonomy is the centrepiece of Kant's view of morality. He refers to autonomy of the will as the ' supreme principle of morality' (Paton, 1956). The person can only behave rationally (and therefore morally) if he or she is free to do so. And the special moral status of reason is denied if autonomy is denied. If persons cannot freely choose between right and wrong action and take responsibility for that choice, then moral judgement and moral behaviour become impossible. So autonomy is for the Kantian the central characteristic that the worker must respect in treating the client as an end rather than a means. It has priority over care, utility, community and even need as judged by those other than the person concerned. Autonomy by contrast is consistent with duty and rights. The difficult part is to ensure at a policy and practice level that one person's autonomy does not compromise another's autonomy. Kant himself was mainly concerned with the individual's duty to respect others' autonomy as part of treating them as ends.

The existentialist view

Existentialism has an unambiguous commitment to autonomy. It follows Kant in viewing the person as being entirely endowed with the capacity for choice, and in viewing the freedom to exercise that choice as being an essential prerequisite of morally significant action. Macquarrie (1972, p.177) suggests that 'there can be few themes, if any, nearer to the heart of existentialism than freedom'. However, existentialists take a rather different view of the possibilities of freedom, in the sense that they regard the exercise of choice as being something that is an existential necessity, not just a moral necessity, and argue that the exercise of choice is possible in most circumstances even where there may be constraint of the heaviest kind, such as a threat to life attached to certain choices. In that sense the freedom to choose is something that is there in all situations, and must be acknowledged and owned by the person. So choice is always possible, and always necessary.

Positive and negative autonomy

The established philosophies tend to focus disproportionately on the idea of negative autonomy – the principle that if nobody tries to stop me from doing what I want, then I am autonomous. The concept of positive autonomy – the range of choices that are actually available to me, assuming nobody tries to restrict my freedom – gets less attention. Negative autonomy clearly has great relevance to community care because it is concerned with not forcing people to do what they don't want to do and, when we are dealing with people in a vulnerable and dependent situation, that is a central concern. However, community care may also be about increasing people's options, and that 'positive autonomy' is something that needs to be considered, not least in the context of justice. Choices are a good, and can be considered in terms of distributive justice.

Motive and meaning

There is another dimension which utilitarians, Kantians and existentialists tend not to take account of, and that is the 'internal' space within which I make choices. The danger of the established philosophies is that they lead us to frame choosing-behaviour within one single consideration – pleasure, passion, duty, self-creation. We know that motivations and personal justifications for the choices that people make are much more variable than that and are influenced by many other considerations. In that connection it is useful to consider the question in the context of specific moral systems embedded in specific communities and cultures. If we look at diverse moral systems in the context of culture, community and religion, we find many belief systems about the options that are available, as well as the options that are desirable and right (Triandis, 1990). The objective limitations that exist around us and restrict our freedom are matched by beliefs we hold about what is possible – not only what choices are available but whether I have any right to make those choices (desirable or otherwise) and whether the exercise of that sort of autonomy is morally acceptable, irrespective of the rightness or otherwise of particular options. In other words choosers are not 'unencumbered selves' in the sense that Benhabib (1992) uses the term. They have personalities, cultures, identities (relating to gender, race and so on) and are in reality embodied in specific situations which will constrain both options and choices.

Is autonomy an illusion?

The contrasts between the views discussed above lead us into the first major issue that we must address with regard to autonomy. Is autonomy a real phenomenon in the first place? If we are mistaken in thinking that we are capable of being autonomous, then the idea of autonomy must lose its moral importance, and it becomes pointless to attempt to safeguard one's own or others' autonomy. We cannot have a right to a good which is illusory. I shall consider some aspects of experience which seem to argue against the reality of autonomy.

External constraints on autonomy

1. There appear to be limits on my autonomy because of physical laws, however much I may will them to become possible for me. My autonomy does not run to being able to grow wings and fly, or travel through time.
2. There appear to be limits on my autonomy because of social or economic circumstances. My autonomy does not run to being able to become extremely rich, talented, popular or powerful.
3. There appear to be limits on my autonomy because of the particular rules of the society I live in. My autonomy does not run to rifling my neighbours' safe and murdering them in their beds.
4. There appear to be limits on my autonomy from the particular hegemony that I inhabit, which involves being manipulated by various forces beyond my control. I am manipulated as a consumer, through advertising and through constraints on my buying options. I am manipulated as a citizen of the polity through a limited political culture and constraints on my political options.

Some of the above considerations relate to probability. None of the actions that I identified in points one to three above as beyond the limits of my autonomy are inconceivable. The actions in one above are reasonably characterized as impossible but it is conceivable that they will become possible in the future. The probability that I shall do them is extremely low. The limit on my autonomy in two above is again a matter of probability. Arguably, it is possible for me to become extremely rich etc., but it is extremely improbable.

In the case of point three, four additional elements come into the picture. First, the law will prevent me from murdering my neighbours and rifling their safe. Therefore, there is a conscious desire on the part of person or institution to limit my autonomy, something that did not apply to the earlier points. Second, what that means, in fact, is that the law will punish me afterwards, not that it will stop me beforehand; and it will only be able to punish me if I am caught and convicted of the crime. So, again, we are dealing with probabilities. It is certainly possible for me to perform the crime if I am willing to risk certain outcomes, and it is possible (though perhaps improbable) for me to get away with it. Third, the situation in point three highlights the problem of the distribution of autonomy. If I commit that crime, I am extending my own autonomy at the expense of my neighbours' autonomy. I allow myself an option, and they lose everything. Fourth, my own conscience or socialization may stop me from contemplating the crime in the first place. I may in that sense regard the action as 'impossible' for me to do. I shall consider the implications of that later.

In the situation in point four above, I may choose to refuse to be manipulated by the hegemonic system I inhabit. Such a choice would depend upon my being able to resist the cultural power of the dominant system over my thinking. If I am able to make that choice, I may do this by choosing an alternative lifestyle and alternative politics – possibly by joining the Donga tribe. This would to some degree free me from covert manipulation, but the probable consequence would be a good deal of overt harassment. So, again, I am dealing with the probability of certain consequences following from my exercise of autonomy.

Several points arise from this:

1. Autonomy can be considered in terms of the probability of particular outcomes following from particular options. Autonomy must be affected by the probability of those outcomes, and their acceptability to the actor.
2. We can distinguish situations where autonomy is limited through an intentional act or policy, by an individual or institution, from situations where it is limited by circumstances outside anyone's control.
3. We can see autonomy as something that can be distributed and redistributed between people. I can limit other people's autonomy by extending my own.

4. Autonomy rests in part on our belief that we are autonomous – that certain options are available to us. If we do not see them as such – if we see them as impossible, unacceptable or simply inconceivable – our autonomy is affected by this.

We can infer a number of ethical problems from these considerations. These might concern:

1. The distribution of autonomy between people in particular situations, and workers' duty in terms of accepting or questioning that distribution.
2. The morality of actions intended to limit autonomy.
3. The degree to which the individuals' own perception of their own autonomy, on the basis of the acceptability of particular options or outcomes, should be taken by others (particularly the worker) as defining their situation.

None of these considerations seems to me to suggest that autonomy is an illusion. However, so far I have only considered one half of the equation – the availability of options. It can also be argued that we do not make free choices, though the constraints come from within rather than from outside.

Internal constraints on autonomy

Assuming that the outside world offers us options, how free are we to choose between those options? There are strong arguments to support the proposition that human behaviour can be viewed scientifically, as governed by laws. Such laws have been identified in several academic disciplines. Developments in sociology and psychology in the latter part of the nineteenth century and the early twentieth century (largely post-dating the period of Kant and the early utilitarians) have sought to identify forces shaping human behaviour which are to a large extent beyond consciousness, and beyond conscious control. These traditions within sociology and psychology if understood in particular ways, can be seen as offering 'causes' for the choices of individuals. Mabbott (1966, p.110) states that 'from that time [1850] onward, Darwin in biology, Marx in sociology, Pavlov and Freud in psychology, were advancing causal explanations across the frontiers of life and mind'. Traditional Marxism is predicated on a model of historical change that determines the actions of individuals, groups and indeed, whole societies. Humans behave in accordance with their class interests, and consciousness is moulded by the relations of production, but hegemony and ideology hide that fact from the actor. In fact revisions of Marxism since the 1900s have sought to rediscover a place for human agency, but the basic propositions make this a difficult and subtle business. Both psychoanalytic and behavioural traditions in psychology place the mainsprings of action largely outside the control of the rational faculty and, in the case of psychoanalysis, outside awareness.

More recent developments in all these disciplines have to some extent restored control to the conscious and reasoning part of the person, though B. F. Skinner sustained the determinist tradition well into the post-war period (Young, 1993). But the power and prestige of the causal theories in psychology and sociology mean that they still have a significant effect on the way we think about motivation and action in the human services, and Gray (1995) argues that current theoretical developments in social work are to some degree informed by determinism. If we believe that people are in the grip of social and psychological forces beyond their control, how can we regard them as autonomous? Does autonomy simply mean that they are free of the interference of other persons, so that they are left free to act out the forces of history working through them, or the forces of the id? It seems a very limited form of autonomy indeed.

Biological arguments against autonomy

More recent arguments have been put forward in relation to the genetic element in our make-up, which may act as the cause of a number of kinds of behaviour, particularly some forms of criminal behaviour. This connects with discussion that has taken place at various times about other biological factors that affect behaviour, such as hormonal balance. These views have been put forward most often as part of arguments that the actor should be absolved from responsibility for the particular actions in question. These have less obvious relevance to issues in community care at present, but are relevant as part of a wider picture.

Cultural constraints

A more pressing and immediate issue is the importance of cultural and social constraints on people's behaviour. In a multicultural society it is clearly important to understand the way in which culture influences both thinking and behaviour but it is not always easy to make the distinction between influence and causation. Part of the argument for a multicultural approach is that culture confers a world-view and a morality, and to require people to behave in a way that is at odds with their world-view and morality is to harm them and (for the relativist) to require them to behave immorally. However, one might argue also that it is wrong to create a situation where people are disadvantaged through following the precepts of their culture, when the influence of their culture is so strong that it is unreasonable to expect them to go against it. So, where someone has taken an action, on the dictates of cultural tradition, which involves criminal behaviour, or behaviour which would normally be responded to with some sanction, we might argue here that culture is such a powerful influence that it should at least be taken account of in mitigation.

Again, the question arises as to how autonomy can be taken as having any meaning in this situation. How can I exercise free will in making choices and decisions when my thoughts, feelings and actions are subject to such a battery of pressing influences. It would seem on the face of it to reduce humans to machines.

Autonomy and probability

However, when we look closely at the process of scientific explanation, the threat to autonomy recedes somewhat. No theory of human behaviour, however well supported by an accumulation of experimental evidence, can predict with absolute certainty what is going to happen. That is not the nature of experimentation. All that the social scientist can do is to state that there is a particular probability of something following from something else for the predictive theory to be correct. All evidence to support such a theory is partial and probabilistic. It is possible that theory or experiment is faulty but, even if it is not, it deals with probability rather than certainty. The one hundredth time that a particular stimulus is presented to me I may not respond to it in the way that I have the previous 99 times. So truly scientific attempts to predict my behaviour do not determine my behaviour, because built into the method of prediction there is room for the unpredicted. Therefore such predictions do not deny my freedom. Neither Marxism nor psychoanalysis are, as it happens, based on experimental evidence, so though their propositions are intended to be widely generalized, they have relatively little predictive power. Behavioural psychology and sociobiology, by contrast, have attempted to study human behaviour in a systematic way, but predictive models are none the less incomplete. So, while we may accept that many factors influence human behaviour (including the choices of individuals) we can never say that they determine it. There still seems to be room for autonomous action.

Explaining human behaviour

To say that human behaviour cannot be predicted is not to say that it cannot be explained. Does explanation compromise autonomy? If I can explain your actions in a way that does not accord with your explanation, what does that say about your autonomy? It is possible that I can see a pattern in your behaviour that you are not aware of, that I can see that you do X whenever Y happens. I need not claim to predict that the same thing will happen next time, or to say that you have no choice but to react in that way. All I need to do is to say that your behaviour is explicable by reference to factors which you are unaware of, or are unwilling to acknowledge. So those faculties that justify the existence of autonomy are not in control of your actions. In that sense you are not autonomous.

However, this assumes that your explanations for your own behaviour are in some sense incorrect and fail to take account of the true dynamics that are operating under the surface. But we can never be certain about knowing 'true dynamics' given the difficulties of comprehensively making sense of human behaviour. Every action can be explained in several different ways – focusing variously on moral justification, motivation, options and opportunities, circumstances and triggers – and these different explanations need not conflict with each other. The number of details and circumstances that could feature in an exhaustive explanation of even a simple action is enormous. If you can offer a reasonable explanation for your action, which includes rational and coherent connections of circumstance and motivation, and it is not fabricated, it makes no sense for me to say that the shortcomings in your explanation mean that you do not know why you performed that action and that you are not in control of your actions. That is not to say that I have to accept your explanation as honest. You may give me a false explanation in order to disguise your true motives, but the fact that you are deliberately fabricating an explanation requires you to know what your honest explanation would be, since it is that which you are hiding.

Therefore, the ability to explain human behaviour without reference to the individual's conscious decisions likewise does not compromise autonomy, because it does not exclude the individual explaining his or her own actions in a way that does allow for choice.

AUTONOMY AND CONSENT

So far, I have sought to establish that whatever its limitations, autonomy has some meaning both in terms of the options available to people in our social system, and in terms of our ability to make choices from among those options. Despite this, it is clear that there are some instances where our social and legal systems countenance the denial of autonomy to particular people in particular situations. If we can establish why some people are not regarded as autonomous, we can perhaps be clearer about why the rest of us can be so regarded.

In health and social care one of the areas where the problematic nature of autonomy is most clearly highlighted is that of consent, particularly consent to treatment. The requirement that treatment can only be given with the informed consent of the patient is a recognition of the right of the individual to be autonomous, at least with regard to their own body. However, that right is not always supported. It is worth considering why that is.

Invalid consent

There are situations where law and practice invalidates the individual's consent to treatment, on the grounds that they were not truly exercising autonomy when apparently giving that consent. This implies that truly autonomous consent can be recognized and distinguished from invalid consent.

Criteria for consent

The literature on consent tends towards a view that valid consent must be voluntary and informed, and that the consenter must be competent to consent (see for instance Beauchamp and Childress, 1994; Buchanan and Brock, 1990).

The voluntariness of consent requires that the consenter is free to decide for or against the option under consideration, and that they know this to be the case. Where the consenter does not believe themselves to be free – where they believe, however mistakenly, that they will be prevented or punished – then it could be argued that their decision is not voluntary.

Consent must be fully informed. In the community care context this must primarily involve knowledge of options and knowledge of the consequences of each option. Options increase autonomy, but only if those options (and their consequences) are known about. If they are not, they are not available, autonomy is impaired and the validity of consent is compromised.

Finally, the individual needs to be competent in order to consent. This is the most difficult of the three requirements. Buchanan and Brock (1990) explore a number of definitions of competence, each with different requirements. The most minimal of their definitions of competence only requires that the individual be able to communicate their decision. A more demanding definition would involve the ability to understand the nature of the decision they are making. This really means having the capacity to understand and make use of the information that is necessary to make the decision – to understand options and consequences. A more demanding definition yet is that the decision should be reasonable. This requirement raises difficulties about bias and subjectivity in the person assessing competence. Buchanan and Brock express a preference for a process view of competence, which focuses on the *way* the decision is arrived at, rather than the outcome of that process. The difficulty with this is that it is more difficult to reliably identify the nature of a person's reasoning process than it is to identify the outcome.

Invalid withholding of consent

There are situations where law and practice permit negative autonomy to be suspended, so that the individual can be treated or detained against her or his will. The area of health and social care where this impinges most strongly is that of the compulsory admission and treatment of people suffering psychiatric illness in certain circumstances. Here the law explicitly permits that such action may be taken against the individual's wishes. However, the same principle applies to children. The requirements of information and voluntariness are not on the whole particularly relevant here. People are not compulsorily admitted to hospital because their refusal of consent is ill informed or because they are subject to duress in so refusing. The operative principle here is clearly competence. Competence that is impaired to a particular degree provides the general justification for such interventions, though other factors are required as well – specifically, in the case of compulsory psychiatric treatment, that the individual is subject to or a source of danger.

Problems with information, voluntariness and competence

Information

How much information is enough? This is the problem that arises wherever a valid consent is sought. Most life-decisions of any importance are likely to have complex ramifications. Predicting the consequences of a decision concerning health treatment or care, or complex legal transactions will require expert input. In some areas research evidence might need to be considered and the probability of particular outcomes judged. The amount of information that could be taken account of in relation to some major pieces of medical treatment is colossal and may be beyond the competence of one individual professional, let alone the user. How is it possible in these situations to claim that the user's decision is informed? How can we judge a minimum acceptable level of information? Clearly there is a level at which we can understand the relative likelihood of particular outcomes from our decisions and we may see this as sufficient, but we may often not understand the mechanisms whereby these outcomes will come about, if come about they do. We may suspect that our collective view of an acceptable level of information in informed consent is that which would allow the majority of the population to feel that they are exercising autonomy.

The other problem with information is its potentially burdensome, even harmful, nature. This may be because it is painful, bringing unwanted and frightening news. It may be simply that it is tedious, complicated and vexatious. Whoever has control of that information, and in particular control of the giving of it, has the power to cause that individual a good deal of pain, confusion or fatigue. A number of questions may arise in this sort of situation. The most obvious concerns the balance between utility and autonomy, which reflects, among other things, a tension between the priorities of utilitarianism and those of the Kantian emphasis on individual responsibility. Alongside the burdensome nature of information is its unpredictability. In the case of information hitherto unknown to me I cannot know whether I want it or not until I have it, and I will not know what its impact on me will be until I know what it is – and then it is too late. It is a resource, and a burden, which cannot be relinquished. Once I know something it is, in normal circumstances, impossible for me to unknow it. I may suffer amnesia, but that will be a chance event beyond my control. I may manage to put unwelcome knowledge out of my mind – out of my conscious awareness – for much of the time but that does not mean that I cease to know it. I am stuck with that knowledge. So transmitting information is a permanent change and, if that change turns out to be for the worse in some important respect, it cannot be reversed.

This means that the exercise of autonomy can be doubly costly. We may make bad decisions. But we may also need to use information that permanently burdens us with pain, anger or loss, in order to make the decision in the first place. It may be that the emotional implications of that information are not particularly conducive to a 'rational' use of autonomy in any case. Do I then have a duty to make use of all relevant information in making decisions, however painful that information may be, or can I claim the right to make decisions on the information that I have at that time, and which I choose to include?

Voluntariness

There are some difficult questions about what constitutes choice. If someone excludes a particular option from their range of choices because their priest has warned them of the wrath of God if they so choose, is their exclusion of that option voluntary? If the same person excludes that same option because her husband has threatened her with a beating if she chooses it, is the decision to exclude that option voluntary? We might be more likely to say that the former is voluntary and is an exercise of religious freedom, while that latter is not. Likewise someone may exclude one or more options because of the fear of ostracism by family or community. On a more mundane level, they may exclude certain options because of financial considerations. In all of these cases we can frame the decision as freely made in the context of predicted outcomes, desirable or otherwise, and equally we can frame them as being heavily constrained, to a degree that the notion of free choice is compromised.

The traditional approach to health care ethics might allow us to accept consent given under some or all of these constraints, on the principle that all human activity is subject to constraint, and the professionals' main concern is to ensure that they themselves, or their colleagues, are not contributing to that constraint. I may accept that a patient is being pressured into giving consent by other persons or circumstances. However, I ought not to exert any pressure myself. If I do, the consent is compromised.

The ethics of social care are more demanding. The British Association of Social Workers' code of ethics (BASW, 1986) enjoins the social worker to work to maximize the users' choices, not simply to refrain from limiting them. The user cited above, pressured by priest, spouse, community or material constraint, is arguably short on choices and perhaps has a legitimate claim to be helped to widen those choices. This does not necessarily entail that the worker ought not to accept decisions made under constraint but it implies that such decisions are in some sense morally problematic.

Competence

This requirement produces at least as many difficulties as the other two. I have already outlined something of the range of different requirements suggested for the individual to count as competent – from the bare ability to communicate a decision, to a mode of reasoning. In the context of this lack of consensus the most obvious danger from an ethical standpoint is injustice – that there will be inconsistency in the way the concept of competence is applied to people in different situations, or people in different groups, and that those inconsistencies will reflect inequalities of power. People with certain labels (learning disabilities, mental health problems, confusion) are most likely to suffer injustice in this situation, in that they are more likely to have their competence questioned and scrutinized because of that label, while the rest of us carry on making decisions as incompetently as we like.

Though it is arguably unjust, it is clearly a simpler matter to claim that competence is compromised because of an impairment that can be expertly diagnosed – a specific illness or condition – than to question competence in someone without such a labelled characteristic. The latter situation forces the questioner to be clear about their definition of competence and about what constitutes evidence of its presence or its absence. If we go beyond the simple requirement to be able to communicate, and focus on characteristics of thinking and decision-making we need to decide whether we are concerned with the general competence of the individual or the competence with which this particular decision is made. If I choose to decide whether to give or withhold consent by the toss of a coin, does that mean that I should be treated as incompetent? I am not making a reasoned decision. Does it then matter why I chose to toss a coin? If the decision was so finely balanced that it defeated all weighing of options, perhaps a resort to random chance is rational in this one-off situation. But what if I believe that the world is so chaotic that all decisions should be made in this way, and proceed accordingly as a matter of normal practice. Is my consent then competently given? Or if I choose from sheer caprice to make my decision by tossing a coin on this occasion, knowing the risks of a bad decision, am I more or less competent than someone who attempts to make carefully weighed decisions but, through forgetfulness, fails to remember all the factors to weigh? It may well be that coin-tossing in these situations will be regarded rather differently in a middle-aged lecturer than in a 15-year-old trying to decide whether to agree to the termination of her pregnancy.

As soon as we look beyond those labels that have traditionally been regarded as compromising competence, we encounter these problems. It could be argued that, logically, the same problems of agreement and definition ought to arise with the confused elderly, the mentally ill and those with learning disabilities. If they do not, perhaps we should suspect injustice.

AUTONOMY AND INFLUENCE

To what degree is it acceptable to seek to influence someone in their decision-making? We may believe that there are clearly preferable options among those available to a user and that we ought to work for those options to be the ones chosen. We are after all under a duty to make the best use of our knowledge and abilities. To put these at the user's disposal by offering advice on the advisability of particular courses of action seems a reasonable expression of that duty.

Clearly there are various ways in which this might be seen as compromising the autonomy of the user. If I am in a position to provide resources or help, my advice may be seen as a test of loyalty or compliance. It is not unusual in ordinary relationships for the ignoring of advice to be taken amiss. Certainly there is often an assumption that accepting advice is a condition of further help – that we help only on our own terms. So this may be the user's expectation. Presumably in this case he or she is wrong but does not know that. There may also be an assumption that the genuineness of the desire or need for help is being tested – that if he or she feels secure enough to ignore my advice his or her situation cannot be so bad. There are a lot of ways in which advice can be seen as carrying a significant freight of power.

Counselling skills and autonomy

However, there is another dimension to this issue. The process of helping a user come to a decision can be seen as a professional activity, and it is normally seen as legitimate to use whatever skills the worker has available to do this effectively. These may be communication skills – exploring the areas that the person is unclear or uncertain about, giving information in a clear way that the other person is going to retain – or they may be more specific counselling skills – skills of clarifying the person's feelings, bringing out areas of feeling that may not have been fully acknowledged. These skills are helpful and highly facilitative, but they also confer a certain amount of power. Thompson (1990) argues that a number of commonly used counselling skills promote dependency rather than autonomy. The worker who helps to release and explore pent up feelings in a particular area of a person's life may be in a position to loosen resistance to particular courses of action based on the denial of those feelings. Decisions can be motivated by a number of things, and one of these is a desire to keep certain feelings and experiences at bay.

So my refusal to allow a home help into my house might be a reaction to my sense of loss of competence and self-sufficiency as a housewife. The worker who helps me to recognize and talk through those feelings is also probably making it more likely that I will agree to the home help. That may well be in accordance with my assessed needs but is it in accordance with my autonomy?

UNWANTED AUTONOMY

We have worked, so far, on the assumption that autonomy is desirable, something to be maximized, but we can also see autonomy as a burden, something that people may not wish for in some situations, and we can identify situations where people show a real desire to leave decisions and the accompanying responsibility, to someone else. How should we regard autonomy in that context? Do people have a duty to exercise autonomy where they do not wish to? The existentialist view approximates towards that analysis. Or is it part of the definition of the person, as in Kant's view? This raises bigger issues concerning the relationship of the State to the citizen. Traditional liberal political theory has been predicated on the assumption that the State is 'always a necessary evil, a potential threat to the liberty it exists to secure' (Schwartzmantel, 1994, p.42), that it has a legitimate jurisdiction over only a part of the individuals' autonomy and that the individual should not, and will not wish to, surrender any more than falls within that jurisdiction. It is not geared to dealing with situations where some citizens want the State to take over more of the citizens' autonomy than the State wishes.

Unwanted autonomy and community care

This problem can be seen clearly in the present government's policies with regard to community care. The development of those policies means that the option of having institutional care for a significant part of one's life is being removed, so fewer people have the prospect of ceding some of their autonomy to others in that situation, through choice or force of circumstance. This accords in many respects with professional practice, in that professional goals in this context are geared to promoting client autonomy, and the codes of conduct of nursing, social work and occupational therapy all emphasize this. Therefore the provision of service to the individual user will be characterized by an emphasis on this process, given the political and professional commitments to this. And a question must arise as to the degree to which the propulsion of individuals toward autonomy can be justified ethically.

This issue arises in a range of situations where people with impairments or difficulties of various sorts are encouraged to take greater control of their lives, and to exercise autonomy to a degree that they may feel unable to do or have had no expectation of doing. In the first category may be elderly people in residential care who feel a loss of confidence in caring for themselves. In the latter category are a range of groups who have been institutionalized and who, under community care policies, are being encouraged to move back into the community and become more autonomous. This could be partly an issue of the ability of individuals to exercise autonomy, and the constraints and limitations that may impinge on this. We have considered this issue to some extent already and will do so further but, at this point, the issue is one of volition. How far is it justifiable for policy-makers and professionals to pressure individuals who feel unwilling to take on the requisite degree of autonomy, to do so?

Let us consider it from the users' point of view. People who have been effectively treated as incompetent to varying degrees over a period of several years, and have become accustomed to this, are being told that they must now begin to exercise autonomy. Paradoxically they are being told this in a sense while in a non-autonomous position, both psychologically and practically. So the exhortation to become more autonomous is likely to be experienced as an instruction. The choice to agree to this programme may therefore not be made in a way that we would regard as fully autonomous. And there is evidence that some of them do not want to choose that option. For instance Crosby *et al.* (1993) found that a third of their sample of people discharged into the community from psychiatric hospital said that they had not wanted to leave hospital. Does this cast an ethical shadow over the acceptability of this process?

There is clearly a logical paradox in exercising one's autonomy to hand part of it over to someone else. It is the kind of action which, if universalized, would produce exactly the sort of self-contradiction that Kant saw as the sign that an action is morally flawed. The contradiction concerned is that of taking away someone's power to act on their own wishes by acting on their own wishes. Ultimately it is a paradoxical act. If everyone were free to give up their own liberty then nobody would be truly free because they could deliver themselves into bondage on a whim. If they were free to retrieve their liberty whenever they wished, they would not in truth have ceased to be free, and would not in truth, therefore, have been able to give up their freedom. So it is irrelevant whether another person agrees to take over the exercise of their autonomy. They cannot because it is impossible.

So we have a Kantian argument against this. The issue here would centre round competence – anyone who is competent to make such a decision would be acting wrongly in doing so. It could be added that anyone who competently does this does not thereby absolve him or herself from responsibility for what befalls him or her in the hands of an incompetent guardian. On the contrary this person is responsible for the results in so far as he or she made a choice to put him or herself in the hands of the guardian. The person may be absolved in so far as he or she was deceived or kept in ignorance about the implications of what he or she was doing but in so far as he or she was informed, he or she remains responsible. So the act is not only paradoxical, it is impossible. However, that involves a rather simplistic all or nothing view of competence and it assumes that we are concerned with decisions made by people with full liberty, whereas we may be dealing with desires expressed by people with less than full liberty who are not in a position to make such decisions.

It could be argued that reluctant users are having autonomy imposed on them, not seeking to transfer it elsewhere. In many cases the transfer took place long before. Autonomy is now being transferred back at the initiative of those authorities who took it from them originally. However, this does not change the paradoxical nature of the users being reluctant to take back their autonomy. If their autonomy is genuinely theirs again, refusal to accept it amounts to using that autonomy to refuse it – a contradictory action.

Two considerations apply to this:

1. It is not easy to be certain how autonomous a user in an institutional setting truly is. I suggested earlier that a decision is only voluntary if the person making it knows that they are free to do so and free to do the opposite. So the user who agrees to take more responsibility for his or her life – within and, perhaps later, outside the institution – may be doing so because he or she believes he or she has no choice. The user who clings to the institutional routine may paradoxically be acting more autonomously than the user who accepts a programme of return to autonomous living.

2. The user who autonomously demands to remain institutionalized may have a legitimate claim on institutional care, even if he or she cannot reasonably demand to be deprived of his or her autonomy. The fact that the initiative for this change comes from the authorities rather than the user might be seen as implying certain obligations on the authorities. The user might argue an implicit commitment on the part of the authorities built into the long-term care regime – a commitment to providing indefinite care. Such a claim is probably not sustainable, but the unilateral imposition of a change of this magnitude in the relationship between care authority and user must imply some special obligation to the user to provide adequate support.

AUTONOMY, INTEGRITY AND PRIVACY

The concept of autonomy also connects with two other important ideas, of bodily integrity and of privacy. To be physically free to move around seems to be basic to autonomy. However, if I use my freedom to stand too near to someone else and make them feel uncomfortable, that might start to impinge on *their* freedom. If we are in a crowded underground train and we are jammed together like sardines, we are all in effect restraining one another's physical freedom, but we are not doing it deliberately. It is a side-effect of our decisions to travel on that train. We seem to be able to accept that this is morally legitimate. If we grew up in a culture where it is normal to stand very close to people, to touch them a lot, to hold them during conversation and so on, we may view that rather differently. Again if the intention is simply affiliative and communicative, and not in any sense restrictive, we would not wish to condemn the action.

It is clear that the context of behaviour is important in shaping its significance for autonomy. For instance, if I stand in the doorway of a colleague's office when they are alone and there is nobody else on the corridor and make no sign that I am going to move even when my colleague makes it clear that the conversation is over, am I then impinging on the autonomy of the other person? He or she could tell me to go. Perhaps he or she is afraid to do so because he or she thinks it might trigger some more threatening behaviour in me. Let us suppose, for instance, that I am known to have a short temper. Does that add to the threat? My physical behaviour is not overtly restrictive and my conversation is not overtly threatening but in that particular social context my overall behaviour may be experienced by the other person as threatening. If I am male and she is female this will alter the context, and the significance of my behaviour. So the range of ways in which even immediate physical autonomy can be impinged upon is considerable.

Physical restraint

We regard deliberately physically restraining someone as a more extreme action, and generally more reprehensible, than unintentionally physically restraining them, as on the underground train. We also regard it as more extreme than restricting their options in other, non-physical, ways such as my bank manager withdrawing my overdraft facility. Its impact in terms of the importance of options restricted by that action may be less than the loss from losing my overdraft. But we feel that there is something more fundamental that has been violated. Physical restraint does not simply prevent us from walking down this road rather than that one. It takes away from us a basic power over our own bodies, which includes who and what we allow to touch us physically, that seems to be a more important loss of autonomy.

Privacy

The right of privacy is part of autonomy. Rieman (1976) argues that privacy is essential to personhood. It involves me being able to decide who has access to what aspects of me and my life, both in terms of my physical being and physical space, and also in terms of some other things, such as information. Other writers see privacy as being reducible to other rights – for instance, Smith and Allen (1991) see it as reducible to freedom and justice. In a famous legal judgement in the USA, Warren and Brandeis saw it as deriving from rights to life, liberty and property.

Privacy and information

How do we apply the principle of privacy to information? I know at least where my body is located and what space it occupies and requires for certain functions and activities, but how do I identify information that constitutes part of my private space? I might want any document that concerns me to be under my control. But that document might concern a lot of other people as well, and it might be impossible to untangle the different elements so that the bit about me can be kept confidential. Also, information about me may be vital to the well-being of others. Do those who hold that information have an absolute duty to withhold it from those who need it – perhaps for survival – simply because I choose not to let them see it? Do I have the same power over that information as I do over my own body? In many situations that information is owned by someone else who holds it and needs it for their own purposes. That is certainly often the case for users who are in a position where agencies hold information concerning them. So how can we find an ethical ground for decisions concerning confidentiality of information?

1. We can see information as the subject of promises and undertakings. Where users are giving information as part of the process of assessment it could be argued that the information is given on the promise that it would only be used for the purpose for which it was given. From a Kantian point of view autonomy and promise-keeping are both powerful principles, which underpin the principle of confidentiality in that they oblige the recipient of information to use it only for the purpose for which it was given.

   However, there are clearly situations where duties to other people conflict with the promise-keeping duty and though a strict Kantian might regard the keeping of the promise as binding, others' interests, which may be more pressing, have to be considered. Also, this principle benefits the source of the information at the expense of its subject, who may be a different person.

2. We can see information as part of an 'informational self' which forms a kind of penumbra around our physical self, delineated by the concept of privacy. This perhaps gives the subject of the information some rights over it, whoever the source may have been.

   However, there are problems with this concept. Our 'informational self' cannot be separated from that of other individuals. If I am HIV positive then my partner is likely to be at risk if we are having unprotected sex. That fact is part of my partner's informational self and yet I have control over who knows it, if I have just had a test. A good deal of our informational self is public anyway. We are public beings both physically and socially. Social norms require us to reveal numerous things about ourselves. The only way to be completely invisible is, paradoxically, to be a vagrant. If I have a home someone is going to know about it. 'Normal life' requires a good deal of disclosure of that sort. Does this mean that there is a distribution of information which is acceptable through being normal?

3. We could view information as property, over which certain individuals have something akin to property rights. However that does not tell us who should have what rights; should it belong to the giver of the information, its keeper or to whoever the information concerns.

   Information does not behave like most goods that can be owned as property. If someone has wrongly come into possession of some information, they cannot simply return that information unused as they could return any other good. Likewise I cannot examine the information to see if I need it, and then return it if I do not need it. Once I know something, I cannot unknow it, and the knowledge may place a responsibility upon me that I cannot divest myself of, however much I may wish to do that. Information sometimes seems more like an infection than a good or a gift.

4. We could see information as a source of harm, and claims to restriction as resting on the danger that its propagation will injure me. However, it would be difficult always to predict the likelihood, nature or degree of such harm and the degree to which precautionary claims to restriction 'just in case' are acceptable. Also, if I am only claiming protection from harm as a basis for confidentiality, my claim to confidentiality is weakened if its maintenance harms someone else more than

breaking it harms me. There are also some sorts of information that are either innocuous or complimentary, and are not going to have any such effect in any case. In practice we do not use that as an exception from confidentiality.

Each of these four bases for confidentiality benefits different individuals, and each has different strengths and weaknesses. The fourth base – that of harm and utility – seems to command the most support in the literature. Smith and Allen (1991) reject the property base and, indeed, the general principle of privacy, in favour of protection from harm. Beauchamp and Childress (1994) also appear to favour the utilitarian basis. However, the idea of harm can be extended further than simple utility. Edgar (1994) argues that loss of confidentiality is itself harmful, whatever the practical results, because it represents loss of control over the self's boundary and harm to the competent social self. So his definition of harm connects closely with the idea of privacy and personhood.

In terms of a professional practice that is going to command some credibility in the community, it is arguable that all these principles need to be balanced. Such a conclusion ensures that conflicting arguments will emerge in many cases and will not be resolvable finally – but that is the nature of ethics.

REFERENCES

BASW (1986) *A Code of Ethics for Social Work*. Birmingham: British Association of Social Workers.

Beauchamp, T. L. and Childress, J. F. (1994) *Principles of Biomedical Ethics*. New York: Oxford University Press.

Benhabib, S. (1992) *Situating the Self*. Cambridge: Polity Press.

Buchanan, A. E. and Brock, D. (1990) *Deciding for Others*. Cambridge: Cambridge University Press.

Crosby, C., Barry, M., Carter, M. F. and Low, C. F. (1993) 'Psychiatric rehabilitation and community care: resettlement from a North Wales hospital', *Health and Social Care in the Community* 1(6), 355–64.

Edgar, A. (1994) 'Confidentiality and personal integrity'. *Nursing Ethics* 1(2), 86–95.

Gray, M. (1995) 'The ethical implications of current theoretical developments in social work'. *British Journal of Social Work* 25(1), 55–70.

Hampton, J. (1990) *Hobbes and the Social Contract Tradition.* Cambridge: Cambridge University Press.

Mabbott, J. D. (1966) *An Introduction to Ethics.* London: Hutchinson University Library.

Macquarrie, J. (1972) *Existentialism.* Harmondsworth: Penguin.

Mill, J. S. (1946) *On Liberty.* Oxford: Blackwell.

Paton, H. J. (1956) *Groundwork of the Metaphysic of Morals.* New York: Harper.

Rieman, J. (1976) 'Privacy, intimacy and personhood'. *Philosophy and Public Affairs* 6, 26–44.

Schwartzmantel, J. (1994) *The State in Contemporary Society.* London: Harvester Wheatsheaf.

Smith, J. W. and Allen, R. (1991) 'Privacy, medical confidentiality and AIDS', in J. W. Smith (ed.) *AIDS: Philosophy and Beyond.* Aldershot: Avebury.

Thompson, A. (1990) *Guide to Ethical Practice in Psychotherapy.* New York: Wiley.

Triandis, H. C. (1990) 'Theoretical concepts that are applicable to the analysis of ethnocentrism', in R. W. Brislin (ed.) *Applied Cross-Cultural Psychology.* Newbury Park: Sage.

Young, R. (1993) 'The implications of Determinism', in P. Singer (ed.) *A Companion to Ethics.* Oxford: Blackwell.

CHAPTER 4
Responsibility

INTRODUCTION

In this chapter I shall explore the significance of responsibility as a moral linkage between government, agency, worker and user. I shall focus on three main areas: different meanings of 'responsibility'; the responsibility of government and the State; and links of responsibility between agency, profession, worker and user.

DIFFERENT MEANINGS OF 'RESPONSIBILITY'

Our first difficulty with the idea of responsibility is that it is not one idea but several, so our first task is to identify the different concepts which might be referred to as 'responsibility':

1. Responsibility may be synonymous with duty. If we say that people in the community have a responsibility to ensure that their neighbours are safe and well, we probably mean that people in the community have a duty to do that.
2. Responsibility may be synonymous with credit or blame for a particular state of affairs. If I say that a particular worker is responsible for administrative mistakes concerning a user, I may simply mean that that worker is to blame for the mistakes.
3. Responsibility may be synonymous with accountability. If I say that I am responsible to the user, the profession or the agency for the quality of my practice and the services I provide, I probably mean that I am accountable to them. It is not clear how accountable I am, however, if I cannot be held accountable, and though my employer can hold me accountable, and my profession perhaps can, it is not clear how the user can do that.
4. Responsibility may be synonymous with control. If I say that I intend to take responsibility for my own health from now on, a

duties to a fellow citizen – duties of recognition and mutual aid. The worker doubtless hopes and expects that his or her community care activities will express and build upon his or her duties as person and citizen. There may be times however when the worker's community care responsibilities appear to conflict with those basic duties. We shall return to this issue later.

I shall spend a good deal of time considering the moral status and goals of the employing agency, and its corporate obligations to the user and to others. I think this is important in understanding the position of the worker and the manager, in terms of obligations. However, I begin by considering the significance of the worker's professional role in defining and explaining his or her obligations.

The worker's professional obligation

The worker who is assessing, providing or mananging community care, is often part of a body which has its own moral agenda, the profession. Professions are not agencies – they are not agents who have an active role in service delivery. Their goals have a steady-state quality and are in that sense more consistently conservative. Membership has a peer dimension, and their decision-making activities are primarily regulatory. Their main concerns are the maintenance of professional standards, and the replenishment of the profession. It is therefore worth considering the individual's relationship with his or her profession, and the implications of that relationship for the individual's relationship with the outside world, and, in particular, the user.

First, the profession. If I am a member of a profession, that means that I have joined an identified group with a code of ethics and a body of knowledge. If I join the nursing profession I gain registration under the aegis of the United Kingdom Central Council for Nursing, Midwifery and Health Visiting (UKCC). There is a transaction involved. I receive a seal of approval from the profession that allows me access to certain situations.

In return I see myself as under a duty not to discredit that approval. This duty can be underpinned morally by Kantian concepts of promise-keeping and truth-telling. Entry into the profession implies a commitment to certain behaviours and certain principles, and arguably there is an implicit claim and an implicit promise which I break if I do not maintain commitment to these standards. This also applies to my relationship with users and other members of the public. Membership of the profession implies a promise to the user, that I will act in a certain way toward them because I am committed to certain principles. If I fail to do that, then again I am being dishonest. I am breaking that promise. Ozar (1987, p.158) argues in relation to nursing that 'one reason why a professional is obligated to judge and act in a particular way is that he or she has made a commitment to do so. The act of commitment is like the making of a promise or making of a contract'.

Confidentiality provides a good example of this principle. If I enter the nursing profession, I am commiting myself to the UKCC code of conduct, which includes a commitment to confidentiality. Patients therefore have reasonable expectation that I will respect confidentiality within the terms of that code. My membership of the profession is itself a message to that effect. If I break confidentiality I am breaking a promise to the patient and I am effectively lying. So the professional code of conduct is not the only yardstick of right and wrong. The issue of right and wrong is located also in my adherence to the code, in the light of its significance in the transaction.

It is also the case that where I break my profession's code of conduct I am harming my colleagues in that profession. The practical effect of breaching the code is that users are less likely to have confidence in other members of that profession. Users may suffer as a result of that through the loss of a viable and acceptable source of help. Adherence to the profession's code can therefore be justified in rule utilitarian terms. The profession has a legitimate claim, on the users behalf and on its own, to its members' adherence to the code, on the basis of avoidance of harm and on the basis of keeping a promise.

The worker's obligation as an employee of an agency

I said above that the profession is not engaged in delivering services, though its individual members are. However, the agency clearly *is* engaged in delivering services – that is its function. It is an actor in a transaction with the user in a way that the profession is not. So a question arises in this context which did not arise in relation to the profession: does the worker-as-employee have any obligation to users at all, or is the worker simply carrying out the obligations of the agency? I shall suggest three positions on this which may cast some light on the issue:

1. One position would be that the real moral relationship exists between the agency and the user. The agency has obligations placed upon it by the State and by the law, and the

worker-as-employee is simply the agency's agent in carrying out its obligations. The agency enjoys certain advantages from employing an agent who has professional skills and professional ethics, because it helps to ensure quality of service. But the worker is acting on the agency's behalf and whatever direct obligations that worker has to the user in a professional role, his or her obligations as an employee of the agency are entirely to the agency.

2. A second position would be that the agency and the worker cannot be separated from each other. The worker can sometimes influence agency policy, and often can influence agency practice. So he or she is party to aspects of both. There are ways, albeit limited, in which the worker might be able to avoid applying agency policies and practices he or she regards as unethical. So the worker is responsible to the user directly in his or her employee role for partaking of the agency's activities.

3. A third position would be that the agency cannot be said sensibly to have any obligations at all, or to be accountable to the user, in moral terms. Though the law recognizes corporate responsibility, the moral responsibility for supposed agency actions is distributed among all those individuals who were involved in deciding and implementing those actions. Most of these individuals will be employees of the agency, from director downward, though a few at the very top (board, elected members) will not be in that role.

The moral status of the agency

Our views on these positions will depend on the moral status of the agency. In particular they will depend on whether we believe it is possible for the agency to have moral responsibilities (that is, to have moral duties, to be accountable and blameable for wrongdoing). If it cannot, then position three above is the only one that is tenable. If it can, then positions one and two become tenable.

As the agency is a particular kind of organization, we may ask first whether it is possible for any organization to have moral responsibilities and to be the focus of moral responsibilities. Is it possible, in fact, for any organization to enter into those sorts of moral transaction? In Chapter 1 I introduced French's (1984) argument that organizations might be seen as having corporate moral responsibilities on the basis that they have the necessary decision-making machinery and corporate continuity to be viewed as a corporate 'person'. However, this is not by any means universally accepted, and other writers, such as Freeman and Gilbert (1988), argue that the only moral activity in the corporate context is that of individual persons. In coming to a view on this issue we might be influenced by the fact that the law recognizes the existence of corporate personhood and corporate responsibility in certain contexts. However, to say that this concept is workable and appropriate in the legal system is not in itself a reason for seeing it as valid in ethical terms. For the rest of this discussion I shall treat the idea of corporate moral responsibility as a usable but problematic concept.

Distribution of moral responsibility within organizations

Positions two and three above ascribe some responsibility to the individual employees. This suggests that they are accountable and blameable (by the user or others) separately from the employing agency. However, we need to consider how that responsibility might be distributed among individuals in the organization.

The organizations which we are dealing with in the context of community care are of several sorts – municipal and state bureaucracies, quasi-independent state bodies such as NHS (National Health Service) trusts, voluntary organizations of many different structures and private commercial bodies – all of which have different structures and bases.

The two groups of people we might consider within the agency structure are those who make corporate policy (elected members, directors, boards, senior managers) and those who implement those policies (the rest of the body of employees). It is clear that a simple unidirectional hierarchy of power is not a realistic model of modern organizations. Lower-level employees can influence the shaping and pacing of policies, and to some degree block and sabotage the decisions of senior managers. Directors can be made to feel as powerless as front-line workers in some situations, but if everyone adheres to their contract of employment senior managers will have a good deal more power than everyone else. Lower-level employees can only block and resist in ways that are risky for themselves. Senior managers can retaliate in ways that are much less risky for themselves. That is a real difference of power. I would argue that this produces a real difference in responsibility in terms of duty, accountability and blame. In terms of duty and accountability Kant's principle that ought implies can – that we can only have duties to do things in our power – implies that directors, elected members and senior managers must have more extensive moral duties in relation to the broader activities of the agency, than lower-level employees. I shall consider blame further later.

If I believe that the organization can carry corporate moral responsibility, I could still see myself as an individual employee being held accountable by users in three ways. One relates to my use of whatever influence I have within the agency, which may be large or small. The second relates to my choice to work for the agency and put my skills and talents at its disposal. Again, that must be tempered by the alternative options available to me. The third relates to the way I perform my tasks as employee, in those interstices where my managers are unable to control or know about my every action because they are not there when I am engaged with the user. All of these could be associated with duties – to influence my employer, to use my talents and to perform my day-to-day tasks in a particular way. However, what is not clear is whether any of these responsibilities could be regarded as arising from my role as employee. I must perform them in that role. But they could equally be seen as personal/citizen responsibilities, or as professional responsibilities. The key to my employee responsibilities lies in my relationship with the agency, and the degree to which that has a moral element. To consider that question we need to return to the moral status of the agency.

The moral goals of organizations

If we take position one or two above, we are ascribing some corporate moral status to the agency, and perhaps also corporate moral responsibilities. If we do this, we must find a way of establishing what those moral responsibilities are, and to do that we must consider the agency's corporate moral goals – the purposes for which the agency was created. In whatever way organizations resemble persons, they differ profoundly in one respect: in the western world-view persons exist 'for themselves', whereas organizations are created for a purpose. In the case of formal organizations such as community care agencies the purpose defines the organization, and it could be argued that managers and workers within them have no power or mandate to act on the agency's behalf outside of those purposes.

We can make a distinction here between organizations which have explicitly moral goals – churches, political parties, some community and pressure groups – and those which exist to pursue goals of self-interest such as commercial organizations, where the impact of morality is likely to be expressed primarily in the restrictions placed on its activities by law. This is not a simple categorization because some bodies that are commercial in structure and activity none the less have been brought into being, and are focused in broad policy commitments, by moral goals. This would apply, in varying degrees, to ethical investment companies. There is an issue also as to how far pressure groups and self-help groups are focused on moral goals, and how far their agenda is self-interest for particular groups. However, it is possible to identify differences of degree.

The kind of goals that an organization works to achieve must have some bearing on the kind of moral obligations we might place upon it. A purely commercial organization might be restricted by certain basic requirements embodied in the law. Beyond that, we may feel it is acceptable for that organization to distort the truth in advertising, and to seek to drive its competitors out of business. These activities are necessary parts of commerce in a capitalist economy and are part of the *raison-d'être* of commercial bodies. We might condemn the system that creates them, but it makes no sense to condemn them for doing what they exist to do. However, if the Child Poverty Action Group were to behave in that way, we would be far more likely to condemn that behaviour.

State community care agencies were created for purposes which express moral principles. In that respect they have been similar to churches and political parties rather than commercial undertakings. Reforms in the 1990s confuse this picture by importing what appear to be commercial goals into these agencies. Competition between NHS trusts is now a reality and that constitutes a real shift in moral goals. Local authority agencies are less affected by this. For as long as the primary duty is to users, and there is no introduction of a shareholder role or equivalent to demand maximization of profits, the basis of moral goals remains.

The focus of agency moral obligations

If the organization has responsibilities (in the sense of duties) they are duties to somebody or other. Often organizations stand in a complex relationship to several other bodies or individuals who are affected in various ways by the organization's activities. Some of these others stand in a specific relation to the organization, defining the organization's goals and purpose. Stewart (1983) offers a list of the kinds of relationship which a local authority has with the local population, including the electoral relationship, ratepayer (now taxpayer) relationship, user relationship, constraint relationship (where the local authority is enforcing regulations), collective, demand and participative relationships (where the local authority is respectively pursuing local interests, responding to organized local demands and engaging the local population in active political participation). A health commission's profile must be simpler, since there is no electoral relationship and the taxpayer relationship is routed through central government.

For our purposes I am suggesting a simplification of this list into two kinds of relationships between authority and population and adding to this the authority's relationship to central government. I shall refer to the two kinds of relationship as those with 'constituency' and 'consumer'.

Constituency

The constituency is the body of people whom the organization in some sense represents, on whose behalf it acts and which gives that organization its legitimacy. The constituency confers upon the agency its moral purpose and goals. In the case of the local authority, this encompasses Stewart's (1983) electoral, taxpaying and collective relationships, and potentially also the demand and participative relationships. However, central government is in my definition part of the local authority's constituency. As an elected body the local authority has a representing relationship with the electorate of its area, but in another sense it is also an agent of central government and is therefore acting on behalf of a national constituency. In the case of a health commission the local population is part of the constituency only in a rather weak sense, through Stewart's demand and (perhaps) participative relationships. Central government forms the strongest component in their constituency. In the case of voluntary organizations, membership would be the constituency. In the case of commercial organizations, the constituency would consist of shareholders.

Consumers

Consumers are those people for whom the agency's services are intended – those who partake of Stewart's (1983) user relationship. In the case of commercial and voluntary organizations it is often the case that the consumers are different from the constituency. For commercial bodies there is a clear distinction between shareholders and consumers. A reasonable moral expectation from the consumers' viewpoint would be quite different from that of the shareholders. With a voluntary organization it is not so clear. For some such organizations membership and leadership are not coterminous with the groups they seek to work for. The Child Poverty Action Group would be an example of this sort of relationship. However, as a lobbying group, there is likely to be some commonality of goals between constituency and consumers. Groups which both lobby and provide services – such as MIND – have a more complex relationship between constituency and consumers, who in some instances overlap.

In the case of state organizations the relationship seems rather different. Local government represents, arguably, the aspiration of the local constituency to provide a service to itself. It represents citizens making a decision to support a policy that will benefit others and may benefit them also. Randall (1995) argues that the political and moral relationship between local constituency and user has been weakened by the 1990 reforms, and is being replaced by a quasi-commercial relationship. None the less it survives sufficiently to be a significant part of the moral landscape. Health commissions have a quite different relationship to consumers, being more comfortably integrated into the agenda of central government.

Stakeholders

Alongside constituency and consumers are other bodies and individuals affected by the activities of the organization. For a local authority social services department these may range from suppliers of hand-towels to people living next door to a children's home. The term 'stakeholder' is often used for this relationship. For most organizations relevant to our purposes this will include employees, and I shall deal with these separately later in the chapter. It will also include other organizations in the purchaser–provider relationship. The organization's obligations to these people and organizations are not defined by the organization's moral goals, as we cannot expect them to share those goals. Some will. For instance a voluntary organization may share the goals of a local authority or health commission. But the permissible relationship between those bodies is defined from outside (by government and statute) and has been shifted recently from moral or political alliance towards a contracting relationship – the same sort of relationship which a statutory agency might have with a commercial agency (see Lewis, 1994).

So we must look elsewhere for moral yardsticks. The law places limits on what corporate actions are permissible in regard to any other person. If we can apply the same general moral principles to corporate action as we can to individual action, in terms of duty, responsibility and blame, we may for instance, be able to place the same requirements of truth-telling on a corporation as we might on an individual. Green (1994) argues that corporate moral duties to stakeholders are generally constituted by honesty, fairness, respect for confidentiality, privacy and safety. These correspond closely to the Kantian duties of respect, honesty and promise-keeping which we can ascribe to individuals, and are in a sense equivalent to the sort of moral duties we might ascribe to people when they are not in a specific (e.g. professional, employee) relationship to one another.

Community and carers

Some groups and individuals need further consideration. They are affected by the actions of the agency because their lives impinge on the lives of users, and agency action to help users may have implications for their situation. We may include neighbours, friends and relatives of users in this group.

The question is, does the agency have a duty to people in this category which is comparable to its duty to the consumer, to the constituency or to stakeholders; or do we need a further category? These people (relatives, friends, neighbours) are likely to be members of the community, and of the local electorate. I have argued in Chapter 1 that 'the community' is too nebulous a body to function as a defining boundary for moral obligations. Therefore, I would argue that we cannot reliably base agency obligations upon community membership. Membership of the local electorate makes the individual part of the agency's constituency, but that individual is only part of the constituency in that political role, where she is contributing to political decisions through voting. It does not mean that he or she can make an individual claim in relation to other needs on the basis of that membership.

Can we view them as consumers? They may benefit from the agency's services in a number of ways, in that they may experience some easing of the strains and demands of a dependent relative or neighbour because the agency is providing some of the necessary care. In that sense their needs might be met alongside those of the user. We might argue from the other side of the coin that neighbours and relatives could be seen as collaborators rather than users, because they will often be sharing the tasks of care with the agency. I am not sure that this precludes the consumer role. Users generally share the task of care with the agency, in the sense that most users are able to care for themselves to some degree and the caring process is one of collaboration with the agency. One can be a collaborator and a user at the same time.

But I think there is another reason why we cannot see friends, neighbours and relatives as consumers in most situations. The crucial element in the consumer role is the agency's obligation to respond, in so far as it is able, to the assessed needs of the consumer. The needs of friends, relatives and neighbours with reference to the user, in respect of support, relief from stress and so on, do not fall into this category. The agency's obligation to respond is only invoked in their case if they 'qualify' to become users in their own right. So, however much a caring neighbour may 'need' professional care for a confused person so that he or she is relieved of the stress of caring and monitoring, that need in itself is not what the agency is responding to. The agency is responding to the need of the confused person. The neighbour's difficulty in providing necessary care will be part of the assessment of risk, but the neighbour's own need does not evoke an obligation on the agency's part.

We can make an exception to this argument where the individual can reasonably be defined as a 'carer' – a person who probably lives with the user, and whose efforts and dedication may save the agency considerable resources. In fact carers can reasonably claim that agencies have specific obligations to them, as the Disabled Persons (Services, Consultation and Representation) Act 1986 (HMSO) does require local authorities to 'have regard' for carers. Although the 1990 National Health Service and Community Care Act (HMSO) does not have any equivalent clause, Mandelstam and Schwehr (1995) point out that government guidelines following the Act state that carers can be assessed. The Carers (Recognition and Services) Act (HMSO, 1995) will also provide carers with a right to assessment. The moral obligation arising from these formal commitments are less extensive compared to those for users, but they certainly exist. Respite care is a good example of a situation where the agency is actually providing for the carer's needs rather than those of the user.

In trying to be more precise about the moral obligation of agency to carer we might argue that the agency has an obligation to provide the most appropriate care for the user. Where the most appropriate care is provided by the carer, the agency clearly is responding to its obligation in supporting the carer through respite care. It is still the user's needs that provide the focus of agency obligation, but this principle provides a moral basis for agency support to carers.

However, there is another dimension to this which might encompass a range of people from full-time live-in carers to interested neighbours. The 1990 National Health Service and Community Care Act obliges agencies to make use of community resources in responding to the care needs of users. In practice part of that 'making use' involves negotiating collaborative roles between formal agencies and informal carers. This can be interpreted as enabling agencies to enter into agreements with carers and other helpers which (following Kant's principle of promise-keeping) place the agency under a degree of (at least) moral obligation. Such agreements are being made (Manthorpe, 1994). In that sense also it is arguable that agencies can have direct obligations to carers. These obligations will not be based on meeting carers' needs, though they may involve that to some degree, so it does not reclassify carers as consumers. Agency obligations, in each case, will depend upon what has been agreed between the parties involved.

The worker's obligation to the agency

We have considered the moral status, goals and responsibilities of community care agencies. Let us now consider further the relationship between the organization and the employee. Whether it is possible to owe a moral duty to an organization depends on our view of the organization. If it can bear corporate moral responsibility then, arguably, it can also be the focus of moral responsibility. It is quite possible to owe a legal duty, particularly in the role of employee, to an organization, but the moral relationship depends on our view of French's (1984) argument. If we accept the argument, we can have a moral relationship with the organizations; if we do not, we may still have obligations to the other people working in the agency, as an aggregate of individuals.

Working from a view that the agency has a corporate moral identity, the contract of employment can be seen as a mutual promise, which on the Kantian principle ought not to be broken. Green (1994) refers to the 'promissory relationship' of the employee to the employer which he sees as requiring a loyalty beyond the dictates of utilitarianism. There is, arguably, a moral obligation to work for the salary paid, if that is the agreement, and if part of that agreement is to pursue the goals of the organization, then there is a moral obligation on the employee to do that. For instance, if my employer makes explicit to me that I am required to adhere to its policy of anti-discriminatory practice as part of my terms of employment and I sign in the knowledge of that information, I would in Kantian terms be committed to that practice. If there is no such explicit element in the contract the matter is less clear. Am I by entering into employment implicitly committing myself to the employer's goals? If I join the production line at Ford, does that mean that I am morally committed to Ford's attempt to lobby the USA congress against environmental legislation? That does not seem to make much sense. I am morally committed to doing what I have contracted with Ford to do. If employment in community care has additional requirements beyond the contract of employment they are likely to come from professional rather than employee obligations.

There may be other bases for a moral commitment to the employer, particularly in the context of community care. One possibility lies in the fact that there may be shared moral goals between employer and employee. In a situation where I am working for an organization which in my view is engaged in morally praiseworthy activities, there is a good argument for showing loyalty to that employer. This may be based on my commitment to principles, to constituency or to users. If it makes sense for me to seek to achieve an outcome which I believe to be morally right, and I believe my employer's activities and intentions have the same goal, it could even be argued that I ought to show loyalty to my employer in that situation if I am in that way helping to achieve the right outcome. A Kantian view might suggest that I have a duty to support my employer in those goals, as I have to pursue those goals. That support is in itself part of the process of pursuing those goals. The utilitarian argument would be that if my support helps my employer to maximize happiness, it is right for me to do so. And it may be that it is right for me to do so even when there are other disagreements between myself and my employer. It may in that context be right for me to allow my employer to get away with behaviour that I disapprove of, if I think a serious challenge on my part might disrupt my employer's activities to such a degree that shared goals are threatened. So the issue of collusion and complicity is brought into focus here.

The practical arguments above – maximizing the achievement of shared goals, maximizing happiness – still hold good even if we do not accept that the organization has a corporate moral identity. The ostensible duty or commitment to the agency in that context is a duty or commitment to maximize the practical likelihood of certain goals being achieved. In reality it does not represent a duty to the agency in itself. We equally could reframe the organization as a group of people who happen to offer the best prospect of achieving certain goals. Our real moral duty in that context is then to the beneficiaries of those goals – the users and the community.

Conflicts of responsibility

I have argued that it is possible to have a moral relationship with the agency even if we do not accept its corporate moral status, and it is certainly possible if we do accept that. This suggests that the agency has a legitimate moral claim on the worker.

However, there are situations where that claim becomes problematic – for instance where the agency requires the worker to implement policies or practices which seem to conflict with the requirements of the worker's professional code of ethics. In that situation a crucial factor must be the focus of the duty. The agency is evoking a duty the employee owes to the agency itself. The professional code of ethics defines duties owed (mostly) to the user, not to the profession (though there is, arguably, a duty to the profession also). Whereas the agency is a means to a moral end, never a moral end in itself, the user is a person and therefore a moral end. So there is a fundamental priority for professional as against agency obligation. This is not to say that workers are morally required to risk their jobs, disrupt the work of the agency or otherwise risk harm to themselves or others in order to adhere to that prior obligation. Clearly there are other obligations involved as well. But I am suggesting that there need to be good reasons for not adhering to that priority, as failure to do so could be seen as a dereliction of duty.

Not all conflicts involve professional duties. There may be some which involve other moral requirements, including the worker's perceived obligations as a citizen, person, family member and so on. If this involves the agency requiring new practices which conflict with the worker's conscience, the worker may be in a position to argue that he or she signed the contract of employment on the understanding that he or she would not be required to do these things. So a promise is being broken. If this understanding was not made explicit, however, this might be hard to sustain. If the contract of employment could be read as including these activities, it may be that the employer could claim to be acting within its rights. However, if the employer uses pressure such as threats of dismissal in requiring the worker to do things which he or she regards as immoral the employer is, arguably, harming the worker and would be open to moral censure for that.

There are other agency requirements which are problematic because they directly disrupt the relationship with the worker. I suggested that one basis for a worker's loyalty to the agency might be shared moral goals. If the agency changes its purpose, and through that its moral goals, it may no longer share its goals with its workers. Part of the basis for loyalty is lost. If those moral goals were in some sense built into the contract of employment, a larger part of the basis for loyalty is lost.

If the agency openly changes its purpose, and its constituency has been actively or passively party to the change, there need be no betrayal of users and the worker may not have grounds for seeing the agency as acting immorally. However, if the agency management introduces policies or practices which conflict with the moral purposes for which the agency at present exists, we have a rather different situation. Not only are the shared moral goals lost. The worker can argue that in requiring actions which go outside the moral goals and purposes of the agency, management are requiring the worker to act outside the agency's remit. Because the actions fall outside those things which the agency was enjoined to do by its constituency, it lacks the moral legitimacy conferred by the constituency. It may also be seen as a betrayal of consumers. Therefore, management cannot claim the agency's moral authority to require it of the worker. In this situation the worker's responsibility to pursue the moral goals and purposes of the agency has come into conflict with the actual policy or practices of the agency management. Green (1994, p.155) argues that in this situation 'loyalty to larger constituencies or to the long-term interests of the corporation may require employees or managers to engage in forms of ethical dissent and whistle blowing'. Again, resistance or refusal by the worker may disrupt and therefore harm the agency, so there may be a real conflict of duties if the agency is in other respects acting in accordance with its purposes.

Complicity

So far we have considered situations where the agency makes problematic demands on the worker. However, there are situations where the agency may be engaged in morally problematic activities which do not require the direct participation of the worker. The problem then arises as to how the worker should respond to this. In particular:

1. How far should the workers regard themselves as party to their employers action through being employees?
2. How far can they justify non-cooperation or counteraction against employers' action?

Simply being employed by the same body that performs these actions need not necessarily involve complicity of any kind, if the goals and purposes of the agency are acceptable and it is 'backsliding' from those. This is clearly a different matter from when the organization's goals are morally reprehensible in the first place. To become an employee or member of an organization such as the Nazi Party is very different from becoming an employee of a community care agency, as its goals and purposes were of a very different kind, and membership must imply endorsement of those goals. It is only if my role as employee somehow contributes actively or passively to the problematic activities, that I can see myself as morally associated with them. If I have any power to prevent or oppose these within the machinery of the agency and I do not do so then it starts to become possible to link me with the actions, however loosely. Even then a good deal must depend on what is morally wrong with the actions under consideration, and which of the worker's duties might justify attempting to stop them. If nobody is being harmed, it is not clear that the worker need even consider action. If the agency's reputation is being harmed, but users are not, it is still not clear that the worker needs to see him or herself as bearing complicity. If users are being harmed, then the worker's professional duty and duty to agency moral goals might justify action but this again requires a reminder of Kant's principle, that ought implies can. Action may be justified, but impossible or ineffective. If there is nothing that the worker can do, it is not clear that there is anything he or she ought to do.

There may be some actions which are possible but which involve harm to, or betrayal of, the agency (in the sense of breaking the contract of employment), possible harm to the worker but no harm to the user. 'Whistleblowing' may be an example of this, in that it harms the agency's reputation, but does not disrupt its activities to the degree where users are likely to suffer. As the agency is not a person, duties to it must be limited and outweighed by duty to users. Harm to the worker is clearly in the hands of the agency management, who may choose to act decently and not dismiss the worker. However, the worker must calculate the risks.

There are some conceivable agency actions, or agency management actions, which may be so strongly in conflict with the worker's perceived duty to the user or to others that it would justify active disruption of the agency's activities. This would potentially harm the worker through dismissal, and would potentially harm users through loss of services. Owing to the latter element, of harm to users, I am not sure that such action could be justified through professional duty, or duty to agency moral goals, within which any such harm would be unacceptable. Probably the worker would need to look to duty as a person or citizen, and to justify this the agency's actions being opposed would need to be wrong to the point of wickedness, and to be causing considerable harm. In effect we are dealing here with actions which any citizen might see themselves as being obliged to try and stop.

THE ETHICS OF COMMUNICATION

I said at the beginning of this chapter that we can identify a bedrock of person-to-person moral obligations that are prior to any professional or agency roles. I discussed these obligations in a Kantian framework. Now that the moral implications of the formal roles have been explored, it is worth considering a wider ethical framework also for the performance of those obligations. The Kantian categorical imperative remains potentially relevant in all relationships, but Kant wrote in an age before the welfare bureaucracies of the twentieth century existed, and his pre-industrial liberalism sometimes seems naïve in the modern context. I shall therefore introduce here a related set of principles developed by Habermas (1991).

Habermas, like Kant, seeks a moral framework based on rationality – on our power to reason. As a late twentieth century European, heir to Marx and Freud, Habermas lacks Kant's confidence in the sovereignty of individual reason. Instead of seeking rules for individual reflection on moral issues, as Kant did, he seeks rules for interpersonal communication, to help participants arrive at morally valid conclusions. Habermas explicitly intends these to counteract the inequalities and oppressions built into communication in modern societies. The inequalities embodied in welfare bureaucracies are clearly part of this. Habermas's principles require that dialogue should be undertaken with a commitment to communicating what is true, comprehensible, normatively appropriate and sincere. Communication should be honest and non-strategic (i.e. it should not be intended to manipulate), and it should not seek to mystify. Habermas takes full account of the ambiguities and pressures of modern society on individuals in his system, and his principles are intended to regulate precisely the sort of situation where the worker may find him or herself. In that sense they are particularly relevant to the complex overlapping of roles which we have been considering. Though their immediate relevance is to communication between worker and user, they are also relevant to the demands of communication within the agency, since it is within that context (if anywhere) that many of the problems we have been considering must be resolved.

REFERENCES

Freeman, R. and Gilbert, D. (1988) *Corporate Strategy and the Search for Ethics*. Englewood Cliffs: Prentice-Hall.

French, P. (1984) *Collective and Corporate Responsibility*. New York: Columbia University Press.

George, V. and Wilding, P. (1992) *Ideology and Social Welfare*. London: Routledge.

Green, R. M. (1994) *The Ethical Manager*. New York: Macmillan.

Habermas, J. (1991) *Communication and the Evolution of Society*. Cambridge: Polity Press.

Lewis, J. (1994) 'Voluntary organisations in new partnerships with local authorities: the anatomy of a contract'. *Social Policy and Administration* 28(3), 206–20.

Mandelstam, M. and Schwehr, B. (1995) *Community Care Practice and the Law*. London: Kingsley.

Manthorpe, J. (1994) 'The family and informal care', in N. Malin (ed.) *Implementing Community Care*. Buckingham: Open University Press.

Nozick, R. (1974) *Anarchy, State and Utopia*. New York: Basic Books.

Ozar, D. (1987) 'The demands of professions and their limits', in C. A. Quinn and M. D. Smith (eds) *The Professional Commitment: Issues and Ethics in Nursing*. Philadelphia: Saunders.

Randall, S. (1995) 'City pride: from municipal socialism to municipal capitalism'. *Critical Social Policy* 43, 40–59.

Rawls, J. (1971) *A Theory of Justice*. Cambridge, MA: Harvard University Press.

Ryan, A. (1991) 'Merit goods and benefits in kind: Paternalism and Libertarianism in action', in T. Wilson and D. Wilson (eds) *The State and Social Welfare*. London: Longmans.

Stewart, J. (1983) *Local Government: The Conditions of Choice*. London: Allen & Unwin.

CHAPTER 5
Dealing with Ethical Issues in the Team

INTRODUCTION

In this chapter I intend to focus on the management of ethical issues in the working group. I shall not be concerned so much with general ethical principles, or with the resolution of practice dilemmas, as with the processes through which a group of people can apply principles to ethical dilemmas in a way that is acceptable to everyone involved. The group concerned may be an *ad hoc* collection of workers who are particularly concerned with one case, a multidisciplinary team or a larger organization. I shall consider ways of mapping situations that might clarify the issues under focus, the kind of differences of view that might arise between people and ways of managing those differences in terms of the issues themselves and in terms of the interpersonal dynamics involved.

A WAY OF PROCEEDING

I begin by suggesting a way of unpacking a situation to allow everyone as much clarity as possible about what the ethical issues are. A useful outcome for such a process would be to have a list of the major ethical concepts relevant to the situation, the principles that seem to be at issue and the areas where these principles seem to be in conflict. To derive this material, questions need to be asked about the present state of affairs and about available options. Each individual initially would need to go through this process themselves. The kinds of questions relevant to this process might be as follows:

1. What, if any, aspects of the present situation seem to me to be ethically problematic?
2. Why do I think this?
3. Which aspects are more and which aspects less problematic?
4. Why do I think this?

5. How are blame and accountability distributed?
6. How is duty distributed?
7. What aspects of the situation can I legitimately seek to influence?
8. How are my duties distributed?
9. What are the likely consequences of options available to me, or required of me?

Questions two and four are crucial to this. By asking myself why I believe something to be morally problematic, and why I believe it to be more so, or more importantly so, than something else, I have the opportunity to bring out the principles underlying my moral judgements.

AN EXAMPLE

Mrs Patel is in need of residential care and there is an issue in the team about the kind of advice she should be given with regard to available care homes and arrangements for admission. The proprietor of a local private home has, through neighbourhood contacts, found out about Mrs Patel's situation and has approached her directly to encourage her to choose her particular establishment. Mrs Patel got on well with the proprietor, and is thinking seriously about moving in there. The team know the proprietor and believe her to engage in sharp business practice, and to be in the care business purely for financial motives, despite her protestations to the contrary. Her action with regard to Mrs Patel is seen as a minor example of her way of doing things.

Position one

I believe that Mrs Patel ought to be advised against going to that home. I admit that I have no reason to believe that standards of care are inferior to that in other equivalent establishments. It may be that Mrs Patel will be as comfortable there as in the alternatives, but I take the view that we should not be passively condoning the involvement of someone like this proprietor in the business of providing care. Care ought to be provided through motives which include genuine caring and concern for others and, failing that, providers ought to be honest about their motive. The active soliciting of clients is also not acceptable and the proprietor ought not to be allowed to benefit from it if that can be prevented. If Mrs Patel knew about the proprietor's motives and general business practices she may well not wish to go into her establishment in any case. She ought to have the information in order to make up her mind.

Position two

My colleagues take a different view. They believe that it is none of our business what motivation and what general business practices can be ascribed to the proprietor. If we believe that the standard of care in that establishment is as good as that in those of its competitors, we are not failing in any duty to Mrs Patel if we allow her to make her choice on the basis of her contact with the proprietor. Mrs Patel knows she has a choice, and elects to make her choice on the basis of that contact which she interprets (not entirely wrongly) as an indication of the proprietor's zeal. We have no evidence that the proprietor is engaged in any illegal activity, or is likely to go bankrupt, or is in any other way in danger of consequences that would be disruptive to the resident's care. So that is really none of our business.

ANSWERING THE QUESTIONS

What is morally problematic and why?

Let us suppose that I identify the proprietor's general methods, motivation and behaviour on this occasion as being morally problematic, alongside the exploitation of Mrs Patel in that context. Let us suppose that my colleagues also disapprove of the proprietor's behaviour. The proprietor's behaviour is seen as morally unacceptable by everyone. Let us suppose that the difference between us is that my colleagues do not see Mrs Patel as being exploited. Answers to question one above therefore may vary in that respect. When trying to explain why we variously identify these aspects of the situation we may all cite lack of honesty on the proprietor's part, but whereas I identify exploitation as a major problem, my colleagues do not. One difference is that I am concerned with the motives of actions, while my colleagues are concerned with the results. If the result is that Mrs Patel gets as good care as she would get elsewhere, my colleagues do not see exploitation, however falsely the proprietor may present herself to Mrs Patel. I see the very act of presenting a false front in order to persuade Mrs Patel to a particular course of action as exploitative in its essence, irrespective of any consequences to Mrs Patel. So the focus is different – the difference between motivation and consequences – and we already are starting to expose the possible deep structure of our moral disagreement.

Location of blame and accountability

In locating blame and accountability I will clearly blame the proprietor, in that she is in breach of a duty of honesty. My colleagues may regard the proprietor as partly accountable for the outcomes (i.e. Mrs Patel's decision) but will probably regard Mrs Patel herself as being largely responsible for that. The function of dishonesty seems important here. Again, I am emphasizing the intention to deceive. If one party enters an encounter intending to deceive, and presents themselves falsely, the other party is immediately at a disadvantage and, arguably, is unable to act with full autonomy. My colleagues, more concerned with results, may question how far Mrs Patel was deceived about what mattered to her. If she (Mrs Patel) is more concerned about whether she gets on with someone than whether they have motives of care or money, perhaps she was able to make an autonomous decision. She may from experience have come to expect a certain amount of 'front' from people, and not be worried by that. She may assume that protestations of caring ideals are always to be taken with a pinch of salt, but that people cannot be blamed for feeling they have to present themselves in a particular way. She may, in other words, not be at all upset or nonplussed by any of this. My colleagues would in that event not need to be worried either.

The differences in orientation that produce these different answers could be of several sorts. One might be a difference, as before, between orientation towards motives and orientation towards results. Another might be orientation towards general and consistent principles against orientation towards individual situations judged on their merits.

Location of duty and likely consequences

Views about our duties in this situation also differ. I take the view that we ought to intervene to ensure the truth is known, and perhaps prevent a wrong being done, by telling Mrs Patel of the proprietor's general behaviour. My colleagues argue that Mrs Patel is likely to be unmoved by such information and that, therefore, she should not be approached in this way even if we believe the proprietor is acting wrongly. It risks creating problems with the proprietor. If she discovers that this is being said about her, she may justifiably believe she is being slandered, and at the very least the department's ability to work with her in future would be badly compromised. Also, Mrs Patel may take it amiss. In my colleagues' view we ought to act in a way that ensures the best outcomes in terms of well-being for present and future clients, and for the relationships with members of the community. Again we are concerned here with the difference between principles such as truth on the one hand, and consequences on the other.

Working backwards

In practice it is often going to be easier to start with 'what ought we to do' and work back from there. Arguments often start with different prescriptions with regard to action, and it is only slowly (if at all) that we work our way back to our views about the moral landscape of the situation, as addressed in questions one and three. So it may often be that questions eight and nine are where we start.

Practical disagreements

If we expose the hidden structure of our moral beliefs it will not necessarily always expose a moral disagreement. We may find that we are in agreement about the rights and wrongs of the situation. So, in the case of Mrs Patel we may be in agreement about the primacy of consequences in deciding on the right action and we may be in agreement on which particular consequences we most value, but our disagreement is about which actions will produce those consequences. I may believe that Mrs Patel would value our concern in warning her about the proprietor, and that this would improve our relationship with her and lead her to make a different choice. My colleagues may believe that it would do none of these things; and so the disagreement would be one about the predicted results of particular actions. Factual disagreements are not necessarily easy to resolve, but it is at least possible to agree on what would be evidence in support of one prediction as against another – whether it is knowledge of the personality and habits of one individual, or evidence about some general feature of human behaviour. Moral disagreements are a rather different matter. They are likely to express differences of value and principle and differences in the relative importance placed on one aspect as against another aspect of a situation.

It is worth considering at this point what kind of disagreements we might discover. Larmore (1994) maps out a framework for disagreement from a pluralist point of view which is useful in clarifying some of the issues. The pluralist view is that moral right has many facets and aspects, and that some of these conflict. However, it is not simply an expression of culture or belief. On the contrary, morality has sufficient reality to be worth disagreeing about and, therefore, to be worth seeking agreement about. None the less agreement is not always possible. This seems a useful standpoint to use in our present situation where, for both moral and practical purposes, agreement needs to be sought, however diverse the starting-points.

First Larmore suggests that moral frameworks may differ – as for instance between the deontologist and the consequentialist, who think about the business of identifying right and wrong in quite different ways. Second, we may have a conflict between different conceptions of the good; that is, we may agree on a moral framework but disagree about what goes in it. So we may have two consequentialists, one of whom is utilitarian and the other of whom gives priority to justice as defining the good consequences of an action. As it happens we may find that those sorts of disagreements are more difficult to resolve than differences of framework. It is quite possible to arrive by different routes at the same conclusion. When we are focusing on different aspects of a situation we cannot be certain of conflict any more than we can of agreement but, if we are focusing on the same aspect of a situation and are wanting different things from it, I suspect that the likelihood of disagreement may be greater. At the same time the possibility of negotiation and compromise is probably also greater.

The other two areas of disagreement that Larmore identifies are of ideals and of obligations. He cites liberty and equality as ideals which often conflict. Though individuals have different priorities in respect of these, it is as often the case that we experience that conflict internally.

Relationships between conflicting values

Larmore also maps some of the relationships that might be identifiable between conflicting values in a situation. In some cases those values are commensurable – that is they are 'rankable with respect to a common denominator of value' (Larmore, 1994, p.67). It might be, for instance, that the justice-oriented consequentialist and the utilitarian emphasize their respective definitions of good because they each believe that that particular 'good' – i.e. happiness and justice respectively – are ways of maximizing human well-being. We might be able to agree on a ranking relationship between justice and happiness on one level, and well-being on a deeper level.

However, there are other cases where values are not commensurable, but are based in different principles even though they clearly compete on the same level in a given situation. Larmore uses the example of a conflict between different duties – the general duty of promise-keeping (which is universal and, in Kant's terms, rational) and a much more specific duty arising out of friendship. Take a situation where I have made a promise to a stranger which conflicts with the urgent need of a friend. The two duties of promise-keeping and friendship might be seen to conflict on equal terms. We might have no difficulty in agreeing on the importance of both duties, but in many situations I shall have to choose between them.

In the light of Larmore's ideas, we can consider how moral disagreements might be dealt with in a way that leads to an agreed course of action, as follows:

1. It might emerge that the conflicting values being expressed in the disagreement are both comparable and commensurable. So adherence to one principle is actually based on adherence to a deeper principle which may not have been articulated yet. For instance, adherence to promise-keeping might be based on a deeper principle, of respect for persons. It may be that the 'surface' principle of keeping promises is the one that I can articulate and is a conscious part of my thinking and feeling when dilemmas arise; the notion of respect is one which is relatively inchoate and unarticulated, and only vaguely in consciousness. Perhaps to renegotiate and develop a clearer idea of the individual's wishes, rather than continuing rigid adherence to a promise, is more strongly in accordance with the principle of respect. I might thereby change my mind about the right course of action without violence to my moral commitments. My colleague, who supports renegotiation on the same foundation of respect for persons will then be able to reach agreement with me.

2. I might be persuaded that an action which accords with a principle I value, conflicts with another principle which I value equally or more. In some cases realization may be based on having the consequences of my action pointed out

to me in a way I had not foreseen – in which case this is really a factual and not a moral matter – but in others it might be a question of seeing my action in a different moral framework, rather than a different factual one. So an action which I intend to enhance and support autonomy might be reframed as an action which withholds and denies care. If I value both equally, the recognition that I am doing the latter may lead me to decide not to do the former. In that situation it may be that care and autonomy are comparable, but not necessarily commensurable. So, it is clear that they are competing on the same level and are defining the same aspect of the situation, but they cannot necessarily be worked down to the same underlying principle.

3. It might emerge that we are using language in rather different ways, and that we mean the same thing but use different words. This is more likely to arise when the disagreement is over the way we want to describe a situation rather than when it concerns the appropriate course of action. It is possible to mean different things by the same word, and to believe we agree when we do not. This creates particular difficulty if we disagree on actions but are unable to pin down a disagreement of principle because we think we agree on the key principle – only to discover that we mean something completely different. Words like 'responsibility' are often mutually misunderstood. Where I might think my colleague means 'blame', when he says 'responsibility', he might mean what I mean by 'autonomy'. Or we may be talking about the same thing. My colleague may use the word 'deserve' to mean the same thing I mean when I say 'has a right to'. On the other hand we may be referring to the same aspects of a situation using different words denoting different ideas. What I might refer to as someone's needs, a colleague may see as his or her desires. Clarification of these kinds of problems is not going to help resolve a disagreement about courses of action in the first instance, only about descriptions of a situation, but from changes in description sometimes come changes in prescription.

PATTERNS OF DIVERSITY

How can people with strongly different moral views work together in areas where issues of disagreement are likely to be prominent in the shared practice? In order to be able to do this we need two kinds of information: some ideas about the kind of diversity which we need to manage; and strategies for managing it. First, then I shall consider some information about the sorts of diversity which may be part of our deliberations.

Professions

The first dimension I shall consider is that between professions. There is some evidence to support the view that professional membership has an effect on practitioners' values and moral descriptions of situations they encounter in their work, and that this will lead members of different professions working together to disagree on some issues (Wilmot, 1995). I have expressed this with great caution because it must be clear from experience that members of the same profession often disagree with each other, and members of different professions often agree. Other factors cutting across professional membership clearly have a great effect on moral standpoints, but that is not a reason to dismiss professional values and ethics as irrelevant to the individual practitioner.

Of those involved in community care, obvious candidates for working together are nurses and social workers. The small amount of research evidence identified and reviewed by the writer tends to suggest that social workers' values and moral beliefs are oriented towards general principles such as rights, while nurses values and beliefs are more oriented towards individual respect and individual care (Wilmot, 1995). This evidence relates to the expressed beliefs of practitioners. However, it can be seen that the codes of ethics of the two professions pull them in the direction of rights-based, collective and egalitarian values for social work, and individualist, respect and care-based values in the case of nursing. The professional literatures differ in similar ways. That is not to say that these elements have a decisive influence on the beliefs or actions of practitioners. However, in so far as they do have influence, they will be in different directions. A study by Dalley (1993) showed differences between social workers and district nurses in views of the responsibility of families for the care of elderly relatives. Where, for instance, an elderly patient's relatives were unhappy about taking on more responsibility for caring for that individual, the social workers were more ready to see the individual's care as a state responsibility, while the nurses were more ready to see it as a family duty of care. This is commensurate with the patterns of professional values I have mentioned. A nurse who sees moral issues in terms of individual care and duties may well react rather differently to the situation of the elderly person and their family from a social worker who sees situations in terms of rights and fair distribution. The social worker is likely to take more account of the State's role in providing care in order to distribute the burden of care as fairly as possible across the community, and the unfairness of the additional demand upon this particular group of relatives. The nurse by contrast is more likely to think of the individual need of the patient to be cared for by someone close, and the duty of care that binds many different kinds of relationship.

Age and gender

Clearly our experience as members of major groupings (in terms of gender, age, class, culture and so on) must have some influence on our moral beliefs. Age and gender are closely connected in terms of evidence in this respect. The classic study of moral thinking at different stages of maturation, that of Kohlberg (1981), sets out a sequence of stages through which we progress in developing authentically moral (as opposed to prudential) responses to moral issues, and increasing levels of moral autonomy through that process. Therefore, childhood tends to be characterized by criteria of personal well-being – avoidance of punishment and achievement of personal satisfaction. More convention-oriented responses gain ground during adolescence – relating to approval, acceptance and maintenance of the social order. These carry over into adulthood, at which stage some people achieve a greater degree of autonomy, and develop either a contractual or a conscience-oriented view of ethical issues. This model provides the basis for a number of analyses. Initially, if we accept the research as valid, it provides a model for moral development, and a way of identifying the different moral perspectives of people who are in different positions in that trajectory.

However, Kohlberg's work has generated interesting ideas through its limitations as well as through its achievements. In particular his findings generated some interesting issues with regard to gender, which have helped to produce a new branch of ethics focusing on gender. Kohlberg's results suggested that men are more likely than women to approach problems from a standpoint of rules, whether individually or contractually developed. Women are more likely to view moral problems in the context of relationships and social processes. Kohlberg's scheme placed the latter at a lower level of moral development than the former, relating to convention and social order rather than to autonomous moral principles. However, this has been argued by a number of writers to show not that the 'womens way' of looking at moral problems is less developed than the 'mens way', but rather that Kohlberg, as a male writer in a patriarchal culture, is valuing the typically male way of thinking about ethics more highly than the typically female way. What the study shows is that there are different ways of thinking about moral problems, and that these correspond to some degree with the different sorts of experience and learning provided by the experiences of growing up male and female respectively in a western society. Kohlberg is seen as having misinterpreted the moral accounts given by some of his female respondents as reflecting dependency on convention and approval when making moral judgements, whereas an alternative reading would be to see these subjects as taking account of different factors – particularly the social context of relationships. Gilligan (1982) was the first to offer this response to Kohlberg's material, and has set the terms of the subsequent debate.

We are left with two frameworks arising from Kohlberg's work. One is that which he intended – a sequence of developmental positions. The other is what he did not intend – the opening up of important differences between the moral perceptions of men and the moral perceptions of women in American society, possibly in parts of British society as well (bearing in mind the cultural specificity of much of this). For our purposes it does not matter whether Kohlberg's stages are developmentally sequenced or not – whether they are stages (or levels) or simply different ways of responding. What matters is that they give us a framework for understanding different responses in the people with whom we are in contact. We may, then, be able to identify responses that are effectively pre-moral responses (though these may often be disguised as something else), responses that are convention-oriented, and responses that are autonomous. So, my desire to protect Mrs Patel from a dishonest home proprietor may be based on a view that such dishonesty threatens the social order, and goes against my conception of social behaviour and therefore should be opposed, or it may be based on a personal commitment to honesty which is independent of social convention. My orientation may not be immediately obvious. Certainly when we ask what the ethical problems in the situation are (question one above) that orientation may not be obvious. It is only when we ask why we see the situation in that way (and perhaps have to repeat the 'why' question several times) that this orientation may emerge. It may be that different orientations lead to the same conclusions – that convention and personal principle direct us in the same way. Where they lead in different directions, however, it is going to be difficult to resolve disputes reflecting those differences. If we are speaking from different orientations, we cannot even argue about the same things. Factual evidence will have quite different relevances, and moral principles will be understood as different things.

However, because a particular response represents a particular orientation, it does not mean that individuals are not capable of thinking from a different orientation. Adults often make decisions on pre-moral orientation, but that is not to say that they are unable to make decisions on conventional or autonomous moral grounds. Kohlberg shows that a level of moral autonomy as defined is achieved by a proportion of the population in adulthood, but the rest of the population engage in styles of moral thinking which to varying degrees are dependent on external rules or forces.

Culture

The other major areas of difference are those of culture, religion and community – differences which reflect socialization into different systems of values. Those differences will always be mediated through personal experience, and often through other differences of experience, such as the gender difference discussed above. Nobody is a prisoner of their culture but there is, none the less, a real possibility that a group of people representing a diversity of culture and/or religion will find a corresponding diversity of moral perspectives.

There is some reason to suppose that a major division lies between the moral tradition which dominates North America and north-western Europe – individualist, rules based, action focused – and the considerable diversity of other traditions throughout the world. The western tradition seems to relate most closely to what would traditionally be seen as middle-class norms concerning individual rights and responsibilities. Clearly the range of other traditions that we may encounter are diverse. Some are highly individualist. Others are collectivist. Ethical traditions in China and Japan place much more emphasis on obligations to the collectivity and the legitimate claims of the group on the individual, in contrast to the rights of the individual (see Triandis, 1990).

There are alternative views to the universalist individualism of the dominant western tradition, in which all rights and obligations attach equally to all persons, other things being equal. Moral obligations in many cultures are viewed as being specific to particular relationships. They may also take a rather different shape from those recognized in the dominant western tradition. Miller (1991) found that Indians were more likely to see benificence (a duty to do good to others generally) and interpersonal responsibility (a duty to do good to specific others as part of a relationship) as fully moral obligations, while Americans saw these as to some extent matters of personal choice. The Americans gave full moral weight to obligations based on justice. So it is possible to identify differences of framework and emphasis in this context. It is interesting that the contrast that Miller found is not entirely unlike the contrast that Gilligan (1982) found between American men and women – that women tend to place more moral weight on obligations arising from relationships. The dominant tradition seems to be at odds with the moral thinking of a large part of the human species.

Religion

Whereas culture is likely to produce different emphases and different moral frameworks, the influence of religion may in some cases be much more specific. The position of the Roman Catholic church on issues such as abortion, euthanasia and contraception, or the Islamic position on burial, presents the believer with a fairly clear set of injunctions. Sometimes those injunctions are the most specific and conscious parts of a tradition in which, to some degree, religion and culture are combined. If I have grown up in a particular religion that my family and community have followed for a substantial period of time, it is likely that my whole world-view will be influenced by that, and it will not always be easy to unpick the specific requirements of the religion from the general cultural background. If, on the other hand, I am a convert, my position is rather different, in that I may retain many, even most, of the cultural baggage of the communities which have socialized me, with whatever moral perspectives that confers on me, to which I have added a specific set of religious requirements.

MANAGING CONFLICT IN THE TEAM

We now need to consider how all these differences might manifest themselves in the team context, and how they might be managed on an interpersonal and group level. The essence is conflict, and conflict management. The issues that are likely to lead to significant disagreement on ethics are likely to be emotive and in a practical or symbolic sense, to be important. Feelings will be invested in these, and in some cases intense and painful experience may be connected with the issues. The interface between emotion and intellect is important here. I have discussed ethical issues in a context where cognition and analysis are the focal tools for management, but disagreements cannot be managed or resolved purely on the basis of reasoned argument. The management of feelings is crucial to the process.

The team as a group

Let us consider the context within which the issues are being dealt with. Teams are groups. They are a subcategory of that most varied and complex phenomenon, the human group. As groups go, the team's life span is often reasonably long – running sometimes into years. Membership change rates vary a good deal depending on the team's situation. Teams belong to that species of group which exist to perform a specified set of externally related tasks. They are different from friendship groups, or even therapy groups, which exist to provide their members with a certain kind of experience. Teams have a service to provide, and relationships within the team are a means to an end – to ensuring that the service is provided effectively. None the less group maintenance – the ability to keep members feeling positive about the group and about other group members and to keep on wanting to be part of the group – is crucially important in allowing the group's tasks to be performed (Johnson and Johnson, 1987) . In terms of relationships and feelings, we can be sure that most functioning teams will develop a pattern of roles and behaviours over their life span, which will reflect both the external forces impinging on the team, and the internal dynamics between members. These features constitute part of the team culture – the norms and shared beliefs that develop within the minisociety of a group, and in which no two groups will be precisely identical. Within that culture individuals will perform different roles and have different impacts. Leadership will be distributed in various ways – concentrated or diffused – and power will be likewise distributed in different ways depending on the kind of power that each member is able to exert in the group – based on formal position, expertise, knowledge, status in the outside world, ability to reward or punish other group members, or simply personal force or charisma.

Practicalities of conflict management

Within the team's culture and history will be a set of group norms concerning conflict. Johnson and Johnson (1987) argue that the ability to openly acknowledge conflict is crucial to the success of a group. So the ability to ensure that a group is well maintained through conflict allows it to deal with that conflict in a way that optimizes task performance. Denied, repressed conflict takes up group energy, and focus on the task is lost. Conflict that is openly acknowledged and managed increases group cohesion even where disagreements are not resolved; it also releases group energy for task performance. This analysis, though well supported by research (Baron *et al.*, 1992) , tends to conflict with real-life group dynamics as they develop in many situations. Groups have a life cycle, and the development of a sense of group identity can at some stages in the groups life cycle show itself as a strong desire for group consensus, a fear of anything that threatens that consensus and resentment to any member manifests such a threat (Bion, 1961) . The most successful groups are those which are able to work through that fantasy of group homogeneity, and to accept and value the individuality and differences between group members, so that communication within the group is directed specifically at individual members rather than generally to 'the group'. However, in order for a group to cope with the demands of diversity and difference, it needs to be able to cope with the resultant conflict.

Conflict management takes time. Issues of conflict are often confused. Usually there is a mixture of issues of principle and personal feelings and resentments mixed together, and these need to be teased apart. One issue leads into another, often unexpectedly. As Payne suggests 'substantive conflicts easily lead to emotional conflicts, and emotional conflicts tend to lead people to find issues that will divide them' (Payne, 1982, p.78). Where this is the case, disagreements of principle and negative feelings both need proper expression, and that requires not only a willingness to allow those expressions by other group members (who may disagree or feel threatened) but a willingness and ability to listen effectively and actively, and facilitate expression. This is personally demanding, and is clearly an ideal that no real group of people will achieve all the time. It also requires an amount of time that no working team is going to be able to spare in one session, unless they are resourced to take team 'time out'. Often matters can only be dealt with in small 'bites'.

It is also important to acknowledge that conflict is not a process that involves pairs of individuals, with the rest of the group listening and mediating. Group conflict is likely to draw in most or all group members in one way or another. This is not to say that everyone will take sides, but simply that most or all members will have some feelings evoked by the conflict, will identify with fellow members more overtly involved, either openly or covertly, and may well experience conflict arising out of the original issue, and feelings about the behaviour of other participants or about some aspect of what is being said. The situation which most stable working groups find most alarming is a clearly delineated split, where two parts of the group take opposite sides of an issue in a way that makes it difficult for group members to perform a mediating role. That is certainly a very difficult situation, but it is only the most pronounced of a wide spectrum of different mixtures of involvement in group conflict. It is normal, for instance, for alliances to be formed on particular issues in groups. This does not mean the group is lacking in cohesion. If those alliances are consistent over a number of issues, and amount to the existence of consistent subgroups, there may be more grounds for concern about cohesion. Having said this, it is sometimes unavoidable for the emotional survival of people in the group that they have consistent sources of support. If for instance there is a minority of Black members or a minority of women members, it is quite possible that given commonalities of experience, and given that one shared experience is likely to be marginalization, it ought not to be read as a necessary sign that the group is 'unhealthy' if those minority members provide one another with a degree of consistent support. This is far more a comment on the 'health' of wider society; the crucial point is that the rest of the group is able to recognize this as a legitimate meeting of need by group members.

ETHICAL PROBLEMS AND PRINCIPLES IN CONFLICT MANAGEMENT

For the rest of the chapter I shall concentrate on ethical issues arising from the business of managing team conflict, and on some principles that might offer a moral framework for that process.

Freedom to change and pressure to change

An important question concerns the legitimacy of pressure to change one's moral beliefs. I have suggested that from a relativist viewpoint pressure on someone to do something they think is immoral could, arguably, be seen as immoral itself. However, if we can truly change a person's view, are we doing them any harm? This might depend partly on the degree of freedom we ascribe to people in relation to their beliefs. If I am so deeply embedded in my beliefs that I cannot be said to have any choice over what I believe, then any action on the part of another to change my beliefs will involve some element of manipulation, or perhaps even duress. If I am at liberty to change, then the process is under my control. Which way we view it must depend on our own perspective.

I have suggested that nobody is the prisoner of their culture – that people are capable of forming independent views that conflict with aspects of their own culture and socialization. But if the individual concerned simply disagrees with that view, and believes him or herself unable to deviate, this person may see him or herself as being pressured and manipulated even if that is not my intention. Do I still seek to persuade this individual? On the other hand if he or she sees him or herself as having chosen his or her moral code, does that in any sense affect my duty to respect this person's beliefs? I may respect freedom to choose what he or she believes, and as part of that hold him or her responsible for those choices, and their behavioural consequences. For instance, if the person chooses to convert to a religion that in his or her opinion requires him or her to regard homosexual relationships as sinful, what claim does he or she have on the respect of others for that belief? This individual chose the package, knowing its implications. Have his or her colleagues then no right to express negative views towards his or her position? Does that make his or her position different from someone who grew up in a religious and cultural milieu that led him or her to be socialized into homophobic attitudes? The latter could apply to a large part of the population of this country, but many people have overcome that socialization – perhaps partly because we have also absorbed other values which conflict with homophobia and which provided a firm moral ground to stand on in discarding homophobic beliefs. Where those conflicting values are not part of someone's culture, do they then carry less responsibility for their homophobia?

Justice in conflict management

The principle of justice has been considered in a number of forms as being a requisite of the management of moral disagreement. Hampshire (1978) has argued that there is a bedrock conception of justice that is likely to be applicable to most moral disagreements. We are concerned here primarily with the procedural idea of justice – the opportunity to be heard and to put one's point of view without duress or limitation, and the commitment on the part of others to give attention to each person's case and to subject it to clear and open scrutiny and argument. The enemy of justice in this context would be anything which might unnerve, disorient or unequally limit the ability of the protagonists to put their case clearly (which ought to include an opportunity to think through their case clearly beforehand), and any responses in the process of argument and analysis which are intended to confuse, conceal or mystify. The deliberate use of impressive-sounding but faulty arguments would count here, together with the deliberate use of impenetrable language. Feelings are likely to be present and a proper feature of the encounter, but any intentional use of strong expressed feeling to strengthen the impact of one's own case, and even more to unnerve the opposition, can reasonably be seen as unjust. All of these have underpinning them a principle of equal access to a hearing, which is the main component of procedural justice.

However, to operate this principle, we require that the protagonists value justice more highly than they value the prevailing of their own point of view. If I am arguing against someone who appears to be a Nazi, I may feel that the defeat of those views is more important than adherence to justice in the argument. That might be because I suspect that if he wins the argument now, justice within the team and justice for users will soon be a lost cause. So it is nonsense to adhere to justice with the foreseeable result that justice will be destroyed. It may simply be that I regard the values I am defending (given that there is no common ground and it is therefore an all-or-nothing situation) as more important than justice. To conduct an argument in a just way requires that the participants decide to do that, and probably requires that the decision is made with some real sense that it is the right thing to do. There are always arguments available in favour of abandoning justice in the argument because what is at stake is more important than how it is discussed. The team needs to have decided that this is not what it believes in this case.

Accommodation in conflict management

In a plural society it is necessary for people with different beliefs to work together, and to be able to jointly arrive at and jointly own decisions. A question arises as to whether that process requires any general values which cut across different sets of moral beliefs. To put the matter a different way, is there an argument for taking a different position in relation to our own beliefs in a plural society from the sort of attitude we might take in a more homogenous society? Wong (1994) identifies the concept of accommodation as a value which is morally commendable in its own right, because of its relevance to situations of difference. Accommodation in Wong's formulation involves a number of elements including an empathic effort to understand the reasons why other people have arrived at their particular moral beliefs, a willingness to look for practical areas of agreement – or at least compromise – rather than focusing on basic principles that are irreconcilable in theory, and a willingness to have one's conceptions of the good stretched at the margins through the influence of different conceptions. Wong sees accommodation as necessarily reciprocal, and accepts that it will often be less important as a value than values that are being disagreed over. It is clear that in any case we must decide for ourselves the weight that we give to the value of accommodation in our own discussions. It is possible, I think, to conduct discussions in a reasonable way without any commitment to accommodation. I shall discuss that further below.

Communicative ethics in conflict management

In the previous chapter I introduced the ethical principles for communication developed by Habermas (1991). They represent an attempt to develop a rationalist ethic relevant to our knowledge of psychology and interpersonal dynamics, and if they command a reasonable degree of credibility among the protagonists, they offer an ethical structure for argument and discourse. The requirement to say that which is comprehensible, true, normatively appropriate and sincere may seem rather like being against sin – we can all agree it is right, but where does it get us? However, it actually excludes a huge amount of interpersonal behaviour of a strategic and tactical kind. All strategems in argument and all manipulation of relationships are outlawed under this principle. All is most emphatically *not* fair in ethical dispute. Roderick (1986) suggests that part of the value-base of these principles is respect for the subjective experience of the other. So, however much we may disagree with the other person's argument, and wish to expose its weaknesses, we need to accept the integrity of the perceptions and experience that lies behind that argument, and work on the basis that it is authentic and the result of choice. So if I say 'you are only saying that because you are a woman/a nurse/Black/catholic/middle class etc' I am failing to show respect for that subjective experience. I am explaining the other person's views away to my own satisfaction, but denying the other person's choice of those opinions at the same time. Clearly there is something of a tightrope to be walked here between acceptance of the differences of belief and experience resulting from group differences such as culture, gender, race and class on the one hand, and a predisposition to explain people's beliefs on that basis on the other. It is in part the ability to distinguish between influences on an autonomous person, as against psychological causation which denies autonomy.

Habermas sees communicative ethics as an antidote to the inauthentic and oppressive communication characteristic of modern societies. He also sees it as an expression of humanity and rationality, and as a way of arriving at better moral judgements than those we started out with. Habermas is not a relativist, and believes that some moral judgements are better than others and are worth pursuing. It can be strongly argued that adherence to Habermas's requirements is likely to facilitate the testing of moral propositions. And on a practical level it is advisable to have clear rules for a process which potentially involves challenge and change to deeply held beliefs that we may see as having imperative significance for our behaviour. It is reasonable to require that when people enter into discourse of this special significance they do so with the protection of rules. However, in practice it may be equally appropriate for the team to agree its own ground rules for discussion, which may differ from any of these. In the end no principle will be adhered to without the consent of the team. That is the bedrock requirement.

REFERENCES

Baron, R., Kerr, N. and Miller, N. (1992) *Group Process, Group Decision-Making, Group Action*. Buckingham: Open University Press.

Bion, W. R. (1961) *Experiences in Groups, and Other Papers*. London: Tavistock.

Dalley, G. (1993) 'Professional ideology or organisational tribalism? The health service–social work divide', in J. Walmsley (ed.) *Health and Welfare Practice*. London: Sage.

Gilligan, C. (1982) *In a Different Voice: Psychological Theory and Women's Development*. Cambridge, MA: Harvard University Press.

Johnson, D. W. and Johnson, F. P. (1987) *Joining Together*. Englewood Cliffs: Prentice-Hall.

Habermas, J. (1991) *Communication and the Evolution of Society*. Cambridge: Polity Press.

Hampshire, S. (1978) *Public and Private Morality*. Cambridge: Cambridge University Press.

Kohlberg, L. (1981) *Essays on Moral Development*. San Francisco: Harper & Row.

Larmore, C. (1994) 'Pluralism and reasonable disagreement', in E. Paul, F. Miller and J. Paul (eds) *Cultural Pluralism and Moral Knowledge*. New York: Cambridge University Press.

Miller, J. (1991) 'A cultural perspective on the morality of benificence and interpersonal responsibility', in S. Ting-Toomey (ed.) *Cross-Cultural Interpersonal Communication*. Newbury Park: Sage.

Payne, M. (1982) *Working in Teams*. London: Macmillan.

Roderick, R. (1986) *Habermas and the Foundations of Critical Theory*. Basingstoke: Macmillan.

Triandis, H. (1990) 'Theoretical concepts that are applicable to the analysis of ethnocentrism', in R. W. Brislin (ed.) *Applied Cross-Cultural Psychology*. Newbury Park: Sage.

Wilmot, S. (1995) 'Professional values and interprofessional dialogue'. *Journal of Interprofessional Care* 9(3), 257–66.

Wong, D. (1994) 'Coping with moral conflict and ambiguity', in L. Foster and P. Herzog (eds) *Contemporary Philosophical Perspectives on Pluralism and Multiculturalism*. Amherst: University of Massachusetts Press.

CHAPTER 6
The Encounter

INTRODUCTION

The next four chapters are intended to illustrate the application of the principles of ethics to specific situations in community care. My intention is to focus each chapter around one situation, and to bring into that situation as many of the ideas discussed earlier as seem relevant. I shall start with what is in many ways the most basic situation – an encounter between worker and user – and I shall focus in turn on the following areas: the ethics of the relationship; justice in assessment; supporting the user's autonomy; confidentiality; and the user's obligations.

SITUATION

Mrs Smith is 80 and lives alone. She is a widow, and her son and daughter both live in other parts of the country. She has managed to care for herself until recently but is becoming increasingly affected by arthritis, and there is now a good deal that she cannot do for herself. Recently she had a fall and, although she was not seriously hurt, this unnerved her, and she decided to ask for help. Let us imagine that Angela, a community care worker, is visiting Mrs Smith to make an assessment of her needs. Although Angela may well consult other professionals and organizations, Mrs Smith is her main source of information concerning her needs. The crucial process of defining need and justifying services provision will take place primarily between Angela and Mrs Smith. Most of the other interests and commitments involved in that process will be present only by proxy, represented by one of the two protagonists. So the ethical questions will focus around what takes place between them in the first instance. Most of those questions, inevitably, will arise primarily for Angela, because our project is concerned with the behaviour of the professionals, the organizations, the formal machinery of community care provision and those who operate that machinery.

However, we can start by considering how we might view these two individuals in the roles and situation that bring them together. What is the moral significance of this situation, and these roles?

THE ETHICS OF THE RELATIONSHIP

The ethics of the encounter

There are certain requirements that are basic to person-to-person relationships irrespective of the particular role the protagonists are in. An obvious basic requirement must be respect for life and physical integrity. There are exceptions to this, as with the encounter between executioner and condemned or between enemy soldiers in battle. Arguably in the latter instance morality has in any case broken down, perhaps in the former case also in the view of many people, but in most kinds of encounter such life-threatening actions would only be morally justifiable, in the eyes of most people, for self-defence. Otherwise it is immaterial whether the encounter involves professional, economic or personal roles. There are certain requirements the breach of which would be regarded by most observers as immoral. No relationship can entirely absolve its protagonists from some universal requirements.

The most useful moral account of relationships available among established philosophies are those of Kant and Habermas (1991). Kant's is the most comprehensive, with its emphasis on treating people as ends. Habermas's principles of communicative ethics, emphasizing commitment to truth, appropriateness, sincerity and comprehensibility, has the advantage of being recent, with a post-1945 political context. Both sets of principles, drawing on ideas of truth-telling and non-manipulation, focus on an honest acknowledgement of the basis of the relationship that has been entered into and the requirements of that relationship.

These principles can apply even in relationships which do not seem to lend themselves to high moral principles. For instance, if I am a used car salesman following Kant's or Habermas's precepts I could communicate to the customer an honest acknowledgement that I shall be seeking to maximize the price they pay for the car I sell them, and minimize the price I pay for the car they trade in. If that is acknowledged, then I am arguably treating my customer as an end, because the relationship is not founded on deception, and my *bonhomie* and banter need not be mistaken for true benevolence.

However, we would expect a very different way of implementing Kant's and Habermas's principles to be visible in the interaction between user and worker in a community care situation. Recognizing the other person as an end must be a richer and more complex process for Angela than for the used car salesman, because Angela is responding to richer and more complex aspects of Mrs Smith's personhood. Also there is clearly a difference between a situation where, as with the used car transaction, honesty about the nature of the transaction is accompanied by an assumption that both parties can look after their own interests once the facts are known and a situation where (as in some community care situations) that cannot be assumed, and there may be a duty on the worker's part to actively support the user's autonomy.

Is this truly a person-to-person encounter?

I have suggested that we can draw upon a basis of person-to-person morality to make sense of this encounter. However, this is not simply an encounter between two individuals. It is also an encounter between agency and user, in that Angela is representing the agency. How far, then, should we see the ethics of the encounter as involving two persons, and how far as involving a person and an organization?

We would expect the agency to operate on the assumption that Angela will carry out its policies and practices rather than her personal desires. In that sense Angela is the instrument of the agency. However, if she has the status of professional – if she is subject to a professional code of ethics – that will counterbalance the agency's role by emphasizing her individual agency and responsibility. I suggested in Chapter 4 that membership of a profession could be seen as involving an implicit promise to adhere to certain principles and behaviours. The very nature of that promise is that it is freely entered into. It can also be broken in a number of ways without the individual being in great danger of detection or sanction. The individual professional in this situation has a choice as to how she acts, and in that sense she is properly part of a person-to-person encounter. Mrs Smith may know nothing about the UKCC (The UK Central Council for Nursing, Midwifery and Health Visiting) code of conduct or the BASW (British Association of Social Workers) code of ethics, and she may have only a vague idea of Angela's professional status. The person-to-person nature of their transaction does not depend on that. If Angela is aware of the commitment implicit in her professional membership, and of her choices in terms of adhering to that, this is sufficient.

However, the personal nature of the encounter does not depend on professional status. An employee who is not subject to a professional code of ethics is still something much more than the instrument of the agency. The worker is choosing to put her skills and energies at the agency's disposal. She is also making choices about how she does this. It is in the nature of this work that the worker has a good deal of freedom in interpreting her role, and the agency has in practice only limited control or sanction. So on these bases also Angela is personally responsible to Mrs Smith for her behaviour.

The agency and the relationship

None the less, it is clear that the agency is deeply involved in the relationship between Angela and Mrs Smith. Alongside her personal and professional responsibilities, Angela has certain duties to the agency based on her employee status, including a duty to do what she is paid to do. This has a moral element involving justice and promise-keeping on both sides. The making of an appropriate relationship with Mrs Smith is part of what Angela is paid to do. Does that mean that the relationships belong to the employer, as a loaf of bread that a baker bakes at the behest of his employer belongs to that employer? The employer dictates with whom the relationship is made after all. But a relationship between two individuals cannot become totally subsumed into the stock-in-trade of an agency. It is also a real and independent event, belonging to the two individuals. Still, if that independent event develops in a way that obstructs the goals of the agency, the agency can claim that Angela is failing in her duty to it.

An example

Let us consider an example of this. Let us suppose that Angela realizes that the agency will not provide services sufficient to meet Mrs Smith's needs, so she advises Mrs Smith to go to her local councillor to complain about the lack of services being provided. The agency might claim that Angela is failing in her duty as an employee. Angela's contract of employment is unlikely to include any clauses that enable her to act against her employer's interests. To do so may be seen as a breach of that contract and, in Kantian terms, a broken promise. If the agency is an entity that can do wrong, presumably it can also be wronged. We need to consider then whether Angela can justify wronging the agency for Mrs Smith's benefit.

Professional duties

The key to that question lies in Angela's professional role. Angela's professional duties to Mrs Smith are different from the duties she performs towards Mrs Smith on behalf of the agency. They are duties laid on her by her professional code of ethics, and I have argued that they can be seen as promises made directly to the user. If the most appropriate expression of her duty to help Mrs Smith obtain what is her right, or maximize her autonomy, would be to advise her to make the aforementioned complaint, then this would be in keeping with principles (ii) and (iv) of the BASW code of ethics (BASW, 1986) (assuming she is a social worker). Her commitment to adhere to those clauses, to seek to maximize justice and autonomy, can be seen as involving a promise to Mrs Smith, and a duty to keep that promise. Mrs Smith is a person and an end in herself, whereas the agency is neither, therefore I argued in Chapter 4 that the duty to the user should take precedence.

Angela may also believe that it is in the true interests of the agency to suffer some embarrassment on this matter, in order to be propelled into providing the services it was created to provide – to pursue its real moral goals.

However, in reality it may not be as simple as that. Angela may fear that complaints of the sort mentioned might be used by Mrs Smith's local councillor for anti-agency political manipulation and, therefore, are likely to be harmful to the agency and its true aims (the aims she shares). In that event perhaps it is justifiable in terms of professional ethics to choose not to advise Mrs Smith to make such a complaint, on the basis that this harm to the agency may involve harm to users generally. However, this conflicts with the professional duty to enhance Mrs Smith's autonomy by widening her options, of which this would be one. Angela, on that basis, ought not to fail to mention that option, though she clearly ought equally to mention other options if such exist. Mrs Smith can then decide herself, though she may well want, and have a right to expect, some advice on what is most likely to work – Angela will know more about that than she does. If Angela is giving her the benefit of her own knowledge, should that include a suggestion that the councillor concerned will simply use a complaint to discredit the agency in order to justify budget cuts and privatization next year?

I suggested in Chapter 4 that the political relationship between the machinery of local government and the local population is ethically important because the local electorate is part of the agency's constituency and confers legitimacy on its actions. It completes the circle of responsibility which involves a local community taking care of itself. A decision to discourage someone from using that representative machinery, however faulty it may be, runs the risk of denying that link of responsibility. It ignores the structural link, the shared responsibility, between agency and population. That seems dangerous, even though strictness in this context may well be risky.

The relationship and the team

We also need to consider Angela's relationship with her team. How far does that impinge on her relationship with Mrs Smith? Let us suppose that Angela's employer wishes her to regard herself as bound by team decisions and to be accountable to the team. Again this might also be a professional duty in terms of the code of ethics.

If she is part of the team, we can reasonably hope that she is in a position to influence decisions that are made, but she may still be outvoted or overruled. If the team has made a decision about procedures and practice that Angela decides is detrimental to Mrs Smith, what should she do? For instance, if the team made a decision about the speed at which different kinds of cases would be processed and it was clear that Mrs Smith belonged to a category that would be delayed longer than other categories, what would Mrs Smith's legitimate expection be if she knew what was happening? Would she have a right to expect that Angela would, if necessary, act against agreed practices for her client's benefit? It may be very difficult to act effectively here. Angela's skills of argumentation may be limited, as may her stamina and will-power. If she says to Mrs Smith ' I think this practice is unfair to you, but I am bound by a team decision,' is that sufficient in terms of her duty to Mrs Smith?

It could be argued that no agreed practices are going to be perfect and that there will be disadvantages for some people in any conceivable practice agreed by a team. From a utilitarian point of view, if those practices are believed to be the most effective in terms of maximizing well-being, then perhaps Angela should accept that Mrs Smith is not entirely advantaged and take the broader view. However, at what point can we argue that the smooth working of the team, which is going to be in the interests of most users, should take precedence over the well-being of an individual user? The main justification for the smooth working of the agency is that it benefits most users. Working relationships need to be maintained for utilitarian reasons, it might be argued, as that will be in the interests of everyone in the long run. That may sometimes be sustainable from evidence but often I suspect it is very hard to prove, and quite likely to be simply untrue in some cases, where user well-being is sacrificed for the sake of working relationships.

If Angela takes a Kantian view, she will be faced with conflicting duties. She will recognize her obligation to Mrs Smith as an individual, but she may also feel that she has entered into an agreement with the team with regard to the way those issues are dealt with – an agreement which can also be counted as a promise. Which promise then takes precedence? Again, the professional commitment comes to the fore here, emphasizing the duty to the user, as against duties to colleagues. As fellow employees, Angela's duty to the team is part of her duty to the agency. As fellow professionals her duty to them may well be in part a professional duty, but her code of ethics (if she is a nurse, social worker or occupational therapist) will state clearly the prior duty to the user.

The relationship and other people

We need to consider whether Angela has duties to other people in the community which might impinge on or compete with her duty to Mrs Smith. For instance, let us suppose Mrs Smith has a neighbour who has helped her with shopping and other tasks. Mrs Smith promised the neighbour a small payment for these services, but because of an argument between them she has refused to keep that promise. The neighbour asks Angela to take up her case with Mrs Smith. If Angela feels that the neighbour has a good case, and Mrs Smith seems to be behaving unreasonably, should she (Angela) give any attention whatsoever to the neighbour's interests or is her concern exclusively with Mrs Smith?

I have suggested that agencies have constituencies as well as customers, and that for a local authority agency, at least, the community and its individual members could be seen as part of the constituency. However, that does not mean that Angela has any specific duty to the neighbour on the basis of her employment. If the constituency requires that the agency organizes its services in a particular way, with users forming a specific category in terms of duty, then it meets the constituency's requirements to focus primarily on the agency's duty to users, to the exclusion of others. Angela doubtless has a duty to the agency to behave reasonably towards members of the community, for the sake of the agency's position, but she does not have an employment-based duty to individual members of the community.

In professional terms her code of ethics may well refer to her behaviour towards other members of the community but, again, the codes likely to apply in community care make clear that the user – by whatever name – is the focus of specific duties. Relatives and neighbours may reasonably expect Angela to adhere to the ethical requirements of her code during her operation within that status. However, that would also implicitly require them to accept that Mrs Smith, defined as client or patient for the purposes of the code, has a special status.

From Mrs Smith's point of view, the user role has involved her entering into a relationship with Angela and the agency which her relatives and neighbours have not. So in terms of keeping agreements Mrs Smith has a special claim. Because she is making herself vulnerable to Angela and the agency in terms of revealing information about herself, she has a claim to special consideration as the other side of that transaction. She is allowing her life to be subjected to interventions and skills which she does not fully understand, and cannot necessarily always monitor. This, again, as a matter of reciprocity and respect for persons suggests some special consideration.

JUSTICE AND INJUSTICE IN ASSESSMENT

We now need to consider the justice issues and arguments that might arise in this situation. I shall focus here primarily on procedural justice in the process of assessment.

I argued in Chapter 2 that considerations of justice apply to the way distributive decisions are made as well as to the outcome of those decisions. I also argued that users have a right to a fair assessment on the basis of equality of moral worth between persons. Mrs Smith has a right to a fair assessment, and a right to fair consideration on the basis of that. What she has a right to in terms of provision is going to be much more dependent on what is available, as individual welfare rights are not practically sustainable outside of a particular system's ability to deliver. I shall consider further rights and justice in terms of the outcome of assessment in the next chapter.

I shall concentrate here on the way Mrs Smith is assessed. Equality of treatment is a central part of procedural justice, and all the requirements below are intended to support the principle of equality:

1. Angela would need to use the same method of assessment as is used with other users being assessed for the same range of

services. Only in that way can we have a reasonable expectation that users are not being disadvantaged by differences in the method of assessment.

2. Mrs Smith needs to know that she is being assessed, and when the assessment process is happening. The basis upon which the encounter is initiated must be explicit. If she is not made fully aware of that, she cannot fully exercise her autonomy in her own interest, and is not being treated as an end; she is being deceived.

3. Mrs Smith needs to know what services are available. She is being assessed for a range of services. If a user does not know what is included in that range, she is not fully cognizant of the basis of the encounter and, again, cannot fully exercise her autonomy in her own interest.

4. Mrs Smith needs to know what information is relevant to the assessment. This again enables her to use her autonomy in her own interest, by giving relevant information. It also allows her to safeguard her own privacy by not giving information that is irrelevant. Without that knowledge, users will not necessarily be able to judge whether large areas of personal life and history might or might not be relevant to assessment. A sense of open-ended pressure to give personal information clearly does not help the user to guard her privacy.

However, we cannot simply treat all users as fully able to pursue their own interests in assessment, once allowed to. For some users that ability is impaired for cognitive, psychological or other reasons. Therefore, in addition to all the above requirements, there must be a professional commitment and ability on the part of the assessor to ensure that the user's disadvantages in that respect are compensated for, and that a user with impaired autonomy is enabled to give as much and as relevant information, with as much advantage to him or herself, as a user without such impairment.

We must also require that other differences do not influence outcomes in an unjust way. That depends on the ability of the assessor to be free of prejudices and stereotypes which make expressions of need couched in the terms of one culture or identity more eloquent than those couched in another. This clearly relates to the relevance of equal opportunities and the issue of having assessment methods which are as free as possible from cultural bias.

AUTONOMY

How, then, does Angela support Mrs Smith's autonomy? If she assumes that Mrs Smith is fully competent, she must none the less acknowledge that, first, her practical autonomy may well be a good deal less than that of most of her fellow citizens. Power is unequally distributed. But it may also be the case that Mrs Smith sees herself as having little control over her life. Her physical mobility is limited, she is relatively poor and isolated and she is aware of the low status accorded to her and her wishes by others (perhaps including her family). She may also have experienced a lifetime's socialization into a culture which emphasized the inevitability of certain events, and the appropriateness of bowing to that inevitability. She is faced with a combination of factors which may make the idea of open-ended autonomy and responsibility a rather dubious one from her point of view. Her morality may be based on adherence to socially sanctioned rules and norms, or rules sanctioned by God. Kantian, utilitarian, existentialist or relativist perspectives on the part of the worker may not make much sense to her. She may adhere to a morality which focuses primarily around relationships with and obligations to family, both living and dead.

So what can Angela properly expect of her? How far is it legitimate to seek to encourage any change in her perspective – moral or practical? How far should Angela follow a conscious strategy based on specific values – for instance, of empowerment? We considered in Chapter 3 the mutual impact of persons on each other, and the limits that might be set on that in the name of autonomy. We know that there are powerful interpersonal processes which make it largely impossible for people not to be influenced by one another. We know that there are physical boundaries which are easily breached without intention, and that this breach can have a negative effect on an individual's fragile sense of autonomy. Angela's very presence in Mrs Smith's home, in an official capacity, may already be having that effect. Is Mrs Smith's nervous compliance during the assessment interview actually a manifestation of a profound sense of powerlessness and invasion? If Mrs Smith is in relatively infrequent contact with members of her family, the sense of significance and moral purpose that came from those relationships may also be weakened, thereby making her more vulnerable. Angela's code of ethics will enjoin her to respect the user's autonomy. If she is a nurse, it will be couched roughly in those terms. If she is a social worker, the injunction will be more specifically to help her to increase the range of her options – to go beyond passive autonomy towards an active widening of the range of initiative – and empowerment. Mrs Smith may be keen to learn about new options and possibilities, and to exercise her choice. On the other hand she may find the process of broadening options frightening because of the uncertainties that it injects into her situation, and because of the new exercise of responsibility that such choices involve. She may find it painful because of the implication that she has missed the opportunity, perhaps for many years, to take up certain options simply because she was not aware of them. There may be a considerable loss of utility in being presented with choices. It may not have an empowering effect at all.

For Mrs Smith's autonomy

A sense of inadequacy in the face of choices and responsibilities is a common experience, so there is no reason to see it as seriously problematic in Mrs Smith's case. To move into a situation where one is negotiating aspects of one's life with a care agency is for most people a major life transition, and inevitably it is going to be stressful. But people make major life decisions at other times of life with much less experience than Mrs Smith has, relating to work, relationships, education – often under great pressure and in considerable stress – and nobody absolves us of those responsibilities. It is reasonable to expect Mrs Smith to make the necessary decisions. It is not reasonable to expect anyone else to decide things that Mrs Smith should decide for herself, for good or ill.

Against Mrs Smith's autonomy

We might argue against this that Mrs Smith's autonomy is a sham in any case. Her life has not equipped her for decisions of this sort. She has always been propelled in particular directions by the close supportive pressure of family, neighbourhood and social habits and norms. The 'normal' thing to do has always been made explicit to her; the 'right' thing to do has usually also been made clear. She has not had dilemmas in the full sense of the word. The oppressions of her situation have limited her options to a very narrow range in any case. It is unreasonable to expect someone who has grown up in a culture, and in a political situation, where individual autonomy has meant very little, to start exercising it in her eighties to suit the demands of a community care worker's code of ethics, or political ideology.

Achieving a balance

Both these descriptions of the situation are likely to be exaggerations, and to run the risk of serious injustice for Mrs Smith. Kant's model of the autonomous person seems at times to consist of a disembodied mind, without feelings, relationships or involvements, making decisions on the basis of reason. This misses a good deal of the reality of autonomous decision-making. In this situation the communitarian perspective, recognizing as it does that moral choices are not made in a social vacuum, perhaps has more to offer than Kant's individualistic and disembodied philosophy. The appearance of a careful and conventional life lived in a network of close family and community relationships and norms may disguise a number of dilemmas survived and difficult decisions made. The fact that the decisions appear to have been in the direction of maintaining convention and the social order does not constitute proof that Mrs Smith has not exercised autonomy. For most of us most of the time liberty is the liberty to do what our culture and social norms encourage us to do. Liberty is having the option of doing otherwise, and usually deciding not to. Let us suppose, for instance, that 50 years ago Mrs Smith discovered that her husband had been unfaithful to her, but that she decided not to leave him or demand his departure. Her decision to stay with her husband, perhaps for her children's sake, may look now like the action of someone imprisoned in a cage of internalized patriarchal injustice. However, it could equally be seen as a choice made in the face of real and possible options. To do the 'normal' thing, to be influenced by the opinions of her neighbours, to try to live a Christian life in so far as she understands what that amounts to, are painful and demanding exercises of choice.

Choosing to choose

On the other hand, it is not realistic to suppose that Mrs Smith will necessarily feel fully committed to making new and unfamiliar choices. I have suggested that there are situations where we appear to choose to give up our autonomy. Usually these are situations where we lack the knowledge to make a decision, and what we are doing in many cases is engaging the expertise of others to help us to do this. We may wish that we could hand over full responsibility to another, at least for a while. But for as long as we remain competent in general terms, and capable of understanding the advice we are given, we are not really relinquishing our autonomy, because the other person's apparent power is being exercised only with our permission. However, we may feel overawed by the expertise of the expert and insufficiently confident to question their advice. Let us suppose that Mrs Smith feels irritated by her doctor's patronizing attitude to her but still feels unable to question his advice, or even to report adverse effects from it to him. The exercise of autonomy is costly, sometimes in material terms, sometimes in emotional terms, and the costs of autonomy are very unevenly distributed. For Mrs Smith it is a huge effort to disagree with an official figure – particularly one with the trappings of middle-class status and power. She finds it more difficult to disagree with the doctor than with Angela. This in itself leads to difficulties. It seems quite legitimate for Angela to encourage Mrs Smith to empower herself – to argue, to reject advice. Her skills and training enable her to help Mrs Smith do this. Her style of offering advice likewise makes it easy for Mrs Smith to question it. This is empowering practice. However, if Mrs Smith is at the same time unable to say no to the doctor, does Angela's careful work have any meaning at all? If Mrs Smith feels constrained to follow the doctor's advice, the autonomy she demonstrates with Angela may seem rather meaningless.

Power and persuasion

The issue of power brings up the issue of influence. If Angela is a trained and experienced worker she may well have counselling skills. I discussed in Chapter 3 the degree to which the use of such skills for persuasion is legitimate in a professional relationship. It may partly be a question of the way this is done. Let us assume that the doctor uses his authority to tell Mrs Smith what he thinks she should do. He has the weight of class, status and professional power on his side, and does not have to worry about finding a way to shift Mrs Smith in the way he wants her to go. He tells her. Angela is less advantaged by class, status and power (not to mention gender) and ethically inhibited from direct persuasion in any case. On the other hand Angela may have very strong and legitimate views and feelings about what is likely to be beneficial to Mrs Smith, and what is not. Must she then conceal these feelings and thoughts entirely? It is not clear that concealing a strong view is showing respect for Mrs Smith as a person, treating her as an end. It is not clear either that the kind of relationship that is appropriate here excludes that sort of expression. Nor is it clear that it is unlikely to maximize Mrs Smith's happiness.

Mrs Smith may well be used to strenuous efforts at persuasion, or at least forceful and unambiguous advice, from friends, neighbours, family and other professionals. In cultural terms such advice can be seen as proper, a sign of friendship, commitment and interest, morally laudable. The way in which those views impact on Mrs Smith presents us with our ethical problem. We see it in the case of the doctor, using his authority. Any profession with a commitment to empowerment, would be ethically at odds with itself using the weight of power and status, given that this is likely to reinforce a lifetime of disempowerment for someone like Mrs Smith.

Skilled persuasion

The other problem lies in the method of communication. I suggested in Chapter 3 that the use of counselling skills to persuade constituted a mismatch of method and purpose. A method which gives the expert an advantage in unravelling the more vulnerable and confused parts of the user puts that user at a considerable disadvantage in terms of being able to use her rational faculties to evaluate what is being said to her. However convinced the worker may feel of the rightness of the advice, the user loses a vital bit of autonomy here, and is not being respected. So we have a problem. Our difficulties are added to in a situation where the user appears to be caught in a web of oppressive social relationships which are pushing her in a particular direction, or holding her immobile when things need to move. If the rest of Mrs Smith's world is doing this to her, and thereby making it impossible to help her, it seems disabling for Angela to do her job with one hand tied behind her back. It is one thing to encroach on Mrs Smith's own autonomy by using position or skills to persuade her; it might seem a rather different matter to countervail against the influence of other people over Mrs Smith, by persuading her more effectively. Clearly the danger here is that Mrs Smith's personhood and respect are entirely lost as she becomes an object of competitive power play.

Honesty and courtesy

Perhaps the honest expression of opinion breaches what Mrs Smith regards as courtesy and good manners. It seems a sound principle to remain within bounds of the other person's conception of courtesy and civility. It also adheres to Habermas's (1991) principle of normative appropriateness. In cross-cultural encounters one can never be sure of the line between social etiquette and moral principle and where there is even relatively limited cultural difference a relativist approach would seem to argue in favour of such observation. It is not easy to make a distinction between cultural norms and individual habits of defence and denial which actually prevent the receiving of uncomfortable feedback.

Another dimension to this issue is the basis of the relationship as it is understood by the participants. If a degree of honesty going beyond social convention is not explicitly negotiated, then one could argue that an implicit promise is being broken. It has something of the impact of some of the techniques of counselling and psychotherapy – breaking through conventions and defences and making the user thereby unusually vulnerable and suggestible. In that sense it can constitute a further skewing of the power differential.

INFORMATION AND CONFIDENTIALITY

If assessment has been conducted in an appropriate way, then Mrs Smith will be aware that she has given Angela a certain amount of personal information for an agreed purpose. Assuming that information is recorded, and is used for the agreed purpose, we need to consider what should then happen to it. In particular we need to consider what legitimate say Mrs Smith might have in that and what, if any, responsibility Angela might have towards Mrs Smith in reference to that.

I argued in Chapter 3 that we can look at control of information in four ways. We can regard information about somebody as being something that the person has some rights over. Such rights might be pseudo-proprietorial, or analogous to rights over personal physical space, or claim-rights arising from promises made by the person obtaining the information. We might also regard information about someone as a potential source of harm from which the person should be protected. Such harm could include loss of privacy resulting from the information becoming widely or publicly known in a way that is culturally inappropriate.

Perhaps the information given by Mrs Smith will not do her any harm whosoever hands it falls into but, if it falls into the wrong hands, she has none the less suffered a harm through loss of privacy, which is a loss of autonomy. Also, we can put a Kantian argument, that the information was given as part of an agreed transaction for an agreed purpose. Any dissemination of that information outside that purpose breaks a promise. However many other reasons might emerge for giving it to someone else later, the fact remains that any such action would be promise-breaking, and in breach of a duty in Kant's terms. Other agreements – for instance, that 'this information will help us to help you' – might be seen likewise as conferring some rights, at least of veto, of that information being used for any other purpose.

Mrs Smith breaches her daughter's privacy

We may have situations where the same piece of information breaches the privacy of several people at once, or in some other way constitutes a potential harm or breach of rights for several people. In the case of Angela and Mrs Smith this could arise in a number of ways. Mrs Smith could give Angela information about herself that also involves other people. In that case do all those people have rights over it? If we are talking about a group of private citizens, such as a family, we can see a conflict of interest arising out of their interlocking and interdependent privacy. Let us suppose that Mrs Smith's late husband, as well as being unfaithful to her, was also frequently violent to her and her daughters. Mrs Smith may gain in terms of well-being from being able to talk about this experience (and part of that experience must have been to watch helplessly while her daughters were abused). Her daughters may not wish any of this to become known outside the family; and it is as much part of their biography, their 'informational space', as it is hers.

Is Angela's duty to respect privacy confined to Mrs Smith in this instance? She is the user. Angela has entered into no agreements, explicit or implicit, with anyone else in the situation, but Angela's position has indirectly given her access to information about other people which is not in the public domain. That power, based on her professional role and agency role arguably gives her some duty to the other people involved, not to harm them by breaching their privacy – that is, by making it possible for others to have access to it. It might be impossible to disguise the identities of these other people in the record, because of the nature of their relationship or involvement with Mrs Smith. We could work on the basis that it is Mrs Smith's responsibility who she tells about whom. The worker, and the agency can then concentrate on ensuring that no information is recorded that is not in some way beneficial to Mrs Smith. The professional and the agency can legitimately prioritize Mrs Smith's needs over those of her daughters because she is the user and she is the prime focus of their duties. However, accepting that there are some duties to other members of the community in both agency and professional frameworks, one such duty might well be to avoid recording any information about them that is not going to help fulfil duties to the user.

A neighbour breaches Mrs Smith's privacy

Let us imagine that Angela receives unsolicited information about Mrs Smith from a neighbour. By receiving it (unless it is sought and obtained by agreement with Mrs Smith) Angela is colluding with a breach of Mrs Smith's privacy, though the responsibility for that breach is the other person's. If it adversely affects Mrs Smith's prospect of help then Mrs Smith is suffering another harm and arguably has a right to protect herself, despite the third party's requests 'not to tell her'. Arguably Mrs Smith ought to know. The principle that she has some right over it (in this case to know about it) because it concerns her and is part of her 'informational self' is augmented here by the potential or actual harm that may result. This incidentally also provides a strong argument in favour of users having access to their records.

The nature of information creates some dilemmas for Angela in this situation. She may already know enough about the neighbour to suspect that the information may be damaging to Mrs Smith's interests. If she does suspect this when she learns who is in the waiting room or on the phone, should she be willing to receive the information? Is it ever right simply to refuse to know about it? Once known, and believed, it cannot become unknown again – it is an irrevocable event. However, it is possible that the information will be of vital importance. It may allow someone – Mrs Smith or someone else – to be protected from harm. Therefore, from a utilitarian point of view there is a strong argument for hearing it, just in case. Again we encounter the other oddity of information – we cannot decide its utility until we have heard it. There is also a need here to balance the value of truth (if we discover that Mrs Smith has been lying, for instance) as against other values such as privacy and care.

DOES THE USER HAVE ANY DUTIES?

Nearly all of the discussion so far has concentrated on the worker's duties. We need to consider whether the user has any duties in this situation and if so, to whom.

I argued at the outset that we can view this encounter morally as between two persons, despite the role of the agency in the transaction, and the duties of persons towards one another are not entirely dependent on the roles they are in. In principle then, if we follow Kant or Habermas, Mrs Smith ought to behave in an honest and non-manipulative way towards Angela, as Angela should towards her. She ought to treat Angela as an end and not seek to harm her.

The difficulty arises when the user appears to be in breach of these moral requirements. Where the worker is in that position we can point to identifiable and sometimes enforceable requirements. Criticism and even negative consequences are seen as legitimate. However, it is not clear what if any response is legitimate where a user is acting thus. Neither worker nor agency have a legitimate role in enforcing moral standards in the community. I have argued that desert does not play a legitimate role in the distributive justice of assessment or resource allocation. An immoral user, therefore, presumably ought not to suffer in terms of provision on that basis.

Some user behaviour can make the encounter unpleasant and stressful for the worker, without preventing the worker's task from being completed. Some can make the job difficult or impossible. An example of the latter would be dishonesty in providing information for assessment. Some user behaviour can make the worker's position literally untenable. An example of this would be abusive or, even, violent behaviour to the worker.

It could be argued that behaviour that makes the encounter stressful is not something from which any negative consequences should follow, as the tone and quality of interaction is affected by so many unmeasurable factors of interaction and perception that it is often difficult to make a fair analysis of what is going on in the encounter. Where a competent user is being dishonest, it is arguable, I think, that negative consequences for the user may be acceptable, as may negative feedback. A user who deliberately lies in assessment may gain or lose by that process. However, there is always a risk of assessment and subsequent services being disrupted by the clash of true and false information. Where the user is competent, it is not the agency's or the worker's responsibility to take extra precautions against disruption to services resulting from user dishonesty. To do this would be to treat the user as incompetent.

It would seem appropriate also to acknowledge to the user that they gave false information. This is on the same basis, that it is treating the user as an end to offer that honesty. Also, however overwhelming the evidence of dishonesty may be, there is always the chance of another explanation, which the user can only offer if she knows what is suspected.

Three arguments might be put against this sort of response. I shall deal with each in turn. First, there is the argument of non-judgementalism – Biestek's (1957) famous principle that the worker ought not to sit in moral judgement on the user. On this I would argue that the scenario I am suggesting would not involve moral judgement of the user. I am not suggesting that the user ought to be denounced or upbraided, but simply that the untruth should be pointed out, without explicit judgement. The appropriateness of any further comment or feedback – any expression of feeling by the worker for instance – would be a matter of professional judgement of whether it would benefit the user.

Second there is the moral relativist argument. Perhaps the user is working to a different moral code, and does not believe that dishonesty in this situation is wrong. The problem with this is that the process of assessment is predicated on certain ethical principles – particularly justice and honesty – without which it would be a different activity. To engage in assessment involves acceptance of that moral framework.

Third, there is the argument of unequal power. So far I have discussed this issue as if the user and the worker are engaged in an equal transaction. Clearly this is not the case. The worker has the power of the agency behind her, and is likely also to have the advantage in social power arising from class, status and other differences. Control of personal information – and the power to distort that information – is one of the few levers that the user has in this situation. If the worker and agency are fulfilling their obligations, the user need not exert that particular power. Part of the point of regulating this encounter in ethical terms is to ensure that the user does not have to find her own strategy to deal with the power differential. However, if the agency or the worker are not adhering to the principles I have discussed, a different situation emerges. If assessment is carried out in a dishonest or unjust way, the user is effectively thrown back on her own resources in protecting her interests. Dishonesty in giving information may still prove a poor choice in terms of achieving that, but in moral terms the duty to communicate in a non-manipulative way may not apply.

The third situation, where the user is behaving in a violent or abusive way to the worker, ceases in a sense to be an ethical problem for the worker and becomes an agency matter. Such situations would normally fall outside the worker's commitment, and therefore duty, to the agency and the agency would, therefore, have a duty to ensure that the worker is not put at risk in that way. The only exception would be if there is specific agreement between worker and agency that such situations are part of the workers range of competence. This would perhaps apply to certain sorts of residential setting, and would require specific training and support.

REFERENCES

BASW (1986) *A Code of Ethics for Social Work*. Birmingham: British Association of Social Workers.

Biestek, F. (1957) *The Casework Relationship*. Chicago: Loyola University Press.

Habermas, J. (1991) *Communication and the Evolution of Society*. Cambridge: Polity Press.

CHAPTER 7
Providing and Prioritizing

INTRODUCTION

In this chapter I shall consider the application of the principles of distributive justice as they affect four individuals who are in need of help from a community care agency. The areas I shall focus on are: prioritizing and distributing care services; distributing care responsibility between agency and family members; justice in the process of decision-making; and justice in the choice of service-provider.

FOUR USERS

Mrs Harrison lives alone. She is 85 and suffers arthritis. Other than that, her health has been reasonably good until recently when she suffered a stroke. She has made a reasonable recovery but has lost some mobility and also a good deal of confidence. She does not now feel able to use the stairs in her home and has had her bed moved to the ground floor. Her son, Brian Harrison, is married and lives 70 miles away. He visits monthly and says that he cannot make more frequent contact except in emergencies, because of his own family and business commitments. Her daughter, Eileen James, lives 15 miles away and usually visits weekly or twice-weekly. She has three teenage children, and her husband has recently had a heart attack and is off work at present. Mrs Harrison has a network of relationships in the street, and a fair amount of support and interest from her neighbours. However, nobody is in a position to undertake any strenuous practical tasks like cleaning and shopping. She needs help with these.

Mr Khan is 59 and lives alone. He is diabetic and suffers high blood pressure. Although he has shown over many years that he is well able to manage his own care and medication, he has recently started to neglect himself in this respect. He has become forgetful and lethargic. It is not clear whether Mr Khan is suffering an organic problem or whether he is developing depression. He is socially isolated, with very little contact with his neighbours. His son moved to Canada some years ago. He experiences occasional episodes of racial abuse, mainly from children in the locality. As well as neglecting his own health care he is also apparently becoming unable to keep his house satisfactorily, and conditions are becoming poor.

Mrs Brown is 80 and lives with Peter, her 50-year-old son who has moderate learning disabilities. Mrs Brown is suffering from congestive heart failure and is bedridden for much of the time. She is also now becoming confused. Peter has contributed a good deal to the running of the house over the years, but has relied on his mother to make the decisions. He realizes that she is not able to do this now, but does not have confidence in his ability to do it in her place. He has become very anxious about this. They live in an area of private housing with quite high mobility – mostly young families – and have not built up a significant network of relationships locally. Peter suffers from a certain amount of prejudice, and some neighbours now also have difficulty coping with Mrs Brown's mental deterioration. There are no other close relatives.

Here we have three situations where there may be a need for help from a community care agency. All the people involved are in a position where their independence is threatened. Their ability to continue living in the community is at risk and, in each case, the situation is unstable. There are processes which propel it towards further deterioration – perhaps rather suddenly. Such a sudden deterioration may result in institutional care of one sort or another for any of the people involved. A basic principle of community care is to avoid that outcome if possible – to support people in continuing to live in the community – therefore all of these people have some claim to consideration for appropriate help towards that end.

Ethical problems are likely to arise in relation to the availability of resources to help these four people. We know that resources have, on occasions, not been adequate to meet assessed need in a number of places. Help may have to be rationed. For a worker who is assessing these three cases, and for the manager and others involved in deciding on the resources that are provided, the question is not simply one of identifying need. It is also one of deciding whose and which needs will not be met from the resources of the department.

For all three situations it might be that some domiciliary support would be appropriate, with a varying mixture of practical help and social support. For the latter two cases some help with building community networks would seem to be needed as well. In both the latter cases those inputs would need to be informed by a commitment to combatting discriminatory attitudes and behaviour in the community. In the case of Mr Khan an additional effort would be required to ensure that any help given would be culturally appropriate.

PRINCIPLES FOR DISTRIBUTION

The bigger picture

Resources are restricted. Not all needs can necessarily be met, and we must start our analysis of the ethics of the situation by considering why this is. Let us suppose that the local authority and health authority have decided to give some priority to the movement of a group of hospitalized users with learning disabilities to the community. As a result of this, the four people above are a little less likely to get a particular level of care than they would otherwise be. In Chapter 2 I suggested that need, utility, rights and equality were important principles in judging the justice of a particular distribution of goods. I shall begin with need. It could be argued that different needs are at stake here, and that by most standards the needs of elderly people at physical risk are more pressing than the needs of people who may well be lacking in autonomy and social opportunities but who are physically safe, albeit in an institutional (and perhaps institutionalizing) environment. However, if we accept that, institutionalized users, with learning disabilities or mental health problems, will always come at the back of the queue because they are physically safe, whereas people in the community are more likely to be in physical danger and will always come first. Are there ways of balancing this situation?

We may argue that utility is served by putting more resources into the rehabilitation of institutionalized users. If we always prioritize the meeting of safety needs, our attempts to guarantee safety to the elderly become so intrusive as to be counter-productive, and it is more useful to devote some of that resource to doing something that will achieve real enhancement in lives on a principle that is by its nature economical – at least in the long run – because we are aiming to help people to become independent and less in need of care resources.

We can also take account of rights. It could be argued that distributive justice is served by ensuring that those who have a right to a 'normal' social existence have the opportunity to enjoy that. Although in the immediate term we are talking about welfare rights to support and help, in the longer term we are talking about liberties – the right to live one's own life unmolested. Institutionalized users do not have these, and justice is served by providing them. That may be seen as comparable to the right of our four potential users for a degree of security and support in their lives.

Finally we can take account of equality. There is not likely to be any real equality of circumstance between different groups, but rather equality of opportunity and equality of consideration. Part of that equality is ensuring that we take account of all factors, not just need, in considering this issue. Another is that we take equal account of what is missing from the lives of both groups of users.

It may be, then, that we can argue in favour of this particular distribution of resources, but it means that we have not necessarily got the resources to respond to all the needs of the four users introduced at the beginning of the chapter. Therefore, we must now apply the same principles of distributive justice to their situation.

Need

Need always relates to an end. If I need something, I need it as a means to obtaining or achieving some other thing, usually something more fundamental. The most urgent and pressing needs are for those things which will afford us safety and prospect of survival. So one way of comparing needs is comparing physical risk. Such a comparison is always extremely difficult, involving as it does prediction and probability, but in theory it is possible.

Safety is seldom the only need that is being experienced. For these four users the physical risk is unlikely to be so immediate that it renders other needs immaterial. Doyal and Gough (1991) identify the need for autonomy as standing alongside survival need in moral terms. Maslow (1954) identifies the need for affection as following from the meeting of safety needs in psychological terms. The need to survive as a social being, as a person, will be experienced even in situations of acute physical risk, and whereas sources of physical risk can to some degree be treated objectively, sources of social or existential risk are highly subjective and comparison is highly problematic. How can we compare Mr Khan's depression with Mrs Brown's confusion or Peter's anxiety? We can more easily agree they are sources of need, but which is greater?

Utility

In Chapter 2 I suggested that need and utility were both possible components of justice in deciding between individuals. In a situation such as this, where we are trying to decide where to put resources between new cases who may not be getting anything from us at the moment, the matching of services to needs is crucial. Part of the practice of assessment is to ensure that what is provided is likely to be optimally effective in meeting needs. There may be situations where a high input of resources will produce a relatively low increment of well-being. Let us suppose that Mr Khan's assessment is delayed, and by the time he is visited he has become seriously depressed and self-neglectful, and his physical health is also deteriorating. It might be possible to maintain Mr Khan at his present level and prevent further deterioration by a heavy input of skilled domiciliary and social work support, but that would be highly uneconomical compared with the utility that could be achieved using the same resources on other users where we could prevent the deterioration already suffered by Mr Khan. Equally, it is uneconomical compared with other inputs that could be provided for Mr Khan – for instance, a course of drugs that would actually restore his mental functioning and consequently self-care to former levels much more cheaply than intensive domiciliary support can maintain him. Utility concerns choices between services, as in this case, but for the worker assessing Mr Khan it is also a choice between users because the service with the highest utility – drugs – cannot be provided by her agency.

Let us suppose, though, that the doctor does not agree about the utility of drug treatment and refuses to offer Mr Khan medication, insisting that it is a social problem, despite the conviction of the community care worker that he has a real psychiatric problem. The worker believes that social support can do much less for Mr Khan than medical treatment, but the medical treatment is withheld. If we are satisfied that social support cannot help at all, there is presumably no justification for providing it. In the real world that will be very hard to establish. The fact is that there is a prospect of preventing further deterioration through domiciliary support. As drug treatment is unavailable then social support becomes the input with the highest utility for Mr Khan.

Rights

All three prospective service-users have a welfare right to the time spent assessing them properly, and to whatever they are assessed as needing, that the agency is in a position to make available – which may be nothing. They have a claim-right to an honest and accurate assessment, and to being properly informed and treated respectfully in other ways. They also have a claim-right to equality of treatment, based on the principle of equality of moral worth, which can be drawn from one of many moral theories. The right to equal treatment must take account of need if it is to be just. It probably should take account of utility as well. So none of these rights will necessarily get any of these people a single hour of home-help time, let alone more extensive services. We might wish to argue that all three households have a moral right to services sufficient to meet their needs, irrespective of whether the agency is able to provide those services. That is rather like the argument that the people of Somalia have a moral right to a national health service. One can argue the right, not least by basing it on the UN Declaration of Human Rights, but it brings us no nearer to finding the resources. To find those resources it is likely that we would have to deprive someone else. Most importantly, the wide reference of such a right makes it useless in helping us to decide who out of the three households should be given priority.

Separate rights

However, there are other rights that might distinguish between the three clients. Let us imagine that a voluntary organization exists to provide support and advice to members of Asian communities suffering from diabetes and circulatory problems. This body could be commissioned by the agency to provide support for Mr Khan. Mr Khan is eligible for the help of this body in a way that the other two people are not. If his needs meet the criteria of the organization, he has a right to their help in a way that they have not. He falls within a category that entitles him to certain services. Again, we might identify welfare rights on his part to whatever that organization is able to provide, and a claim-right to equal treatment with other claimants, in terms of fairness of assessment. The question we might then consider is, what does Mr Khan's right do to the justice of the overall situation between the four?

There is nothing necessarily unjust about different people having different rights. Mrs Harrison may have taken out a private insurance many years ago, which now enables her to pay for private domiciliary help, or she may have inherited money that allows her to do the same. People can create and exercise rights for themselves through the use of their liberties, and these will be different for different people. If the aforementioned voluntary organization is able to supply Mr Khan's needs at no cost to the agency, then in one sense it is rather like Mrs Harrison's insurance allowing her to buy domiciliary help herself.

Equality

I have suggested that equality must link closely to need – equal service must depend on equal need. However, this is complicated by the fact that comparing different needs is extremely difficult. I have also suggested that equal treatment in assessment is a crucial aspect of equality. Mr Khan's specialist provider illustrates this issue. Such an organization might have come into being precisely because the assessments made and services provided by the State are culturally insensitive to the needs of members of those communities, and they were in effect not getting equal treatment with other users. The principle of equality was being breached. The creation of this organization means that Mr Khan can now reasonably expect to get assessments and services equivalent to those received by his White neighbours, so in that sense the inequality has been removed. However, if the voluntary organization concerned resources its services through fund-raising and voluntary effort, we might feel that many members of the Asian communities – those who contribute to that or equivalent organizations – are, in effect, paying twice for community care, because they have already paid their taxes. Therefore, the distributive inequality of services across the population has not been resolved. In our situation it means that Mr Khan is taken out of the equation, and that Mrs Harrison and the Browns are now only competing with each other for services financed partly out of Mr Khan's taxes, which are not used for him. On the other hand if the agency commissions the voluntary organization to provide services for Mr Khan, that is rather different. The common resources of community care are being used to meet his needs, even if the instrument of that is specialist.

DISTRIBUTING RESPONSIBILITY

So far we have considered how the commissioning agency might distribute care for these potential users, on the basis of their needs as assessed. We have not considered other resources and how they might be employed. However, it is clear that there are other possible ways of resourcing those needs which would be acceptable to the agency, if not to the user. Mrs Harrison has a daughter, Eileen James, living not very far away. Social care by its nature exists as an entity across the boundary between that which is provided by professionals, specialists and the State, and that which is part of informal care by family members. The State's obligation overlaps with social obligations based on kinship, friendship, community and other ties. So it is inevitable that we will encounter a situation where the agency can save its resources on the basis that the family will provide care. A number of questions then arise:

1. How far should the agency tailor its response to the distribution of duty rather than the distribution of need? In particular, how far should the agency seek to identify others who have a duty of care, as against their own duty to respond to Mrs Harrison's need?
2. How much pressure should the family experience in this respect?
3. How far should the agency feel any concern, or act on any concern about injustice in the way responsibility for care is allocated in the family?

The relative responsibilities of the taxpayer and the family in providing care for individuals is a legitimate question of distributive justice. This must be affected by a number of contingencies. Am I being justly treated if my taxes are going to care for Mr Khan because his son migrated to Canada, but not for Mrs Harrison because her daughter stayed in the locality? If all families stayed in the locality, perhaps they could all care for their elderly members and I would be paying no taxes for that particular budget requirement. However, I am a son as well as a taxpayer, and I did not stay in the locality. So there is an issue of risks and probabilities here. We don't want to pay for the care of other people's parents but we we don't want to be left with the full responsibility of caring for our own aged parents either, so we spread the risk of getting caught in that dilemma by having a public system of care and accept that a certain level of taxation is inevitable. The level we accept is not enough to spread the risk completely, so some people are still faced with the dilemma. There is not enough to go round. Therefore, I may find myself paying taxes for a state system of social care for the elderly, while providing precisely that for my own parents.

Arguments about family responsibility

An argument can be made based on the notion of reciprocation – that the care I received as a child was given without recompense and its value to me ought to justify some reciprocation on my part. That must depend on there being care and of adequate quality. Given that both those criteria are met, we still have a problem around the fact that I did not voluntarily enter into any agreement about the mutual provision of care, because I never asked to be born to or brought up by these particular people. I could argue that moral debts of this sort should be entered into intentionally or they are not valid. This of course is essentially a Kantian argument, emphasizing a person's freedom to enter into obligations, and it is likely to be unconvincing to many people who may see mutual obligation as a proper part of the moral order. Given the emphasis on individual freedom in the dominant culture in our society, people and communities with that sort of commitment are likely to remain a minority. An alternative is to look for utility. Elderly people may be much happier being cared for by relatives. Does that outweigh the unhappiness that many relatives feel at the prospect of caring for elderly relatives?

Who gets the job?

An issue of equity comes into this question. If we all had to provide a few hours a week of care for our aged parents in relation to our resources of time and energy, just as we are expected to pay taxes in relation to our income I suspect that there may be a real utilitarian argument for promoting family care. The problem is not that we have to provide some of that care. The problem is that only some of us are expected to provide it, while others are not. Avoidance of the burden is not determined by merit. If I am lucky enough for my parents to avoid a period of dependence, either through early death or late vigour, I escape any expectation. If I am lucky enough to have a sibling who is willing to take it on, likewise. Again, if I happen to have emigrated, the pressure is less. The other, more dubious moral quality that is an effective antidote against this burden is the thickness of skin to refuse to take it on, even when my obligation is strongly stated by others. We might argue that there are opportunities to behave badly in many situations, and this isn't unusual. Often we can profit by it. But this is particularly rewarding. If I behave badly to my spouse or children or friends, I stand to lose much more in that I stand to lose those relationships, where our social structure makes this loss very costly. If I lose the esteem of my parents and siblings, I may not lose very much.

In one way the burden is very unfairly distributed. The other way in which the unfairness shows itself is in the distribution of the actual burden of expectation among relatives. It is clear that the burden falls disproportionately on women – the burden of expectation and the burden of actual care. Therefore, the distribution of this burden reflects, in that respect, a reverse picture of the distribution of social power in a patriarchal society. For all these reasons the goods and burdens involved in the care of elderly relatives are distributed in a way that bears no relation to justice either in the process through which distribution decisions are made, or the final pattern of distribution.

Where a care agency acts in effect to reinforce, continue and even extend this inequitable situation, it is not surprising if this is seen as morally problematic. The agency could argue that it is in the nature of informal care, based on kinship, proximity and personal relationship, that it will be distributed in accordance with the contingencies of human society that cannot be regulated by formal notions of justice. People care because they want to or they feel they have to, and we cannot regulate people's felt responses in the context of intimate relationships. On the other hand more has been done to regulate informal and intimate relationships through formal principles in the field of child care, through long-established arrangements such as foster care, and through the more recent provisions of the 1989 Children Act. However, the political support probably does not exist for a similar degree of intervention at the other end of the life cycle.

Let us return to Mrs Harrison and consider how we might feel about withholding services from her because her daughter, Mrs James, is in a position to provide more support than she does currently. We are not simply increasing the injustice suffered by Mrs James. We are also trying to be just to at least three other people – Mr Khan, Mrs Brown and Peter Brown – who have no relatives in a position to offer them any support. By being just to Mrs James we may be in danger of being unjust to these people. Mr Khan and the Brown household may argue that for them it is immaterial where the help comes from. It so happens that Mrs Harrison has two potential sources of help (agency and daughter) both able to provide and both willing at least to consider why they should provide. The other two households have only one potential source. Therefore, the probability of their getting help must be less. That unfair imbalance could be equalized by the agency reducing its likelihood of choosing Mrs Harrison, because of Mrs James's presence in the situation.

Should it make a difference if Mrs James is willing to take on the task? One can imagine a situation where once she becomes aware of shortages and priorities she willingly accepts the responsibility of providing care for her mother. She may be pleased to do so. What is the agency's duty then? By being honest with Mrs James about the situation, the agency is telling her that it does not want to provide help because she is there to provide it. Is there any coercion there, any pressure? She has after all come to the decision herself. If Mrs James had received that information before her mother was referred, the referral might never have happened. If her decision is autonomous, then her autonomy is not being denied, she is not being used as a means and, if she is truly willing and at one with the decision, it may well be that she is not suffering any harm at the hand of the agency. If on the other hand Mrs James was truly pressured, and agreed unwillingly and against her wishes and perceived interests, then the agency is harming her and probably not respecting her as a person. Using Kantian and utilitarian arguments we seem able to distinguish between those two situations, and judge one rather differently from the other.

That is not the whole story. However willing Mrs James is to take this on, we may still be quite convinced that the situation is one of injustice for her, because she happens to be a woman, because she lives nearer, even because she is more compliant, more predisposed for cultural or psychological reasons, to be self-sacrificing in this situation. What is the agency's duty in this situation? One argument is that it does not have a duty to Mrs James beyond what it has to any member of the community. She is not a user and she is not a potential user who is in need. None of the major elements that activate the principle of agency duty are operative. It could be countered that the agency has a duty to minimize inequality and discrimination, rather than to collude with it, but the agency could reply that it has no remit to change the personal balance of relationships already existing. Its duty is to treat its users in an anti-discriminatory way, and it is doing that in this case. The agency might also claim that it is not in a position to make a political judgement on the reasons why someone might be willing to provide care for Mrs Harrison.

I suspect that the first argument, that only users are a focus of duty, is obsolete because of the nature of community care since 1993, which has placed great emphasis on the relationships between commissioning agencies and providers of care, formal and informal. I argued in Chapter 4 that agencies probably have moral duties to carers on the basis of the legislation, which constitutes a promise. I also argued that other duties can arise from specific agreements between agency and specific carers. That is not to say that those

duties will include protecting providers from an unfair and discriminatory situation; but it is more likely to include not treating them in
that way oneself. The problem, of course, is that the issue concerns
the entry of Mrs James into the role of carer. Whatever specific
duties the agency might have to Mrs James as a carer, these only
exist when she becomes a carer and it is her becoming a carer that is
the focus of the problem.

JUSTICE IN DECISION-MAKING

When the assessments are done, the decisions have to be made. Who
gets what? Who should make those decisions? How should we
conduct that process? It may be that I meet with my colleagues, who
have assessed a comparable number of users, and we compare. Our
comparison will enable us to decide who gets what because I can see
that Mr Khan or Mrs Harrison is in a better situation than a large
number of other referred users and, with the stock of resources that
are available, it is clear to me that those others have greater need.
Am I then in any sense failing in my duty to Mr Khan by accepting
that others have a greater claim? Does he have a legitimate expectation that I should advocate for his cause in this, as a barrister might
in a court of law?

I think I have a duty to Mr Khan to undertake a fair assessment. I
argued in the previous chapter that the potential user has a right to
that. That fairness is not being breached if the process of comparison with other claims is itself fair. Therefore, I as worker have a duty
to satisfy myself that the process is fair and to respond if I think it is
not. If for instance I suspect that Mr Khan is in danger of suffering
the effects of racism in the assessment process, then my behaviour
can legitimately change into something closer to advocacy. If I think
the facts of his situation are being reframed in a racist way, then it is
my duty to challenge that, if I accept a duty of fair and equal assessment. It is a duty to Mr Khan but it is also, arguably, a duty in
broader professional terms and in organizational terms. It may well
be a duty to my employer to help to ensure that such practices are
not taking place within its structure. It is also likely to be within the
terms of my professional code of ethics, if I am a nurse, a social
worker or an occupational therapist. Anything in the decision-
making process that appears unjust would justify the same response.
Any priorities that are unacknowledged, covert or do not appear to
relate to any relevant consideration of justice would seem to justify a

challenging response in order to do our duty to the user. So, if the discussion started to take account of character and desert, to consider people on the basis of their perceived moral worth, or the fact that they deserve help because they have done public-spirited things in the past, I would object. I have argued in Chapter 2 that desert is not an appropriate criterion for the sort of goods being distributed in this process and, if my argument holds good, I can properly characterize a discussion that takes account of it as engaged in an unjust assessment.

Is it still my duty to secure a fair assessment for Mr Khan even if it seems that he would benefit from the unfair assessment, rather than lose by it? If my colleagues or managers are sufficiently inept to provide for him at the expense of other more needy cases, can I justify arguing against this? I think that depends on what duty we think we owe the people we are assessing. Duties of care or advocacy may absolve me from concern with justice. However, this would assume exclusivity in the relationship. Kantian duties of respect, truth-telling and promise-keeping imply a commitment to treat other persons likewise with respect and honesty, and that tends to minimize the exclusivity of the relationship unless, for instance, I have promised to be an advocate. That would argue against accepting the unfair advantage of this particular user. Any duty that involves justice (for instance, in relation to equality) would argue for not accepting an unfair advantage. If I owe this user justice, it works both ways.

The decision-making process

We need to consider the way in which such deliberations should be pursued. I have suggested some moral principles for discussion and disagreement in Chapter 5. These involve a commitment to clarity and honesty about the principles or facts that are in dispute, and the avoidance of strategic and tactical behaviour in discussion – for instance, selectivity of presentation, use of deliberately powerful language, alliances and point-scoring to demoralize opponents. I have argued that Habermas's (1991) principle of communicative ethics, alongside the basics of successful group functioning, provide an ethical framework for discussion. Beyond a clear presentation and analysis of evidence, it is hard to see what 'doing one's best for the user' is likely to consist of, other than the manoeuvres that I have just characterized as unethical. Apart from devaluing fellow team members and other colleagues involved, such behaviour also increases the risk of injustice, as it increases the number of active dimensions along which skill, confidence and other crucial characteristics will be unequally distributed. If this were a competitive game of skill requiring participants to seek to defeat each other in various ways, that game could be played fairly as long as all interested parties had agreed to the rules in full knowledge of their implications and of their own skill-level. However, in the process of assessment, such a game could not conceivably be to the advantage of the most interested party – the users. Their agreement would not be forthcoming.

SOURCES OF PROVISION

I propose to use this last part of the chapter to move into a rather different, though related, area. So far we have considered the use and the beneficiaries of resources. But we also need to consider the source of those resources and their nature. In particular I propose to consider the use of private and voluntary agencies in community care, since this is a prominent feature in the post-1990 policy profile.

The commissioning or purchasing agency is charged with the ultimate responsibility for ensuring appropriate services, so I shall approach this from the viewpoint of that agency and its employees in considering the suitability of particular provider agencies and ethical problems that might arise. I shall consider briefly two different sorts of problem: a voluntary agency and a private agency.

A voluntary agency

The first concerns a voluntary agency that is set up to provide a community-based service of day centres, counselling and social support within a specifically evangelical Christian framework. The agency was set up to provide a service for elderly people who are committed Christians and wish to receive community care within that framework. We know that Mrs Brown is a lifelong churchgoer and a strongly committed Christian, and that this agency could provide a suitable care package in practical terms, reasonably cheaply.

Should we use this agency? The main issue must be whether or not it is discriminatory to use an agency that was set up to serve only part of the population. By its nature and purpose it would appear that this agency is discriminatory. I shall consider some points which seem relevant to the ethics of the issue. First, it is clearly acceptable to set up specialist agencies of some sorts, which are going to be relevant to only part of the population. Agencies that specialize in particular kinds of need are a major element in the welfare state, as are agencies providing for specific age groups. All of these exclude large parts of the population in a way that is apparently quite acceptable.

However, to specialize in meeting specific need does not risk discrimination if the agency's service is available to everyone with that need. Life stages are a relevant area of specialization because they are characterized by distinctive needs. Religion is rather a different matter. Religious needs and social needs are different things. However, for most people it is clearly important to receive care that is sensitive in cultural and religious terms. That is a need.

We also need to be clear on what basis this agency selects its users. Is it, for instance, specifically intended for that minority of the population with a specific Protestant evangelical commitment. Will they exclude the rest of the population, including those who have no active religious involvement but may write 'Church of England' when filling in forms? If that is the case, we need to consider whether the minority group they are serving suffer from a shortfall in suitable services compared with the rest of the population. Is this agency filling a gap for a disadvantaged group?

On the other hand, the agency might accept everyone who does not explicitly follow another religious commitment. In that case the 'Church of England' group would have access to its services, but groups such as Moslems and Hindus would be excluded. The indirect effect of this, if not the intention, would be racial discrimination.

In terms of justice, two issues predominate: whether a disadvantaged group is being provided with a service it would not get elsewhere; and whether other disadvantaged groups are being discriminated against in that process.

For the commissioning agency and the worker involved there is clearly a problem of what to do if the voluntary agency is seen to be discriminatory. The real difficulty is around whether a refusal to employ its services for a user would disadvantage that user in an unjust way. If the voluntary agency is providing services for a disadvantaged minority, then the user would be disadvantaged by having those services withheld, but the voluntary agency's policy would be less likely to be discriminatory in any case. If the voluntary agency is providing better services for part of the population that is already relatively advantaged compared with other groups, then not using the agency would be a loss for that user, but it would not disadvantage her, and it would not be unjust.

If the user asks for information on Christian agencies, there is an issue of whether she should be told of this one. To withhold the information would be unjust because it would be dishonest, and it would disadvantage her in making decisions in her own interests. Such decisions may include a choice on her part to pay for her own care.

A private agency

The second situation concerns a private agency. Before considering its detail I shall briefly consider some of the issues arising from the use of the private sector. Commissioning policies may well help to mould the private sector in a way that will not be true for the voluntary sector. Entrepreneurs will set up private concerns in accordance with their judgement of what commissioning agencies are looking for and what they will pay. Therefore, the agency may have considerable influence over the shape of the private sector in its area. Arguably that is accompanied by some responsibility, at least to take cognizance of that influence in its policy-making.

What should the agency look for from the private sector? A utilitarian approach would suggest that the agency should seek simply to use the organizations that can most efficiently provide the service which the agency wants to meet user need. If the agency has to make the difficult decisions about who gets what, it needs to make them in the context of knowing roughly who can provide those services efficiently.

The question then arises as to whether there is a need for shared goals between commissioning agency and providing agency. The commissioning agency will have as a main goal the provision of an anti-discriminatory service. Does that mean that providing agencies should also have this as a main goal? This creates a problem for the private sector because any commercial undertaking must have as its main purpose to make a profit for the shareholders. How might this be resolved?

Let us return to the situation. The private agency concerned provides residential care for older people. The quality of its service is not in question, but it is known that its care staff are being paid at rates well below that acceptable in local authority or trust employment in equivalent activities. It is also known that there is pressure on employees not to join a union.

One result of these practices is that the agency can provide care rather more cheaply than other agencies, and they have benefited from this advantage in terms of contracts. As a result of local unemployment, the agency can still get competent staff, so the quality of care does not suffer. If the commissioning agency continues to use this private agency, it is clearly helping to support and sustain it, and is helping to perpetuate an exploitative employment practice. It is achieving its purpose, but doing so at the expense of the workers in the private agency. What should the commissioning agency do?

The private agency concerned is simply doing more successfully what any private concern needs to do in order to succeed – it is maximizing profits and minimizing costs to the limit that the market will allow. In that sense it is no different from any other private company. If we can argue that the commissioning agency is colluding with exploitative practices in this particular instance, we can say the same, with a difference only of degree, about its dealings with any commercial body. We could say the same about its dealings with suppliers of towels and paper-clips. However, we could argue that, in the case of this one private agency at least, it would be possible to exert pressure in a way that would not be possible in the case of paper-clip manufacturers. Kant's principle that ought implies can might suggest such a response in this case.

We must also ask what duty is the commissioning agency fulfilling in taking action in this case? I argued in Chapter 4 that the agency, though it might be capable of having moral responsibility, does not have the unconditional moral status of a person. The purpose for which it was created provides a major component of its moral base. It is this that defines what duties it has and to whom. I argued that its primary duties are to its consumers and its constituency. Contracting private agencies are neither. Nor are their employees. They can most usefully be defined as stakeholders – groups whose interests may be affected by the agency's actions and who may reasonably expect fair and honest treatment from the agency. It is not clear that using the private agency involved would be a failure of either fairness or honesty. To refuse to use it might drive it out of business, but that would leave its former employees without any paid work. That evidently is not fair to them. To deliberately drive a successful business to bankruptcy for doing what it exists to do through the use of monopoly power evidently is not fair to the private agency. In any case, if there was any risk of loss to consumers, perhaps in terms of choice, from refusing to use the private agency, this would present a considerably stronger argument for continuing to use it.

However, it may be that the agency has a problem with regard to its constituency. For a local authority agency I have suggested that the constituency has two parts, the local electorate and national government. It is quite possible for these to come into conflict with one another. If the local electorate, through its representatives, expresses opposition to the use of private agencies which underpay their employees, the agency has an argument for being influenced by this. It would then have to balance that duty against its duty to the other part of its constituency.

Individual employees of the commissioning agency may be in a slightly different position. If they are committed to a professional code of conduct which refers to relationships with the world outside the user/worker/agency triad, the situation might have to be considered by a different moral yardstick. The UKCC (1992) code, for instance, requires nurses to serve the interests of society, and to justify public trust and confidence in the nursing profession. This code might provide an argument for a nurse, health visitor or midwife not to collude with exploitative employment practices by placing users in the care of this particular agency. However, the emphasis in most codes (particularly those relating to nursing, social work and occupational therapy) is on duties to the user, and any action which disadvantages users would be seen as breaching either the letter or the spirit of the code.

The other possible course of action for the worker might be to inform users who are potential residents of the private agency's employment practices. Professional principles relating to the treatment of users may justify ensuring at least that users know what the agency's employment practices are, if they are considering going into their care. However, there is a conflict here between a user's right to full relevant information in deciding on his or her placement, and the right of privacy of the private agency and its employees. Care staff may not want users to know how much (or rather how little) they get paid, and it is arguable that they are simply being further disadvantaged by that loss of privacy.

A rather different situation arises if the employment practices of the private agency are also racially discriminatory, or discriminatory in relation to some other group. First, this cannot be seen as a legitimate activity for the private agency, as can profit maximization. The argument that it is unfair to drive it out of business would have no force in this situation. Second, neither part of the commissioning agency's constituency could countenance such discrimination, as the Government countenances low wages. Third, such practices would make the private agency's facilities an unacceptable care environment for Black users, or users of whichever minority was being discriminated against. (This would be true even if users were not directly subjected to discrimination.) Therefore, the commissioning agency would be failing to provide appropriate care settings if the private agency were used.

One may argue that a low-wage agency would be nearly as offensive as a discriminatory agency to those users who do not wish to see others exploited for profit, or be exploited themselves. The problem is that combating and eschewing capitalism (which is what would be required) would require a level of social and economic separatism which would be little short of revolutionary, and quite impossible for a public agency. To combat racism and other discriminatory practices is by contrast a realistic and practical goal, and one to which reasonable people of most political persuasions can properly subscribe. Again Kant's principle is relevant: ought implies can.

REFERENCES

Doyal, L. and Gough, I. (1991) *A Theory of Human Need*. London: Macmillan.

Habermas, J. (1991) *Communication and the Evolution of Society*. Cambridge: Polity Press.

Maslow, A. (1954) *Motivation and Personality*. New York: Harper & Row.

UKCC (1992) *Code of Professional Conduct for the Nurse, Midwife and Health Visitor*. 3rd edn, London: United Kingdom Central Council for Nursing, Midwifery and Health Visiting.

CHAPTER 8
Freedom and Conflict

INTRODUCTION

In this chapter I shall focus on the situation of one user, Ted, as he moves from hospital into the community. I shall also consider the options of Katherine, his key worker, and the situation of the community that Ted moves into. I shall make a particular point in this chapter of focusing on the detail of the situation as precisely as possible.

TED

Ted had a disrupted childhood. His father disappeared when Ted was 8 years old, and his mother developed a drinking problem. He spent some time living with his grandmother in an outlying village – this was a stable situation, but fell apart when she died suddenly. Ted spent most of his later childhood and adolescence in children's homes, and in his early teens he started a career of petty offending that continued into his mid-twenties. He later developed symptoms that led to several short spells in a psychiatric hospital in his twenties. He was prone to developing bizarre ideas and, later, bizarre behaviour. He spent some time in secure accommodation, and a period in prison. Ted married in his mid-twenties, and his offending tailed off, but marital conflicts led him to start drinking heavily. His episodes of disturbed thought and behaviour resumed. Then he had several longer stays in hospital and his marriage broke up. For several years Ted appeared chronically ill, and his symptoms tended to re-emerge when he was discharged. He spent longer periods in hospital, culminating in a stay of several years. Ted settled down a good deal during this period, getting used to the hospital routine and becoming a co-operative and manageable patient. However, the capacity of the hospital was shrinking as it ran down its long-stay facilities in the 1970s and 1980s.

BEFORE TED RETURNS TO THE COMMUNITY

Ted has now come to be seen as someone who ought to be in the community. His symptoms are under control, and with adequate support and supervision it is thought that he would be able to function in the outside world. The combination of illness and institutionalization has produced a fairly eccentric character, with a social persona that can be unnerving. He is extremely tall and gaunt and has an air of menacing remoteness which is punctuated by gnomic remarks pronounced in a challenging way. However, Ted is unnerved far more by the prospect of living outside of the hospital again. When it was broached with him that he embark on a programme with a view to moving back into the community, he initially refused and insisted that he was not capable of living 'out there'. 'I'll just go barmy again' is his prognosis.

Katherine, his key worker, is faced with a dilemma in her dealings with Ted. She believes that her role is to help Ted to live his life in a way that maximizes the quality of that life, and maximizes also his dignity and value as a human being. She knows that valuing someone may involve challenging them. To put an easy relationship at risk in order to help someone to grow might be a major recognition of that person's worth. However, she is not happy about dismissing Ted's expressed views as being simply a product of his institutionalization or his mental health problems – as in some sense not 'really' what he feels, or would feel if he were able to free himself from those problems.

Katherine might entertain a range of doubts about Ted's expressed view, all of which create ethical problems. He might be being dishonest, irresponsible, ill informed or deluded. She may think that the result of accepting his preference will be bad for him, unfair to others or unrealistic. How should she respond to these concerns?

We can identify a spectrum of possible positions which Katherine might take with regard to Ted's autonomy:

1. She may start with the assumption that Ted is competent (an assumption in the sense that she does not intend to test that proposition) and that his expression of preference, therefore, is made competently. On that basis she still has three questions to resolve about how she treats his statements:
    - Should she accept the honesty of his statement without testing and probing?
    - Should she accept the seriousness of his statement, likewise without testing and probing?

- Should she seek to support him in sustaining that stance, against pressures from other quarters that may well arise to move into the community?

2. She might work from the basis that Ted is competent but ill informed, that his problems create something of a barrier between him and the reality of the outside world, and that his withholding of consent from this move is not informed. A possible development of this is that he needs more contact with the community before he can make a sensible decision as to whether he wants to stay or go.

3. She might work from the basis that Ted is not fully competent – that his mental health problems and his institutionalization lead him towards unclear and unrealistic modes of thinking, where categories become confused, boundaries lost and his own fears and aggressions projected onto the outside world. Unless he can move forward in this respect he can't make a competent decision about his future.

4. She might focus primarily on what she sees as Ted's benefit rather than on his wishes or his competence. If her best effort at thorough assessment of the situation establishes that Ted will benefit from moving in to the community then perhaps that should be her yardstick for deciding what she should do. Two alternatives arise from this:

   - Persuade Ted that he wants to move into the community, on the basis that his well-being will be enhanced if he makes the move of his own volition. The main task then would be to bring him round to a belief that this is what he wants.

   - Persuade Ted that he has no choice. It may be that Ted's well-being would not be unacceptably compromised if he were to be persuaded that he has no choice but to accept the move. Though he would suffer a temporary loss of autonomy, he has accepted a low level of autonomy for some years. One yardstick for the appropriateness of this decision would be whether he discovers, after experiencing community life, that this is what he wants. The acceptability of the decision may not depend on that, however.

5. She might base her response on distributive justice, on an argument that the policy behind the move towards community care for people like Ted is a good one, in that it redistributes resources in an appropriate way. It is just for

Ted to move into the community because he ought not to be taking up one of the few remaining beds – more impaired users are in need of these. Therefore, it is right for Ted to move out, even if it is not necessarily going to be particularly beneficial for him, and it is right for Katherine to acknowledge and act upon that.

6. She might base her response on acceptance of the historical forces at work. Katherine may or may not feel that Ted will benefit from living in the community, or not be harmed by it but she is also aware that there is little realistic prospect of preventing this from happening. Ted is subject to the effects of social and political forces just like the rest of us; their effects are taking this particular form for him. Nobody is proof against these and no welfare system or professional commitment can protect him from events. So it is appropriate for Katherine to accept this event, just as she might accept for another user that she cannot prevent him or her from being made redundant. Her task is to support Ted through this process and help to ensure that he does not suffer harm from it and that, if possible, it becomes a positive and useful experience.

Let us begin with acceptance of Ted's expressed opinion as a manifestation of his autonomy. What sort of things do we need to consider?

Is Ted telling the truth?

There are sensible reasons for someone in Ted's position to lie about his feelings. It gives him some power in a situation where other sources of power may not be available to him, but is it an appropriate part of Katherine's role to seek to verify the truth of what he is saying? If Ted is lying, it could be argued that he is not treating Katherine as an end – if in fact his intention is specifically to deceive Katherine. In seeking to protect herself from the consequences of such an act by seeking to get at the truth it seems unlikely that Katherine would be acting wrongly. Ted presumably, is at the same time, seeking to deceive Katherine's agency and any other body that is interested in his rehabilitation. Ted might be seeking to deceive those bodies through Katherine without seeking any harm to her. However, that reinforces the suggestion that she is being treated as a means rather than an end, and that her own personhood is being ignored. It is also likely from a utilitarian point of view that Katherine's well-being will be adversely affected by being lied to. This will not always happen, but it would be reasonable for her to fear this. Katherine is therefore probably justified in feeling wronged if she thinks that Ted is lying to her on this matter. However, that still leaves a question open as to what she should do about it.

The other dimension concerns Ted's lying to the organization. In Katherine's role as an employee it may seem justified to work to protect the interests of her employer. There is some equivalence between plain dealing with a person and plain dealing with an organization. Organizations are not 'fair game' for immoral behaviour simply because they are in some sense 'impersonal'. However, it is also true that organizations in this context tend to have a great deal more power than individuals, including considerable power over users, and where organizations are predisposed to use that power in a manipulative way the user may be justified in protecting his or her autonomy and privacy by withholding the whole truth and even, in some cases, by lying.

In that situation someone in Katherine's position may have a difficult choice over the degree to which she seeks to protect her employer from deception. She would have to decide on a number of things:

1. Is it Ted's view of the dishonesty of the agency, or her own, that should guide her conduct?
2. Does she have reason to think Ted is lying? (If she believes with good reason that he is lying, that is rather different from neutrally respecting Ted's choice as to whether or not to be honest.)
3. Will respecting Ted's decision on this impair her or the agency's ability to help him?

Ted's long and chequered experience may unfortunately have cultivated deep suspicion and cynicism, no matter how much standards of care and management may have improved in recent years. However objectively wrong Ted may be, what matters is that his belief is reasonable.

What should Katherine do about this, if anything? If she genuinely believes that the organization is sufficiently moral in its operation for Ted to not need to lie, should she try to persuade Ted of this? One of them is presumably wrong. It could be argued that part of the professional helper role is to stand outside one's own perceptions and to see the other person's point of view, and the frame in which it is located. That might involve Katherine acknowledging that though they have had different experiences of caring organizations, hers is not necessarily more valid than his. If Ted is lying and he is persuaded to acknowledge this and express his real feelings and views, and reveal his real intentions, he has lost an important bargaining counter in his relationship with the agency. In a real sense he has been persuaded to abandon some privacy. For someone who is in institutional care, where physical and social privacy are inevitably limited, psychological privacy – controlling access to what is happening in his or her head – becomes both more difficult and more important. For Ted, keeping his cards close to his chest may be a crucial part of his privacy and autonomy.

I think we have a rather different situation if there is good reason to think Ted is lying. The neutral position is no longer possible in that event. In a sense the verification has partly happened (*vide* the good reason to believe he is lying) and the response to protect from harm becomes more firmly grounded. But there must be an argument for communicating this suspicion to Ted. A pretence of believing what one does not believe is to lie in response to a lie.

Is Ted taking it seriously?

There may be other reasons why Katherine is not sure about what Ted is saying, however. She may wonder how deep and durable Ted's opinions and feelings are. Does he realize the importance of this issue? Are his statements impulsive, superficial, likely to change in any way from one day to the next? There are two questions here. First, does Ted have a right to take this lightly? It could be seen as a legitimate expression of autonomy. Second, does that mean that Katherine must accept that without reaction? It is hard to see how it might be in Ted's interests to take this lightly – in contrast with the situation where it might well be in his interests to lie. It is hard to see how that would alter the power differential in a useful way. Also, it represents an expression of autonomy with possibly rather less weight to it than Ted's decision to deliberately conceal or falsify his feelings. If Katherine succeeds in persuading Ted to come clean and acknowledge that he is not telling the truth about his views or feelings, she is persuading him to throw away an important card in his hand. If she persuades him to acknowledge that he doesn't care about it very much, he is not being persuaded to sacrifice a strategic advantage in anything like the same sense.

If it emerges that he is taking that view (that it is not important), should she then respond by trying to persuade him to treat it with more weight? It could be argued that an unconsidered attitude of insouciance is not an exercise of autonomy in the sense that deliberate concealment is, and that it is more supportive of Ted's personhood – more respect-ful of him as a person – to try to persuade him that it is important to bring his autonomous reason to bear on the issue. However, there are other perspectives. A utilitarian view might be that there is no guaran-tee that the fact that Ted is fully engaged with the issue necessarily means that happiness will be maximized. There is also a view, possibly veering closer to existentialism, which applauds an attitude of insou-ciance about the matter as an expression of authenticity. A commitment to deciding one's own values for oneself, and taking responsibility for this, could express itself in deciding that the issue of accommodation did not matter, and to justify resistance to advice to the contrary. There clearly are different versions of personal empower-ment. However, that position does not justify Katherine forbearing from trying to persuade Ted of its importance. It does justify Ted ignoring that advice.

If the agency is a party to Ted's future, and if his ideas seem grossly unrealistic and carry the seeds of almost certain collapse when implemented, the agency itself will experience some difficulty. It therefore has a dilemma – it has a duty to do its best for Ted's general well-being, but at the same time to recognize and respect his autonomy, privacy and self-respect. In utilitarian terms there could be a strong argument for putting considerable pressure on Ted to discuss and examine his ideas, simply because of the potential for unhappiness for him, and possibly for others, if unrealistic or misconceived plans are implemented or if no forward movement is made at all. If, for instance, Ted insists on remaining in the hospi-tal, only to discover three years later that the hospital is closing and he will have to move elsewhere, possibly with less planning and resourcing, it would in utilitarian terms be a disaster, and would justify some pressure on Ted to face that likelihood now. Help with predicting outcomes would be a basic utilitarian requirement.

On the other hand to pressure him to talk about something he is not prepared to discuss is an invasion of privacy and, at its worst, of liberty also. If Ted does not have the option of walking away from confrontation and challenge when it is offered, his privacy and liberty are compromised. However, it is important that Ted knows that Katherine (who is the one who, presumably, will have to speak for the agency) believes that these things need discussing, and is aware of the importance of this. Without that knowledge he cannot make an informed decision about whether or not he is going to discuss it with her. Arguably he needs to be aware of her strength of feeling on the matter if this is not going to be an invasion of his privacy and physical integrity. Katherine's skill is clearly a crucial factor here. It is possible to encourage someone to explore their thinking without subjecting them to the sort of pressure that can compromise privacy, autonomy and well-being. However, it is unrealistic to suppose that this type of probing can be accomplished without some discomfort for the individual concerned.

Any process which involves the examination of strong beliefs is going to produce some threat and discomfort, and it is a question of keeping this to a level which does not produce the harm I have mentioned, while at the same time pursuing the legitimate goals in respect of the user's well-being. Accepting that some probing may be justified and possible, we need then to consider Katherine's position in communicating with others about Ted's stated feelings. Here again we run up against the advocate role conflicting with the advisory and facilitating roles. As advocate her priority would be to support Ted's autonomy. That might argue for advocacy of his views without subjecting them to any evaluation herself. Apart from the ethical problems of uncritical advocacy generally (does this include advocacy of views that one regards as actively evil?) there is also the question of Katherine's other duties, as an employee of an organization with duties to a range of people, and duties in particular to use resources in a way that meets needs and achieves utility. Her code of ethics is likely to encourage her to support her client's autonomy, but that might involve (for instance) helping him to widen his range of options, which may not be synonymous with uncritical support of his position. The real dilemma is probably not how far she advocates for Ted as much as whether she uses her power to block him achieving what he wants. This leads us on to the next question.

How informed is Ted's decision?

If Ted has been in hospital for several years, and has had little contact with the community, it is likely that he will be somewhat out of touch with the state of things on the street. Part of that might be remediable through straightforward information-giving. For instance, if he has been institutionalized during a period of inflation he can be helped to get accustomed to the idea of higher prices. Other aspects may be matters of skill and experience rather than simple information. He may have false anxieties about a neighbourhood that had a dubious reputation a few years ago but is now greatly improved. His fear of living there, based on recollections of that community, and of what people said about it, might be out of date. He may believe that moving to this neighbourhood would be both a fall down the social ladder and a matter of personal risk. It isn't likely that Ted will be content simply to be 'put right' on all this. This will be hard to accept, and may need some direct experience, or at least something more concrete than a well-intentioned lecture. It would seem reasonable to suggest to Ted an arrangement to visit the area, to look round and spend some time there, before making any decisions. Again, how much pressure should there be on him to do that? The exercise of autonomy requires information, so any individual who wants to maximize their autonomy would usually want to maximize their information – as long as the information is in a form and quality to be usable. However, I suggested in Chapter 3 that the exercise of autonomy also implies choice as to the way decisions are arrived at. If Ted's autonomy is truly to be respected, this must involve respecting his choice as to how much information (and of what kind) he uses.

Let us suppose that, for Ted, the exercise of autonomy in itself is more important than the quality of the decision. It may be that for Ted to establish to his own satisfaction that he is doing something the agency doesn't want him to do, is a good indication for him that he is autonomous in that respect. If he is persuaded in the end to move out, then he can feel no confidence that he is in fact autonomous. 'They' might have made him do it anyway, and in any case 'they' have got what they want. So the reasonable arguments and evidence presented to him by Katherine in fact present a threat to his autonomy, in the sense that he can't be sure that he truly has the option of doing something other people don't want him to do, until he does it. For Ted, whose autonomy has been threatened and denied to a degree most people have not had to live with, this may be an important issue. The difficulty is that from the point of view of utility it may cause him to suffer both practically and emotionally. Autonomy is ultimately unprovable and, therefore, we cannot claim a right to proof of autonomy, even if we claim a right to the autonomy itself. But Ted's resistance to persuasion may be entirely understandable none the less.

Is Ted competent?

We now come to the most difficult of the issues facing Katherine – that of Ted's competence. Let us suppose that Katherine in her conversations with Ted has come across ideas that seem to have elements of delusion. Ted believes that the world will end in a few

years – the basis of this belief is vague, as he seems to have no religious commitment. He believes his dead mother speaks to him and
advises him on whom to trust and whom not to trust. On the other
hand much of what Ted says is thoughtful and sensible, often wryly
perceptive and humorous. So how far can Ted understand what is
going on around him? How far can he understand information and
advice? How far is it morally acceptable to support Ted's exercise of
his autonomy? Are his thought processes, his perceptions, his
emotional responses, of a sort that can allow him the option of
making reasoned decisions? There are situations where incompetence must be clear – where the individual is severely deluded,
demented, hallucinating, impaired or immature. There is much less
problem in agreeing on situations where severe impairments establish incompetence, and identifying situations where it is clearly
justified, and indeed imperative, to protect the individual from the
consequences of his or her actions and decisions. The problem arises
in the marginal cases. Often these cases are people like Ted.

For most of us, for most of our adult lives, our competence is not
questioned, however 'incompetent' we may be, but for people with
certain labels the question is there at all times. Clearly there is an
injustice here. Most of the literature will acknowledge that, though
the law clearly has to attempt a clear dividing line between competence and incompetence for certain purposes, in ethical terms there
will never be a set of firm, final and transparent criteria that can
claim everyone's agreement (see Buchanan and Brock, 1990). There
are many situations, involving many people, where competence
could be questioned, but where its presence or lack could never be
established firmly and permanently. Therefore, given that the issue
of competence in marginal cases is not resolvable, we are left also
with an issue of justice. A level of procedural justice might be
achieved if the same criteria were consistently applied in every case.
Given that this is usually dependent on individual judgement, it
cannot be relied on.

We also have an issue of distributive justice. It is those who find
themselves in positions where someone is in a formal position to
question competence, with labels such as 'mental health problem',
'learning disability', 'confusion' and so on, who are most likely to
have their competence questioned. This is not to deny that many of
those people may actually have serious difficulties with competent
decision-making at various times, but this does not clearly distinguish them from the rest of the population. In that sense, having
their competence questioned is in part a contingency of their social

situation. In terms of distributive justice, the loss of autonomy arising from the questioning of competence (even when there is not a legal sanction for this) is not necessarily distributed in a way that corresponds to need or utility. At any stage where Katherine might feel in some doubt as to Ted's competence to make these decisions, she might then ask herself whether that doubt, if it influenced her own or others actions, might not constitute an injustice. It might well.

However, because the situation is unjust, it does not mean that Katherine should ignore any question of Ted's competence. To say that it is unjust to question Ted's competence does not mean, in this context, that he is competent. The way competence is questioned seems crucial to the justice issue for someone like Ted, and we might identify some justice-based principles here, as we did with assessment. So competence should be questioned in accordance with consistent and openly acknowledged principles which would be equally applicable to those with labels and histories of difficulty as to those without. This is simply the principle of equality applied to such decisions. It is difficult to apply this when there are so many differing definitions of competence, but it seems fundamental none the less. The other principle I would suggest is that competence should only be questioned when applied to a decision of importance, where my incompetent decision is likely to do me real harm. Given the fundamental nature of autonomy to personhood, the burden of proof should always lie with whoever questions its exercise to show that they are seeking to prevent significant harm.

Is it in Ted's interests?

Let us consider a situation where Katherine believes it to be in Ted's interests to follow a particular course of action, whether Ted realizes that or not. Belief about Ted's competence may have an effect on whether Katherine chooses to pressure or manipulate him for his own good. I have already outlined some problems that arise in acting on the belief that someone is not competent. If Katherine seeks to control the situation while believing Ted to be competent, then there is a rather different issue. In Kantian terms she is treating Ted as a means rather than an end in that situation. This is because she is pursuing her own desires and agenda for Ted, rather than respecting his desires and his agenda. She believes that she will be able to make a better decision than Ted. The immediate utility of that action is therefore, by her prediction, greater if she does not leave Ted to decide for himself. However, from an act utilitarian point of view this leaves out the impact on Ted of having his preference blocked. From a rule utilitarian point of view it leaves out the problems arising if we have a rule to the effect that I seek to overrule users' decisions where I think they are bad for them. There are clearly serious problems with this course of action.

Is it just?

Let us imagine a situation where Katherine decides that the policy of community care is one which achieves sufficient good widely enough distributed to justify requiring Ted to comply with its requirements, even if that did not fully respect his autonomy or personhood. The question here concerns the moral nature of Katherine's role in relation to Ted and to others. If she has a specific role, say as key worker, are there special obligations that go with that? I have suggested in previous chapters that there are such obligations, arising from a professional commitment implicit in assuming the role. The agency is in the business of distributing goods as fairly as possible, and it is not necessarily fair for a worker to seek the advantage of a user at the expense of everyone else. It is legitimate for the worker to partake in the agency's goals in terms of fair distribution. The worker's professional obligation likewise does not require uncritical seeking of advantage for the user. It does require certain basic characteristics – particularly respect and honesty. If Katherine believes that she ought to be encouraging Ted to move into the community for the greater good, rather than for Ted's good, then her professional obligations, as set out in her code of ethics, would require her to tell him that. Any attempt to persuade him on any other basis would be deception and would involve treating Ted as a means rather than an end.

Is it inevitable?

Finally let us imagine a situation in which Katherine takes the view that the move towards community care is inevitable and that Ted should be helped to make the best of what cannot be resisted. She cannot necessarily know that it is inevitable for Ted individually, but she can take the view that it is not her job to protect him from something that will sweep most of his fellow patients into the community. Part of the reality of autonomous personhood is that autonomy is limited by social, economic and political forces that propel us in various directions, often against our wishes. Ted is therefore experiencing autonomous person-hood if he experiences those forces. To attempt to protect him is to diminish his personhood. There is a paradox with this. The paradox is that for most of us autonomous personhood does not involve having someone who can decide to expose us to the cold winds of history or protect us from the same. We may be protected or unprotected, by our-selves or others, but no one is deliberately leaving us individually to sink or swim. We may be in a position to resist those forces of our own resources in a way that Ted is not. So it could be argued that Katherine does have a role, offering a compensatory counterweight to Ted's dis-advantaged situation – a substitute for the resources that most of us have, and Ted has not. This would provide some justice in the situation in terms of equality of opportunity.

AFTER TED RETURNS TO THE COMMUNITY

Let us assume that Ted finally agrees, for whatever reason, to move into the accommodation designated for him in the community. Ted remembers the area he has moved into as being particularly run-down, with a reputation for poverty and crime. He dislikes being there and has negative feelings towards the neighbourhood and its inhabitants. He has not fully registered or appreciated the develop-ments over the past few years, whereby the social mix has changed a good deal. In fact he is in a neighbourhood with a strong community life. There are three pubs serving this group of streets, two clubs, a few corner shops, a school and two churches. There is a good deal of new housing dovetailed into the old inner-city area. This has helped to revitalize the area and has led to a socially and ethnically mixed neighbourhood. There are sufficient focal places for the active members of this community to organize voluntary support for Ted and the few similar individuals living in and near the hotel. The pubs are well organized for charity activities as are the churches.

Ted lives in a small private hotel which now specializes in accom-modating people discharged from hospital. The accommodation is not particularly good – he has to get his own meals out, and there are no lounge/common-room facilities in the hotel. On the whole he feels that it is a good deal less satisfactory than hospital.

Ted is in many ways marginalized in the society he inhabits. His parents are dead, his wife is long gone, he knows not where and he has no children. His connections with the social order around him are tenuous and problematic, and he does not experience them as working to his advantage in any respect. However, his experience in hospital led him to develop an inner sense of self-sufficiency, and an ability to keep others at a distance and not to try to engage in relationships which might prove unsatisfactory. Though this might perpetuate Ted's isolation to some extent, it also helps him to cope with the isolation that is a real part of his situation.

Ted's problems in the community

Ted still sees the neighbourhood and its inhabitants as they were 20 years before, and expresses his disdain both verbally and non-verbally with relatively little provocation. This makes him unpopular. He has arguments in shops, in the pub and in the street with people because of this tendency. If his antagonist is sufficiently persistent he will acquaint them with his views about the end of the world, emphasizing their likely individual fate in graphic and eloquent terms. These accounts are tinged with violence, and are spoken with vehement intensity. To be on the receiving end of this is, for many people, to feel as though they have been on the receiving end of an assault – though Ted does not either act violently or threaten to act violently towards anyone. He manages to transmit the resentment of his own inner life without in any literal sense being violent. He is a rather imposing and intimidating figure before he even starts to say or do anything. People are frightened of him and this has the unfortunate added effect of making him a target for those who need to prove that they are not frightened of him. He has suffered some assaults from local youths – nothing as yet that has led to serious injury, but this could happen. As time goes on Ted gets more isolated and unpopular. The owner of the hotel takes little interest in these matters, but he is not immune to pressure from local people, and may wish to gain some local goodwill by getting rid of Ted. Ted's situation is deteriorating and could come to a point of sudden catastrophic change that would be hard to manage in a positive way.

The ethics of Ted's relationship with the community

We need to consider the ethical contours of Ted's situation generally. I shall start by considering the moral relationship between Ted and the community. The community seems to be rejecting Ted, and the results of that may be negative for Ted. So we might ask whether the community has any duty towards Ted in terms of support, acceptance or care. Does it have a duty to provide Ted with the kind of acceptance that might involve accepting some rather strange and frightening behaviour, while still receiving Ted into one's company and one's living and meeting areas?

Duties

I have argued in Chapter 1 that it is hard to see how a community can have such a duty, or (in the case of this community) any duty at all, as a community. This community is not a formal organization with a decision-making structure placing individuals in formal roles and relationships. So the community cannot make decisions for which it can be held responsible. We might argue that the community association can make decisions. It might have a duty to provide care, though it is hard to see how that duty might be sustained unless it is written into its constitution, or at least implied strongly (for instance, if it has a declared purpose of providing for the benefit and well-being of all members of the community). In any case the community association is not the community. A community cannot have a duty which it lacks the wherewithal (in terms of internal organization) to carry out.

It may be, then, that it makes more sense to say that individuals have a duty to people who are members of their community. But again, as I argued in Chapter 1, it is hard to see why membership of the same community confers that sort of relationship, if there is no agreed relationship between roles, as might exist between members of the same organization. How can it be that someone who lives three streets away from me has a stronger call on my moral duty than that of other persons living on the other side of the ring-road, the country or (in principle) the planet? In most contexts where specific relationships are not defined (as they are for instance, in families) it is hard to see how such a claim can be sustained, except in terms of the particular moral norms of that community itself. It makes more sense to say that whatever duties we have towards our fellow human beings are, in general, most effectively and easily performed towards those on our doorstep.

We then need to ask what our moral duties are. Do we have a duty of care; a duty of love; a duty of respect? Kant argues for a duty of respect for persons, and for related duties such as honesty and promise-keeping. Noddings (1984) sees potential in the notion of a duty of care as a general principle, but its boundaries and demands are more difficult to demarcate than those of Kantian duties. Otherwise a duty of care is associated with specific roles and commitments. A duty of love is unlikely to be sustainable by moral principles that are universalizable.

Kantian duties are probably the most sustainable in this context, but it is not clear that their observance will provide Ted with what he needs to survive.

Ted's autonomy and the autonomy of his neighbours

Let us consider the other side of the situation and look at Ted's position. I shall start by working on the assumption that Ted is competent and considering how far the principle of autonomy should be carried, and at what point it is ethically legitimate to place limits on Ted's exercise thereof. In exercising his autonomy he is limiting the autonomy of others, just as they are limiting his, and the more his behaviour breaks social norms, the more that becomes the case. It is quite possible that a number of his neighbours feel that their autonomy is threatened by his behaviour. They may feel that they dare not walk down a particular street or go into a particular pub at certain times of day because Ted is likely to be there and he may subject them to some of his verbal challenges.

This raises some interesting questions. How much of a problem does Ted need to become to people before he starts to place limits on their autonomy? If I fear that I will be assaulted if I go to this pub tonight, that feels like a real limit on my autonomy. An ordinary option is made physically dangerous. On the other hand if I fear that there will be someone there that I don't like, even though I expect that person to ignore me, does that compromise my autonomy? It makes that option less attractive, perhaps, and less likely that I will choose it. But that is not a loss of autonomy, surely? The business of deciding which is the most attractive option and choosing that is part of the exercise of autonomy. Some pubs are more congenial than others because of the people who frequent them. Therefore, if the latter situation does not compromise my autonomy, but the former does (for the sake of argument) where do we place the situation as described, where a disturbing verbal encounter takes place, but without violence or the threat of violence from the other protagonist. Is that situation one where an option is being made inaccessible because of the behaviour of that individual?

Does it make a difference that he is directing that behaviour towards me, which is rather different from him sitting in a corner of the snug ignoring me? His behaviour towards me is, or seems, intentional and directed. However, a friendly greeting would be just as intentional. I suspect that there is something more to it, which concerns the issues of interpersonal boundaries of space, proximity, attention and contact, as discussed in Chapter 3. I suggested then that the ordinary processes of communication which would not usually be seen as threatening autonomy can shade over into a breach of privacy – privacy in the sense of control over who comes close to me, who has eye contact with me, who has my attention and who can make me feel uncertain of my physical integrity, even safety, in that situation. There is a real loss there, a loss of some aspect of autonomy, though it is really loss of control of a situation rather than of oneself. There is a loss of well-being as well. It could be argued that the friendly greeting and conversation in the pub or street may be equally beyond my control, if the other is sufficiently pressing. The unfriendly approach is a far clearer indication that I do not have control of the situation, because it is clear to me, to the other person and to onlookers that in this case it is more probably being imposed on me. So there is a real loss there, with some real moral weight.

Responding to Ted's behaviour

Does the situation described above justify some action to limit Ted's freedom to relate to people in this way? If Ted were to target particular individuals for insulting and directly threatening behaviour, it may be possible to use the civil law to obtain an injunction restraining him from doing this. The law recognizes the individual's right of privacy and freedom from harassment in that respect. Of course Ted is not being either directly insulting or threatening, and it could be argued that the anxiety he is causing is a result of the narrow concept of social normality which his neighbours adhere to. I shall consider the issue of normality later.

One way of responding is to treat Ted as autonomous and to respond in a way that does not, in principle, compromise that autonomy, though it might discourage him from doing this particular thing. Such a response might involve legal action, or simply confronting Ted with regard to his actions. If his neighbours think those actions are morally wrong, one response would be to admonish him. Another might be legal action with regard to harassment. This, if successful, would in effect mean that if Ted persisted in this action he would be punished. This response treats him as capable of taking responsibility for his actions. We then have a question as to whether his actions are sufficiently morally wrong to justify that action. I have suggested that he is in a real way breaching the privacy of his neighbours and, arguably, creating a deficit both in terms of respect for persons and also in terms of utility.

Justice and tolerance

A further question arises at this point. Does Ted's damaging life history place a duty of greater than usual tolerance or forbearance on his neighbours? This is really a question about the amount of disamenity and disutility individuals have a duty to accept because someone has suffered disadvantages. In terms of justice we might consider whether people who have been lucky owe something to those who have not. Certainly luck is not earned but nor, usually, is it actively sought at the expense of others, in this context. I don't seek to put others in a psychiatric hospital in order to keep myself out. In any case if there is to be any balancing up of luck it needs to be truly just and ensure that the worst off gain. As some of the worst off may be Ted's neighbours, while others better off may be gaining through avoiding having people like Ted in their neighbourhood, that is not justice. I have argued that love and care probably go beyond sustainable general duty in most ethical systems, and though they would be morally admirable things to offer Ted at his worst, this does not mean that it would be morally wrong not to do so. The most sustainable duty is the Kantian duty of respect, which in this context probably involves not behaving as if Ted cannot help his behaviour − which may involve admonishing him for it. It may also mean taking action to hold him to account for his actions − perhaps through the courts. Paradoxically a punitive response in this context could be seen as respectful of autonomy. However, in terms of utility the most sustainable response is probably one of avoiding making Ted's pain worse, as long as that does not make anyone else's pain worse.

Normality and relativism

Another important question, which I mentioned earlier, concerns social normality. Human beings have a strong need to live by social norms, and where there is uncertainty about prevailing social norms there is likely to be a high level of stress. Where norms are broken, people tend to react negatively to some degree. So clear norms are, all things being equal, likely to maximize happiness, when compared with norm confusion or normlessness.

Does this need confer any kind of right on people to have their own norms respected by others who do not subscribe to them? From a utilitarian point of view there is clearly an argument for avoiding breaking other people's norms in their presence, and thereby saving them discomfort, distress or fear, but that must depend on there being no greater loss of utility for oneself in doing this. If I find myself in a community where the norm is for elaborate courtesy face to face, and vicious backbiting when out of sight, I may decide that conformity to this is too great a disutility for me to justify the fact that my neighbours will be more comfortable if I join in.

What if Ted regards the day-to-day courtesy of his neighbours as hypocrisy, and feels tainted by any collusion with that? Should we then accept that Ted has a right to his own normality, which includes a set of behavioural norms also, albeit idiosyncratic. That raises the problem of relativism which I mentioned in the Introduction. The relativist view is that we can only judge behaviour in terms of right and wrong by the code of the person whose behaviour it is. There is an issue as to how far that code would be that of a community, culture, religion or other aggregate of people and how far we can allow it to be individual. Ted is to some degree a one-man culture and one-man moral code, but he inhabits a social space. One of the arguments of relativism relevant to community care is that it is wrong to require someone to do something that they think is wrong, even if we think it is right. However, Ted is not simply behaving in a way that his neighbours find odd. He is not simply talking to himself in their hearing. He is engaging them in a social system (which is what a conversation is) which is governed by his norms, and in that sense making it very difficult for people to avoid becoming part of that process. They are being pressured into an encounter which offends their social and perhaps moral norms. In that sense the kind of stand-off that relativism requires is not being achieved here.

Katherine's options

If Ted is competent and not suffering from psychosis, what should Katherine do in a situation where he is being a nuisance to his neighbours? She will have a duty to help Ted settle and support his reintegration into the community. What then if he shows that he is not particularly willing to reintegrate, at least not on the community's terms? Does Katherine or the agency have a duty to him, or to the community in this situation? If Katherine receives repeated phone calls about Ted's behaviour from his neighbours what ought she to do? Arguably she ought to monitor his state, to ensure that he is not becoming ill, and is not in need of anything that he would be willing to have. We then move into the issue of persuasion and pressure. Katherine may feel able to predict that if Ted carries on as he is doing he will suffer some negative consequences from his neighbours. Also she may be able to assess that he is causing a good deal of disamenity and even loss of freedom to some of his neighbours. Should she do more than acquaint Ted with her view on this? Her professional obligation is to Ted, whose needs seem still to define him quite legitimately as a user. No one else in the neighbourhood necessarily falls into this category. The agency's task is primarily to provide community care for people like Ted, not to care for the community in any general sense – and yet the community is part of the agency's constituency.

However, that 'community' is the whole population of that particular local authority or health district, not just the population of the neighbourhood. I doubt whether any community can be seen as the object of duty by an organization (I suggested this in Chapter 1). Individuals may be an object of duty because of their residence in a particular area, but the community as a whole cannot be seen as having that kind of moral status. Therefore, I am arguing that Katherine's duty is to individuals with specified needs. It may be that none of Ted's neighbours qualify for help from the agency and, therefore, from Katherine.

An interesting issue of relativism arises here. If the local community has norms that involve a fair degree of conformity to certain behavioural requirements, it may contrast with a professional culture represented by the agency, by Katherine and her colleagues, which is more likely to be based on a view that human behaviour is extremely diverse, and that a wide degree of tolerance is desirable. It is to some degree the more relativist culture of the professional with which the local community may find themselves in conflict.

Risk

The other major issue is that of risk. Ted's history does not suggest that he is likely to harm anyone, but the content of some of his statements is tinged with violence, indicating that he is having rather violent thoughts. More urgently, he seems to be courting unpopularity to a degree that is putting his own physical safety at risk. A number of risks might be indicated in the situation.

One could argue that the likelihood of Ted acting violently is a 'technical' issue in the sense that some prediction might be possible from the relationship between his history and behaviour, and whatever research has been done on predicting violent behaviour. This is complicated by the fact that Ted is behaving in a very provocative way, therefore the initial violence might come from elsewhere – from someone who is provoked by Ted's behaviour. So we are also having to predict other people's behaviour, and predict Ted's response to others initiating violence. The difficulty of making reliable assessments of likely human behaviour in a situation of this complexity are enormous. From an ethical point of view, if the worker is to carry and discharge any moral responsibility in this kind of situation, that responsibility would need to focus in part on the appropriate ways of using expert or 'scientific' evidence. If, for instance, a psychiatrist predicts that Ted will not behave violently, do we accept that as the verdict of the expert, and work on the assumption that responsibility for that prediction lies with that professional. The problem is that the knowledge stock relevant to such a prediction does not belong to any single profession or academic discipline, and includes a range of diverse and sometimes conflicting concepts. It is not likely that we shall get any statement that can be treated definitively, as one might get a statement from a radiologist about what my X-ray shows or from a plumber about what is going on in my central heating system. This suggests that the individual worker must take some responsibility for the choice of informant and expertise she draws on in such a situation, and also that she may actually have to acknowledge some practical expertise herself.

It sometimes makes sense to attach some of the blame for an event to someone who was in a position to forsee the event and to stop it, but did not. If I leave my car handbrake off when I park near a downhill slope, I may be expected to carry the main blame if the car rolls down and hurts someone, but in what situation can I reasonably forsee that Ted may act violently? The information base for that prediction is very problematic, as I have suggested. I may have a duty to deal with the information at my disposal in a particular way, in order to assess as accurately as possible the likelihood of something violent happening. And the focus of responsibility must be that use of information – has it been fully assembled, has it been exhaustively discussed by everyone with a knowledge or expertise relevant to the prediction? Presumably every one of those individuals has a duty to contribute and engage in that process to the best of their ability. Again there is an issue about the degree to which anyone is responsible for accepting uncritically opinions from other experts when they may think these are ill considered.

The crucial way in which this situation is different from my car's handbrake is that we are here predicting the behaviour of a human being and we must assume, without clear evidence to the contrary, that his behaviour is chosen rather than caused. If we take it that Ted will become violent only if his mental health deteriorates and he develops a symptomatology which includes that behaviour, we can perhaps talk about cause and effect rather than choice, in that the illness may impel him towards violent actions. In that situation some notion of causation might be acceptable, and prediction of behaviour on the basis of symptoms may in theory have some validity. If Ted's mental state has not deteriorated in that sense, but he is none the less feeling stressed, resentful and isolated, we might try to find evidence as to how often men in Ted's situation behave violently. We might find a number of such studies, and average out a probability from those. However, we must assume that Ted will choose to act violently, if act he does, and that he is therefore capable of choosing not to act violently. While he has the choice, it is not clear that we have any right to intervene in the situation because on the aggregate of our research evidence there is (let us suppose) a better than 50:50 chance that someone in his position will behave violently. This does not mean that there is a better than 50:50 chance that Ted will behave violently.

The alternative response would be to treat his behaviour as symptomatic of mental deterioration, and to take action to safeguard his mental and physical health. This might in some circumstances also involve action to safeguard his safety, and/or the safety of others, but this would be to construe his behaviour quite differently, as a manifestation of something that Ted does not have control over and for which he should not be held responsible. Any punitive action, therefore, would be completely inappropriate. The problem is that we might make sense of Ted's behaviour in either framework; as the chosen behaviour of an isolated individual full of resentment and confusion from his disturbed and institutionalized life, or as a sufferer from a psychotic condition whose mental health is deteriorating again. We solve that problem in part by appointing experts to decide whether this is illness or not – thereby using a medical procedure to deal with it. This may be a genuine solution. However, the validity or recognizability of diagnostic categories in psychiatry have been so widely questioned that we must be left in doubt about that solution. The acceptance of this device in practice by many professionals who doubt its validity in principle is one indication of the difficulty of the issue.

REFERENCES

Buchanan, A. E. and Brock, D. (1990) *Deciding for Others*. Cambridge: Cambridge University Press.
Noddings, N. (1984) *Caring: A Feminine Approach to Ethics and Moral Education*. Berkeley: University of California Press.

CHAPTER 9
Policies and Organizations

INTRODUCTION

In this final chapter I shall focus on ethics at the organizational level. In particular I shall focus on the position of a senior manager who must decide on her course of action in three situations where: her employer's policies conflict with her conscience; her employer appears to be engaged in wrongdoing; another organization appears to be engaged in wrongdoing, to the detriment of her employer.

CONFLICT BETWEEN POLICY AND CONSCIENCE

The situation

Jaspreet is a senior manager in a social services department. She has responsibility for planning services and negotiating contracts with provider bodies. She is a member of the senior management team of the department and has a significant amount of influence over the shape that the organization of community care is taking in that authority.

The local authority which employs her does not have a single ruling party. Decisions are made jointly by the Labour and Liberal Democrat groups. Although they have joined in the criticisms levelled at the community care policy by various local government bodies and by their parties, the elected members have on the whole accepted the job of implementing its provisions. This had involved close co-operation with the two health commissions coterminous with the local authority's territory and, latterly, also with the NHS trusts in the area. All these bodies are run by boards and management who are unembarrassedly committed to the Government's policy and keen to implement it both in letter and in spirit. Most senior managers in social services do not have explicit political affiliations, though a few have histories of involvement with the Labour Party. Several have reservations about the Government's policies with regard to community care but these tend to sink under the technical challenge of getting the new system under way, which engages their energy, and (though they might not say so) enthusiasm. The enthusiasm of their colleagues in the health authorities and trusts has rubbed off here.

A number of things are happening. The senior management team are considering two alternative plans with regard to the future structure of services. One would involve entirely pulling the local authority out of providing, uncoupling all the units, centres and homes that actually provide care and setting them up as independent providers. The other plan would involve dividing the department internally into purchaser and provider parts, with a purely contracting relationship between them. There is discussion also of devolving institutional contracting to area levels. Pressure emanates from the larger potential providers for block contracting as high up the ladder as possible, while the small providers are keener on one-off contracting.

Jaspreet's dilemma

Jaspreet sees herself as a socialist, part of the collectivist tradition which gave rise to the welfare state. She believes that human equality of worth can only be properly expressed and protected in the context of collective action, where the more fortunate and the less fortunate in various ways have their interests united, so they work together for common benefit. She believes in spreading the risk of individual misfortune across the population. She believes that it is collectively, in families and communities, that human beings are most able to express their moral nature, and find their true identity as beings which can reconcile the mind, body and spirit in harmony with the natural and material world around them. She sees competition as a means of bringing out the worst in people, and of bringing about the worst results in terms of inequality. It also expresses an ideology of human aggression and selfishness which she sees as one of the most corrupt and corrupting manifestations of western civilization. As a student she supported the Socialist Workers' Party, but later moved to the Labour Party as the most realistic vehicle for achieving socialism. As her career has taken off she has had less time for active politics, and now has none. But her principles remain largely the same. She sees it as legitimate to express those in her work, in the sense that the provision of social care expresses an essentially collectivist ideal even when the rest of the social system has moved towards a more individualistic ideology. However, now even social care is being contaminated by those principles.

This is the nature of Jaspreet's dilemma. She finds herself part (and a crucial part) of a system which is moving in a direction which she opposes in principle. She is in a position where she might be able to slow or modify those changes. She does not believe that she can stop them – the national political momentum is too great. Some of the questions concerning her are as follows:

1. Should she seek to prevent the organization which employs her from achieving goals which it has collectively committed itself to?
2. Should she participate in the implementing of policies that she believes are morally wrong, and which conflict with her political principles?
3. Should she withdraw herself, with her skills, experience and credibility, from a position of influence which she is now in, to an inevitably more marginal position that she would occupy if she took a job which involved her advocating her political views clearly (e.g. pressure group activism, journalism, academe)?
4. Should she, as a single parent, put the material situation of her children at risk by going into an uncertain situation as a result of resigning her job?

The moral questions that arise from these options seem to be as follows:

a. Is the basis of her opposition to the developing policies relevant? Political beliefs have many different roots. I may identify with a group, a class, a tradition, that binds me socially and emotionally to a particular set of political beliefs – even a programme. That does not mean I necessarily think that programme is morally right, or that its opposite is morally wrong. On the other hand I may have a strong belief that the difference between two political alternatives is precisely that – the difference between moral right and wrong. If my political principles are based on ethical commitments (as Jaspreet's seem to be) does that mean that those beliefs morally justify actions which political beliefs based on social affiliation and felt identification do not?

b. Assuming that there is moral justification for Jaspreet in acting on her political beliefs, how does that match up against her contribution to actions which she believes to be wrong? As an employee of the department, how far is she party to those policies? How far is she open to censure if those policies are morally wrong? The issue here is one of complicity. Does employment in a particular organization lead to complicity with the actions of that organization and does the position that one holds, in terms of power and authority, affect such complicity as can be justified?

c. What is the right relationship with the employer? Jaspreet owes certain duties to the department in her role as an employee. Some of those are part of the employee/employer relationship. However, as a member of the senior management team that steers the policy of the department, it could be argued that morally at least she may have obligations that go beyond the simple employee role, and extends into issues of corporate loyalty and collective responsibility of a less formal kind.

Conscientious objection

Let us return to question (a) above. This concerns the basis of conscientious objection, and raises the whole issue of the nature of ethics and morality, and the degree to which it has a special status that sets it apart from other normative and evaluative systems. Do my moral judgements have more call upon my actions than my political or aesthetic judgements, or my social norms?

If Jaspreet's collectivism is a result of her socialization into a particular set of cultural norms, a cultural relativist would argue that it is morally appropriate for her to act on those beliefs, and morally inappropriate for anyone to stop her doing so. However, other perspectives would identify a distinction between commitments based on habit, upbringing and other influences, and those based on moral perceptions. I may have a right to express my social norms within certain limits, but it is unlikely that I have a duty to express them, except within the terms of the cultural framework itself. Certainly from a Kantian point of view there would be a crucial difference between taking a stand on an issue of political affiliation and taking a stand on an issue of moral conviction. The same might be true from a utilitarian point of view, depending on the perceived utility of the policies in contention. If Jaspreet's political commitments are rooted in individual or collective self-interest, it is likewise going to be seen in most philosophies as a matter of right rather than duty, in the sense that self-interest is a legitimate goal to pursue in most frameworks, but not a moral duty. It seems then that Jaspreet needs to consider the nature of her political commitments, and their basis, when considering what is the morally right course of action to take.

Complicity

Let us consider question (b) above, concerning complicity. The issue is, how far does Jaspreet partake of any moral wrongness that attaches to the policies under discussion. Complicity consists in knowing about, and failing to prevent, wrong actions being performed where one has the ability to prevent those actions, or contribute to their prevention.

If I work for an organization that specializes in evil actions and advertises itself as such, my choice to go to work for it would seem to involve some knowing contribution to its evil, even if my motive for taking the job is not evil (assuming I had the option of changing my job). However, we can perhaps work from the basis that community care agencies do not specialize in evil actions and, indeed, advertise themselves to the contrary. I cannot be held culpable for going to work for an organization that ostensibly exists to pursue morally laudable ends, even if it performs immoral actions occasionally and unexpectedly. What is my moral link, as an employee, with those occasional wrongdoings? It could be argued that I have complicity with those actions unless I am actively seeking to prevent them. My position as a component of the organization implies that I am helping it, keeping it running, however much I dislike some of the things it does and however much my role is routine, mechanistic and not directly connected with the immoral activities. I am contributing to the functioning of the organization. But then so are millions of other people, who contribute to its functioning by contributing to the functioning of the State and economy which sustains that organization. Where does complicity end? Should I emigrate?

As an ordinary employee I might none the less be able to justify my employee role because the organization does more good things than bad things. After all, we all do bad things. Should I be checking on my neighbour, and stopping him from pilfering from his employer? To say that I have a duty to seek to prevent all bad actions which take place in any organizational, physical or social space I occupy (alongside many other people) is impractical. If my contribution to my employer's immoral actions is of that sort, it seems unlikely that I can be accused of significant complicity.

However, Jaspreet's role is not of that sort. Her agreement with her employer is not that she will process monthly travel claims which might reimburse people for going to meetings where decisions are made to do immoral things. Jaspreet's agreement is that she will go to those meetings and contribute to making decisions. In that sense her complicity is of a more identifiable kind. However, we still need to consider how Jaspreet can prevent those immoral actions, were she to decide to do so. What do we mean by 'can' here? There are a number of things she might have the means and opportunity to do that might at least delay the policies. She could murder the director. That would hold things up for a while no doubt. She could take a number of illegal actions that would disrupt the work of the department and the management team. Do we discount those from the concept of 'can' in this case? We might feel that we cannot reasonably regard such actions as options but, if Jaspreet had been a member of the inner councils of the Nazi Party, we might think that such extreme actions of resistance would have been appropriate in 1944. Does that mean, then, that it is the wrongness of the actions that are being prevented that provides the yardstick for the kind of actions that might be justified in opposition?

Complicity and utilitarianism

From a utilitarian point of view we might make a calculation of the harm done by the policy being pursued as against the harm, done by the countermeasures taken by opponents of those policies within the organization. An act utilitarian would look at each situation as it arose and calculate that balance in each case. A rule utilitarian would argue that we ought to judge the rightness of disruptive counter-action in terms of a rule – perhaps a rule that opponents of particular policies within an organization should seek to disrupt the organization's activities in order to prevent the policy being implemented – and see whether that rule maximizes utility. It is likely that, in situations where the organization is bent on highly destructive and damaging policies, utility would be maximized by subjecting it to major disruptions. If the organization is overall doing more good than harm, the matter might conclude rather differently. There is also an issue from the rule utilitarian point of view as to whether the disruption should be initiated from within the organization – in this case by senior employees – rather than by opponents outside, or by employees lower down the hierarchy. A rule of this sort might have a very different utility for outside pressure groups or for the rank and file, than for senior managers. While senior managers might be much more effective at disruption, the ability of large organizations in general to conduct decision-making at senior levels in a coherent way might be seriously compromised if such a rule were operative.

Another consideration relevant to a utilitarian analysis is the acceptable level of disutility experienced by the individual who has taken the action. From the individual's point of view the question comes down to one of the degree of risk that can be set against the moral wrongness of the policy. Should Jaspreet risk losing her job, being put in a position where nobody else will employ her in a comparable position – in effect sacrificing her career for the principle? Virtue ethics might encourage the virtue of courage, and commend a morally heroic show of devotion to principle, involving self-sacrifice. Philosophies of the right rather than the good – in other words philosophies such as those of Kant and the utilitarians which are concerned with moral sufficiency rather than moral excellence – would set much more rigorous requirements for actions with serious risk for Jaspreet. A utilitarian would want to be satisfied that the utility being achieved outweighed the disutility. A Kantian would wish to be satisfied that Jaspreet had a duty to follow the risky course of action. How would we establish that? Partly we would have to consider what her duty might be not to cause these problems for her employer. The issue of those duties will be dealt with in the next section. There may be duties concerning truth-telling, promise-keeping and respect for persons involved in this situation for Jaspreet, all of which may propel her towards action against her employer. She could be argued to have a duty to express her real opinion about the policies in question. If she withholds her opinion or her knowledge about the likely full effect of the policies she may be treating those people who will be adversely affected as a means of keeping her job secure, rather than ends in themselves. However, all of that needs to be balanced against her duty to her employer, of which more below.

The other issue concerns duties held elsewhere. Jaspreet has sole care of her three children, whose material security will be adversely affected if she loses her job. Does she have a duty to them? Arguably so in the sense that the creation of a family can be seen as involving a number of implicit undertakings which then ought to be adhered to. However, this does not mean that Jaspreet must sacrifice every principle to avoid causing them any uncertainty. It may be that where her children are competent to discuss matters her duty is to consult them rather than always to act to protect their security, whatever the cost to her own conscience.

Duties to the employer

Finally we must consider question (c) above, concerning Jaspreet's duty to her employer. We first need to ask if there are any moral duties to the employer which transcend the moral problems caused by the employer's policies. There is an agreement between Jaspreet and her employer, which involves on the one hand the paying of a salary, the provision of benefits and of the wherewithal for Jaspreet to do her job, and on the other hand the doing of that job. This is not to suggest that Jaspreet's resistance to the policies means she is not doing her job. It may be that her disruption of her employer's policies advances the department's true purposes and interests, and could be construed as doing her job. Jaspreet may genuinely believe this but the definition of her job, and her employer's interests, is as much a matter for her employer to decide as for her.

At what point does dogged opposition to proposed policies start to breach her agreed status as employee? Is it only when she takes her opposition outside the organization, and leaks it to the press? Is there a stage within the management team where her continued opposition breaches an agreed definition of corporate responsibility? If she recruits colleagues lower down the hierarchy but does not go outside the department, does that breach an agreed or implied boundary round those who should be involved in such discussions?

There seems to be a difference between the persistent and, even, obstinate use of established decision-making channels and structures to oppose a decision, on the one hand, and a deliberate disruption of those channels and breaching of those structures, on the other. It is always possible that any policy adopted by an organization's senior management will turn out to be against the real interests of the organization. If that is the case in this situation, Jaspreet will have done the local authority a service by opposing it, but the disruption of the organization's structures is clearly against its own interests. Its channels and structures constitute it as an organization in a way that specific policies do not. Therefore, the organization's interests are threatened by that kind of response, and such a response could not be seen as falling within the employee's role, though it may be justifiable from other standpoints.

CORPORATE WRONGDOING

Let us move the situation forward. Despite Jaspreet's arguments against the developing policy, the rest of the management team are resolved to carry on developing an increasingly separated system of purchasing and provision. A decision is made to work towards a situation where all residential care for adults is purchased by the department from private or voluntary bodies. All remaining local authority homes will be privatized and those parts of the department which actually deliver services will be separated organizationally from those parts engaged in assessing and commissioning. The relationship between the two parts henceforth will be that of commissioner and provider. As much as possible of the providing part of the department – including day care and domiciliary care of adults – will be hived off into private bodies, some of which will be run as non-profit-making enterprises. The management team are aware that some establishments are likely to be bought by businesses which have already developed considerable interests in the social care market and are looking to expand. It may be possible for others to be taken over by voluntary bodies, though these on the whole have less in the way of ready resources to buy and run establishments at short notice.

The management team want to keep their plans confidential. They know that there will be a period of confusion in the care sector, and to some extent a deterioration in services (if only through the effect on staff morale) and they want to minimize that. This will be exacerbated by the fact that the elected members will need to make their decision on the plans before they are implemented. They know that as soon as the plans are known, even in the most sketchy way, there will be a storm of political opposition from a number of groups in the community and in the local authority machinery itself. This could delay the changes or force compromises that would destroy their coherence. Also they don't want to give anyone any unfair advantages in terms of opportunities to buy what might be profitable businesses.

The director, chair, chief executive and majority leader agree that, given that the management review is widely known about and major changes are expected, silence from the authority will make matters worse. They decide on a press release that will reassure the community and prevent speculation and agitation. The release, when produced and distributed, is couched in language that is misleading, in that its wording can be construed as implying that changes will be far less significant than they in fact will be.

Jaspreet has decided that she will accept the new policy and work within it to minimize the harmful effects on vulnerable users. However, she feels strongly that the community and interested groups ought to be given a clear idea of what is in store, so that they can express their views effectively. The misleading information given by the local authority is unacceptable. However, it is clear to the director that the premature revelation of the plans to the public may well wreck them; so if anyone goes public on this, the policy will be seriously compromised.

Everyone in the management team knows that the public are being misled, and that this damages the relationship between agency and electorate. They also know that there is considerable risk to the department and its policies in the sense that, if the truth leaks out, its reputation will suffer serious damage. How should they act?

This situation is rather different from the one faced by Jaspreet when the local authority was formulating its plans at the prompting of government. However much she dislikes that policy, it is something that clearly lies within the department's remit to implement, and it is therefore a legitimate part of the employer's expectation of her to contribute to this. It is not a legitimate part of the department's remit to deceive the public about that policy. Nor is it a reasonable expectation by the department of its employees to knowingly be part of that deception. This goes against the legal basis and the declared practice of local government.

It could be argued that it is in some sense 'impossible' for a public body to act criminally, because its existence, unlike that of persons, depends on law and in a real sense it 'can' only operate within the law. A criminal act must be an act by the individuals who run or work for the organization, not of the organization itself. Can we apply the same argument to immoral acts, irrespective of whether they happen to be illegal? That is less clear. Organizations do have moral goals, but they do not rely on them for their organizational existence as they do on law. None the less an act of this kind must fall outside the moral goals of the organization, and must fall outside an ethical interpretation of the job description of a senior manager. This would suggest that everyone who knowingly contributed to its implementation has a personal moral responsibility, because it goes beyond their moral duty as employees. If personal moral duties come into play at this point, then truth-telling is one of these. This would suggest that the employee concerned ought to tell the truth about this matter, rather than collude in untruth.

The question of confidentiality needs to be considered. I said in

Chapter 3 that we can see autonomy in terms of privacy, property rights over the information, promise-keeping and harm. I would argue that corporate bodies do not have a right of privacy because that right is a function of personhood. Although we might treat corporations as moral persons for some purposes, they are not truly persons, and do not have a right of privacy. In terms of property rights, where an organization is acting outside its moral remit, that fact cannot be seen as information over which the organization has property rights. It can have no moral rights when it is not acting in accordance with its moral remit. This must be particularly the case when it is wronging its constituency. Promises would not be broken because the organization had no right to seek any undertaking from employees to comply with, or keep confidential, that which went beyond their duty. I shall consider the question of harm below.

To blow the whistle or not to blow the whistle

Duties

In the light of the above, is it right for Jaspreet to publicize the local authority's dishonesty? We may be satisfied that she has no duty to the authority to collude with its action, and that may mean answering honestly on the matter when asked, but does that mean she should take the initiative and publicize the matter? We need to identify whether such a positive act is justified.

The individuals concerned may have other duties – some as citizens and others perhaps as professionals. Those who are members of professional bodies with specific codes of ethics and groups of users to whom they have a professional responsibility could be said to have a duty to those users which they should set alongside their duty as employees. It could be argued that if they function primarily as managers then a residual professional identity should not be used as a convenient escape clause. However, professional identity may be a central part of competence and expertise. Jaspreet may only be able to function as a member of the team, and understand the significance of the policies involved because she has professional training and experience. Therefore, her professional role is part of what allows her to know what she is dealing with, just as much as the briefing papers she gets from her employer.

The other area of duty would lie in relation to anyone who relies on Jaspreet's salary. They also could arguably have a legitimate claim on her considerations, and provide a possible reason for not whistle-blowing. That depends, though, on our view of whether we should simply assume that she will be sacked, or whether we should make some judgement of the legitimacy of that action. If we think it is inevitable, do we then regard that result as Jaspreet's responsibility?

Utility

There is also a different set of considerations to set against the duty-oriented considerations we have dealt with so far – those of utility. What good will whistle-blowing do, as against what harm? Does Jaspreet have a duty to do it even if she forsees that it will actually do more harm than good overall, in that the department's operation will be disrupted, its competence and professionalism discredited and she herself sacked. The former outcomes could well lead to a deterioration of standards of care, and harm users also. An act utilitarian argument would be that if more harm does result (it is not clear what actual good would result as such) then she ought not to do it. However, a complication arises in that much of the harm would result from the way other people respond to her whistle-blowing, and much of that reaction could reasonably be otherwise, in the sense that people could choose to handle it in a way that minimized harm. Jaspreet fears that they will react badly, incompetently and vindictively. Should that come into her calculation of utility, or is that for the other main protagonists to consider in their reflection on how they should act? The strict utilitarian should focus on results, irrespective of considerations of responsibility, but the situation arises because we are only considering the moral choices of one individual. However, until she makes her choice, the other individuals don't know what their choices are. So the difficulty continues to impose itself.

A rule utilitarian might argue that a rule allowing the department's deception may not have utility even though the one-off situation as it stands might argue in favour of letting things proceed. Persistent deception of the community is likely to discredit the system, and change it over time into something far less effective. The problem arises if a rule allowing whistle-blowing is also found not to have utility. That is perfectly possible. Whistle-blowing may be found to be disruptive more often than not, and to cause more pain than it avoids though, again, that might have a lot to do with the way people choose to react to it. We must, then, find a different way of ensuring that the first rule (not to mislead the public) is observed. Utilitarianism does not necessarily provide any straightforward answers to Jaspreet's dilemma.

WRONGDOING BY ANOTHER ORGANIZATION

Another situation

The department is preparing for the transfer of responsibility for long-term residential care of the elderly from the health commission to the local authority. The department is negotiating with the health commission on the timing of the transfer of responsibility and the actual organization of the users who will be affected by this. Jaspreet is a member of the team involved in those discussions and has close contacts with several senior members of the health commission management. Health commission representatives have said that the transfer can begin at an agreed time in the future, so that there will be a period of preparation of resources running into the next financial year – allowing budgetary preparation. This has been said in the formal discussions, and it has also been said privately to Jaspreet by her opposite numbers in the commission. The department's management team feel that they have time to prepare properly and provide a transition of care arrangements which will be minimally disruptive to users.

The health commission comes under pressure from national NHS management to speed up the transition. The commission management fear that a major project for which they are hoping for government funding will be jeopardized if they keep to the longer time-scale agreed with the department. They are aware that the party with the most influence on the local authority are disliked by the Government because of their history and reputation as 'loony left', and are unhappy about seeming to be in an alliance with them to sustain the longer time-scale of transition, so they decide that they cannot afford politically to adhere to the originally agreed time-scale. They decide to go back on the agreement with the local authority. In doing so they realize that they will be cast as the villain of the piece in the media, so a story is leaked at the behest of the chief executive to the effect that the local authority is deliberately dragging its feet over the transfer, creating uncertainty and insecurity for a large number of elderly people who are at present in hospital accommodation. The story is slanted to imply that the social services department is disorganized and slow to take on new responsibilities.

Clearly the local authority will have a political response to make to this, in order to maintain its position. However, there is also a question of what ethical response might be appropriate. This falls into two parts: first, what kind of ethical analysis can we make of the commission's action; and second, what would be an appropriate response by the local authority, and by its personnel as individuals and professionals.

Individual or corporate wrongdoing

Should we be considering the actions of individuals on this issue, or of the corporate body? If these actions are wrong, who acted wrongly? The chief executive? The members of the management team? The commission? We know which individuals made the key decisions and took the key actions. Does that mean that we can focus on those as individual actions rather than as corporate actions? If we argue, as French (1984) does, that an organization that has a clear and identifiable machinery for decision-making can be treated as a moral actor for some purposes, and be held responsible for its corporate actions, this must be an instance where that applies. The fact that we happen to know how the decision was made, and by whom individually, should not alter the argument that the decision was, finally, made by a corporate entity rather than a person in the usual sense.

How should senior managers in the local authority respond? First, should there be any individual response at all? Should it be a matter of any interest to any of the people involved, as individuals, how the commission is behaving; or is it a matter for the corporate body of the local authority to respond to? On a practical level it may be more effective for one corporate body to respond to the corporate wrong-doing of another. However, if corporate wrongdoing is true wrongdoing, falling within the moral realm, then any morally competent being is potentially in a position to judge its action and, where appropriate, respond to it. Therefore, if as a private citizen I am aware of what the commission is doing, I am as competent as the local authority to say that it is doing wrong, and form an opinion on appropriate redress. If I happen to be in residential care, and my situation is therefore precipitately and perhaps negatively affected by the action of the commission, then as an individual I would be in a position where I could quite logically and sensibly make comments and seek redress. If I work for the social services department, and the commission's action does not affect me or anyone close to me on a personal level, the situation would be rather different. As a citizen I can say that I think the commission has behaved badly towards people in residential care, and towards the local authority. As an employee of the local authority, in which role I am likely to have the closest investment in the outcome and the strongest feelings about the actions, it makes least sense to say that I should also individually express my views and take action. This would be to 'double-enter' myself in the moral equation. If it was a legal matter, in which damages were being pursued, individual employees would not seek individual damages alongside damages sought by the wronged corporation, by virtue simply of being employees. There would be no justification for that. The commission has either wronged another corporate body, or it has wronged a group of people who happen to be senior social services managers. It has not done both.

So there is no justification for Jaspreet to denounce the commission in the local press, or to upbraid the chief executive of the commission, on her own behalf. The only sensible exchange is between the two corporate bodies. Clearly this would involve the same people, but not as their private selves. This might limit what Jaspreet or any other individual can do. The logic of my argument suggests that those matters that she only knows about in her role as a senior manager (in terms of the wrong behaviour of the commission) are things that she ought not to bring into any denunciation of the commission's behaviour, as a private citizen, or in any other role. It is only relevant to the exchange between the two corporate bodies. This clearly has major implications for confidentiality for people caught up in this dispute.

The response of the local authority

So far I have focused on the response of the local authority as the wronged party, but we also need to consider how this relates to the local authority's responsibilities generally. How ought the local authority respond as a public body? Let us suppose that the local authority is being so accepting of the commission's poor negotiating practice that it is in effect colluding with the commission, and that this is a symptom of a highly confrontational management style in the commission that bodes ill for other bodies in collaboration with it. Let us suppose that the commission management are able to intimidate the local authority in various ways that would be unacceptable to the general public if they knew about it. All this might only be known to someone in a senior management role. Is there a point at which a moral problem between two corporate bodies becomes something rather different – something where whistle-blowing is required and justified?

If the local authority is failing to resist the aggressive behaviour of the commission, it could be argued that as a corporate body it is failing in one of its functions, which is to effectively co-operate with other bodies; and that effectiveness must include an ability to be assertive and effective in situations where the other organization is acting in an irresponsible way. However, this raises three issues:

1. Is it a reasonable expectation that corporate bodies will be able to fight their corner? In the world of private commerce there is an expectation that corporations will compete. That is a necessity of the market, but also part of the implicit agreement between corporation and shareholders. However, there is no partisan body of people to whom a public body such as a local authority owes a duty to fight and compete. Its constituency (government and local electorate), its consumers and its main stakeholders benefit not from ruthless competition but from co-operation, at least between purchasing and commissioning organizations. In a fully commercial and privatized system that would not be the case, but in the present system it certainly is. So any requirements we lay upon the local authority must be considered in that context.

2. In interpersonal interactions between individuals of equal competence, protagonist A is not blameable for protagonist B's behaviour, where protagonist B behaves badly, in a dishonest or threatening way. Protagonist A is only responsible for his or her own actions, and that may include a duty to warn or help others who may suffer from the results of protagonist B's behaviour, in order to maximize well-being or fulfil a specific duty of care. The problem with corporate bodies is that their actions must be limited by the purpose of their existence – their enabling legislation or charters – as well as their relationships and the likely results of their actions. If the kind of actions involved in restraining or resisting the commission's actions are not part of the local authority's legislative and moral *raison d'être* it is difficult to argue that it should corporately take up the cudgels. The course of action that seems most likely to fall within its remit is to seek to resolve the problem even if that involves accepting the behaviour of the other body, in order that co-operation can continue. If Jaspreet regards that as a wrong response by the local authority, her role is to argue that as part of the decision-making machinery of that body. If she cannot change the local authority's view, she should accept the situation or resign. The issue is between two

corporate bodies, and the participation of individual employees in that moral dispute seems properly to be done as part of
the corporate body. That seems a logical position.

3. At what stage, if any, should the individual employee of the
organization take some action that goes beyond his or her
role as employee? It could be argued that the behaviour of
the commission is something that is likely to affect the well-
being of the community and of users, and it is therefore the
duty of anyone who knows about that behaviour to bring it
to the attention of the public. If the local authority, which
knows about it, is not doing that, perhaps it is the duty of
any private individual who knows about it to do that instead.
However, if that individual knows about it because of his
or her role as an employee, does that limit his or her liberty to make the information public? I argued earlier that
organizations do not have a right of privacy, and that
promise-keeping and property rights to information cannot
apply where the information concerns actions by the organization that conflict with, or go beyond, its moral purpose.
However, in this case it is not clear that the local authority is
acting against its moral purpose. The commission may be
acting wrongly, but that does not mean that the local
authority (the wronged party) is acting wrongly in not
making the matter public. If that is so, the local authority
has a good case for requiring Jaspreet not to publicize the
matter. Jaspreet clearly has a right to argue the matter in her
role within the organization.

On the other hand Jaspreet may believe that other factors outweigh her
employer's rights and her duties to the employer in this situation. She
may take the view that she has other duties which outweigh her duty to
her employer. She may see herself as bound by a professional duty
based on her reading of her professional code of ethics. She may feel
bound by other obligations, perhaps based on promises or agreements.
Alternatively, Jaspreet may simply make a judgement of the harms and
benefits likely to result from her options.

REFERENCE

French, P. (1984) *Collective and Corporate Responsibility*. New York:
Columbia University Press.

INDEX

WITHDRAWN

WITHDRAWN